ONTARIO

Image, Identity, and Power

Peter A. Baskerville

The

Illustrated

History

of

Canada

OXFORD

UNIVERSITY PRESS

OXFORD
UNIVERSITY PRESS

70 Wynford Drive, Don Mills, Ontario M3C 1J9
www.oup.com/ca

Oxford University Press is a department of the University of Oxford.
It furthers the University's objective of excellence in research, scholarship,
and education by publishing worldwide in

Oxford New York
Auckland Bangkok Buenos Aires Cape Town Chennai
Dar es Salaam Delhi Hong Kong Istanbul Karachi Kolkata
Kuala Lumpur Madrid Melbourne Mexico City Mumbai Nairobi
São Paulo Shanghai Singapore Taipei Tokyo Toronto

Oxford is a trade mark of Oxford University Press
in the UK and in certain other countries

Published in Canada
by Oxford University Press

National Library of Canada Cataloguing in Publication

Baskerville, Peter A. (Peter Allan), 1943–
    Ontario: image, identity and power/Peter A. Baskerville.

(Illustrated history of Canada)
Includes index.
ISBN 0-19-541137-4

1. Ontario—History.   I. Title.   II. Series.

FC3061.B37 2002   971.3   C2002-902945-7
F1058.B36 2002

1 2 3 4 - 05 04 03 02

Cover & Text Design: Brett Miller
Cover image: Robert R. Whale (1807–87), 'The Canada Southern Railway
at Niagara' (1870). Oil on canvas. National Gallery of Canada, Ottawa. No. 6185.

This book is printed on permanent (acid-free) paper ∞.

Printed in Canada

TABLE OF CONTENTS

PREFACE

In the million square kilometres that stretch from the rocks of the Canadian Shield to the fertile land around the Great Lakes, from the time of the arrival of the First Peoples, when interaction between cultures commenced, social, political, and economic life has never ceased evolving. This book is about that process.

There are many Ontarios, each with its own history. The impact of place on any individual or group—and their impact on it—is always filtered: by gender, occupation, age, ancestry, the times, circumstances, and relationships with other groups. A miner at Silver Islet on Lake Superior in the late nineteenth century would understand his world quite differently than would a manager or owner of the mine—or an Ojibwa dispossessed of ancestral lands.

Whatever the context, from the family to the province or country, power relations constrict, define, and enable behaviour. Leaders may appeal to regional identity to further their agendas—Ontario's have often excelled at that art—but no politician can represent all interests. Power begets resistance, and the Ontario of those who resisted is as much a part of this history as are the visions held by those in power.

The images in this book give glimpses of the myriad social relations that have infused meaning into the notion of Ontario. Be it a painting, photograph, cartoon, or map, each is a product of its time, a construction to be read. Of each we must ask, Who created it? In whose interest? And if power had been in other hands, how might it have been different?

ACKNOWLEDGEMENTS

No book is written alone. Archivists throughout Ontario responded with professional grace to my many long-distance requests for help. To list every name would stretch the length of this book to the breaking point, and to omit any would be wrong: I thank them all. I also thank Chad Gaffield for early support and especially Michael Piva for his substantive and selfless input. John Thompson, a fellow author in this series, provided helpful comments on the penultimate draft. The challenges encountered in turning that draft into this book could not have been surmounted without the professional editorial assistance of Sally Livingston, Margaret McClintock, Laura Macleod, and Phyllis Wilson. It is to my partner, Fran, that this book is dedicated.

ABBREVIATIONS

AO: Archives of Ontario, Toronto

CMC: Canadian Museum of Civilization, Ottawa

COTA: City of Toronto Archives

CSTM: Canada Science and Technology Museum, Ottawa

NAC: National Archives of Canada, Ottawa

NGC: National Gallery of Canada, Ottawa

NMC: National Museums of Canada, Ottawa

MTRL: Metropolitan Toronto Reference Library

CHAPTER ONE

Change and Exchange: 9000 BCE–1500 CE

$\mathcal{T}$wenty thousand years ago, ice completely covered the land that would become Ontario. Not until some 9,000 years later is there definite evidence of human occupation in the south-central area above the Great Lakes—probably the first region in eastern Canada to emerge from the last ice age. The common understanding of life in the era before the arrival of Europeans in North America is that it was nasty, brutish, and short. Yet the skeletal remains of a small band of people who lived southwest of what is now London, Ontario, some 3,000 years ago suggest that, like much else once thought about Ontario's past, that view requires some rethinking. Evidence of severe dental deterioration—probably the result of chewing hard substances and perhaps of using teeth as tools—suggests that life was indeed harsh for the people of the 'Hind Site'. It was also short: the average age of death was in the mid-30s. But the remains of a child aged approximately 12 suggest that, despite its hardships, life was far from brutish. The boy was poorly developed and could not have walked; dental analysis suggests that his food would have had to be ground into gruel. But

he was not abandoned. The fact that he was buried with other members of his band suggests that his culture cared for and protected those unable to fend for themselves.[1]

Archaeological evidence of this kind is, of course, unusual, and it becomes even more rare the farther back we go. Yet botanists, zoologists, geologists, and even climatologists have all contributed to our knowledge of early life in Ontario, and gradually a picture—or at least a series of snapshots—is beginning to develop. Scholars used to generalize broadly about life in the Palaeolithic era (c. 9000–7500 BCE) on the assumption that the climate and vegetation resembled those of the modern subarctic—a mixed forest-tundra environment supporting little in the way of plant life—and that Palaeo-Indians lived in much the same way that modern subarctic groups do, as nomadic hunters following herds of animals across the tundra. Recent studies, however, have concluded that the Palaeolithic was the period of greatest weather turbulence in the past 10 millennia, and that local landscape features created diverse micro-environments. While average temperatures throughout most of the Palaeolithic period were close to those of the modern subarctic, conditions were likely a good deal less extreme in the vicinity of lakes.[2] Palaeo peoples probably moved within defined ranges of up to 350 kilometres, exploiting seasonal opportunities. In a period of unpredictable climatic conditions, people could not afford to specialize in big game.

Close attention to specific contexts has led to provocative new outlooks on other aspects of Palaeo-Indian life. It is now recognized that, even in the most temperate parts of the region, survival demanded high-level skills. Seasonal migration across varied terrain required more than one means of transport—sleds or toboggans as well as some form of raft or boat—all of which had to be built with tools chipped from local stone. Palaeo peoples also made weapons (such as spear points), implements such as needles for sewing hides and, possibly, tattooing—and children's toys. The care taken in the choice of materials for such implements—often snow-white or blood-red chert chipped from specific rocky outcrops—and in their crafting suggests that their value was not merely practical but cultural or spiritual. Bands often relied on specific outcrops, and this has made it possible to trace the movement of goods. It appears that Ontario's earliest peoples exchanged tools, crafted goods, and raw materials with bands as far away as what is now northern Michigan. In all probability, they also intermarried with these other bands, ensuring a wider selection of eligible partners and, in the process, establishing a type of insurance in the form of a group to whom one could turn for help when conditions proved especially inhospitable.

Beginning about 10,000 years ago, with the end of the last ice age, the Archaic period saw significant warming trends, and by roughly 8,500 years ago, an essentially modern vegetation community was in place; in fact, forest cover extended 2 degrees north of the present tree line. Fluctuating water levels created many marshy zones in which edible plants such as berries and wild rice flourished, and in the south, around Lakes Erie and Ontario, fish became an increasingly important alternative to deer in the diet. Families lived in spruce-bough or skin-covered shelters. Gradually, populations grew and band territories became more clearly defined.

Interregional trade also increased in this period. Employing a technology first developed south of the Great Lakes, bands living along the shore of Lake Superior began to pound, grind, and polish local copper into tools that were traded as far east as modern Labrador and as far west as modern Saskatchewan. With the development of metal technology—a marked advance on the flaked stone tools of the Paleolithic era—a manufacturing and trading pattern began that would continue until the time of European contact. There is even evidence of competition between manufacturing sites. For a time, flint blades manufactured along the north shore of Lake Erie were widely distributed throughout what are now southern Ontario, northern New York state, and Ohio, but flints from Ohio ultimately won out and Ontario's flint industry became an early casualty of 'free trade'.[3]

Grave goods provide scattered evidence both of trade and of spiritual and social customs in the late Archaic period. Around 3,500 years ago, the grave goods of people near what is now Picton, towards the eastern end of Lake

Ontario, included not just Lake Superior copper items but shell pendants and beads from
the Gulf of Mexico. Farther north, people near
Lake Nipigon were buried with various non-
local items, including deposits of red ochre
and green clay. Although the quantities of
goods placed in individual graves varied, and
occasionally women were buried with more
than men, there is no overall pattern to suggest
that societies were structured according to
hereditary rank. Band status was likely egalitarian, and social distinctions probably reflect
some combination of individual achievement,
gender, health, and age, rather than a formal
set of descent rules.

We can only speculate about the significance of such grave goods. What we do know
is that, at the time of European contact, many
North American indigenous cultures equated
red (ochre) with social well-being, white
(shells) with physical vitality, and copper with
spiritual power. The presence of those items in
graves from the Archaic period (considered to
have ended about 1000 BCE) may indicate that
the Iroquoian- and Algonkian-speaking peoples occupying the territory in 1500 had
already been there for more than two thousand
years. If so, this would have direct implications
for present-day land claims, which are often
based on length of occupation. However, most
archaeologists think the Iroquoian culture
emerged slightly later, roughly 2,500 years
ago, and that the Algonkian began some two
centuries after that.

One reconstruction that has been generally accepted is based on the development of
pottery in the early Woodland period (the
Woodland era as a whole lasted from 1000 BCE
to c. 1500 CE). The fact that pottery styles

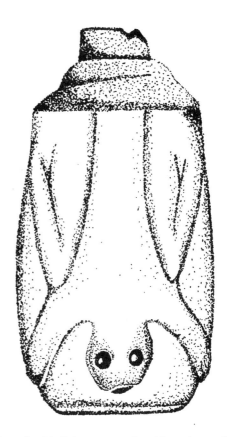

Sucking tube. Medicine men used sucking tubes to draw
evil spirits from their patients. This tube, decorated with a
frog or toad in relief, was made in the Ohio Valley but
found at a 2,000-year-old site on the shores of the Rainy
River in northern Ontario, indicating that links existed
between northern and southern tribes long before the
arrival of Europeans. With permission of the Royal
Ontario Museum © ROM L.S.M.7-1966.

throughout the region above the Great Lakes
were fairly standard suggests that women (the
primary pottery-makers) moved from band to
band through marriage, whereas men (the
hunters who relied on specialized knowledge
of their local ecosystems) stayed with the
bands they were born into. Thus hunter-gatherer societies were probably patrilineal, tracing

Rice Lake Serpent Mound, 1897. Generation after generation, the Aboriginal peoples of the Great Lakes region were buried in large mounds, often over the bones of their ancestors. At Rice Lake, location in the mound and the value of the accompanying grave goods reflected the individual's status in the community. With permission of the Royal Ontario Museum © ROM.

descent through the male line. Each spring and fall, several bands would meet to fish together and conduct the ceremonies, such as marriages and communal burials, that reinforced a general allegiance.

In most cases, the evidence from Woodland burial sites resembles that from the Archaic period and indicates that societies were structured according to a single-family egalitarian model. Yet, in at least one case, a more complex socio-economic structure evolved. Seven con-

centrations of large burial mounds—one measuring some 53 metres long, 7 m wide, and 2 m high—dot the landscape around Rice Lake in southeastern Ontario, an area of rich natural vegetation and abundant animal life. Each constructed on a high point overlooking an expanse of water, the mounds effectively defined a local ecosystem used by a group of between 50 and 100 people. A pattern of successive burials within each mound indicates that bands occupied these territories for generations.

In Archaic times, grave goods had tended to be primarily practical items such as polished tools and weapons that may also have had spiritual significance. By contrast, in the Woodland era the most common grave goods were items such as pipes, cut jaws, drilled teeth, and shaped skulls, which had no apparent practical function. This suggests that the world view of the region's indigenous peoples in that period was primarily spiritual.[4] Certainly the Native practice of gift-giving as a central part of trade, burial, and other ceremonies—much remarked on by early European observers—points to a non-materialistic notion of wealth. In many Native societies, social rank was displayed through conspicuous giving rather than conspicuous consumption.

At Rice Lake, however, there is little evidence of public redistribution of goods. Rather, burial patterns and grave-goods distribution point to clear distinctions in social status. The fact that the privileged individuals buried in discrete sub-floor pits, accompanied by various prized goods, were all genetically related indicates that status was hereditary; the bodies of the less privileged became part of the fill with which the mounds were constructed. When a local leader died, band members would disinter, disarticulate, and rebury the bones of those who had died since the death of the previous leader, in the process adding to the size and, perhaps, the status of their local mound. Even within early hunter-gatherer societies, then, cultural and social behaviours differed.

Why did a somewhat more complex social and economic system emerge at Rice Lake? Rich natural resources would certainly have facilitated long-term residence and the establishment of band boundaries. However, elite status also reflected control of trade. In each of two grave sites, silver items were buried with only one individual, suggesting special access to the trade in that item. The silver, which came from Cobalt, 350 kilometres north of Rice Lake, would have been reworked and distributed through an elite-controlled trade system extending as far away as what is now southern Ohio—the centre of the Hopewellian exchange system, in which Rice Lake had emerged as the northern node. The fact that the Rice Lake culture declined at about the same time as the Ohio, in the mid-third century, supports the idea of interconnection.

Some time in the sixth century, hunters in southern Ontario dramatically increased their efficiency when they adopted the bow and arrow from the Ohio region; an arrow could hit game that was out of range of a spear. A period of even more radical change began around the mid-seventh century, when a new corn variety suitable for short growing seasons arrived in Ontario, along with the technology required to grow it. By 1100, the Iroquoians were also cultivating beans, squash, sunflowers, and tobacco.

With agriculture came a more settled life as bands established small semi-permanent villages. But earlier patterns were not abandoned. Women continued to gather berries, nuts, and wild rice, and at seasonal hunting camps, large numbers of deer would be herded into pens, killed, skinned, and cured before being transported back to the village. Around 1300, however, it seems that the band-based villages of perhaps 200 to 400 people began to coalesce, creating larger, more heavily fortified

Iroquoian women preparing corn. Women cultivated the crops (corn, beans, squash, sunflower seeds), carrying their young children as they worked; soon they were providing most of the food, and hunting—the men's preserve—became devalued. With farming, women adopted a more sedentary way of life, but in winter they still travelled from their villages to transport the meat caught by the men, much as their hunter-gatherer forebears had. From Father François Du Creux, *Historiae Canadensis*, 1664. NAC.

settlements of more than a thousand inhabitants. By the mid-fifteenth century, the population in the region above the Great Lakes had reached its contact level of approximately 60,000, and a good-sized village would have been home to as many as 3,000 people. A single longhouse might be 100 metres in length and house more than 20 families.

The corn that contributed to the settlement process may have accounted for half the calories that people in the region consumed in the fourteenth century. But corn by itself is a poor food source: to release its full nutritional value, it has to be combined with other foods, such as the beans that spread throughout the region in the fifteenth century. The introduction of beans likely contributed to the rapid population growth that began about the same time, but it may not have been the only factor. Unlike people farther south, where longer growing seasons made it possible to rely much more heavily on cultivated crops, those living north of the Great Lakes had necessarily continued to eat a good deal of meat, especially in winter. Certainly they experienced fewer winter famines and significantly lower death rates than most of their contemporaries in North America.[5] When growth did level off, in the latter part of the fifteenth century, one likely reason was the spread of tuberculosis, a disease associated with dense concentrations of population.

Disease was not the only threat. It was during this period that larger confederacies began to form—the groups that would become known as the Neutral and Erie in the southwest and the Petun and Hurons in the southeast—and villages were fortified with multiple rows of palisades, catwalks, and turrets. At the same time, warfare increased dramatically, in the west between the Neutral people and the Algonkian Fire Nation, and in the east between the Hurons and the St Lawrence Iroquoians.

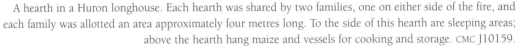

A hearth in a Huron longhouse. Each hearth was shared by two families, one on either side of the fire, and each family was allotted an area approximately four metres long. To the side of this hearth are sleeping areas; above the hearth hang maize and vessels for cooking and storage. CMC J10159.

Contrary to longstanding assumption, then, the violence often blamed on European newcomers actually began some time before they arrived. It was not until the 1580s that the fur trade got underway in earnest; a few trade goods reached the interior from the Gulf of St Lawrence before that date, but the quantity was not sufficient to have prompted competition for locational advantage. The presence of Europeans exacerbated social upheaval among the peoples of southern Ontario, but their arrival did not initiate it. So where should we look for its cause?

The clustered placement and variable size of village longhouses suggest that some band members might have enjoyed greater status than others. And there is evidence that certain families enjoyed special rights to fishing, trading, and farming areas. As yet, however, no evidence has been found to suggest significant differences in material wealth. Perhaps the tradition of conspicuous giving, based on an

Princess Point Vessel, *c.* 600–900. In the Woodland era there was little variation in pottery styles through the Great Lakes region, suggesting that women probably moved from band to band through marriage. On this typical pot, the lines near the neck were made by using a coiled string to press twigs into the clay. As the cultivation of crops became more important, women became more likely to stay with their own bands, and distinctive regional pottery styles appeared. From C.J. Ellis and N. Ferris, eds, *The Archaeology of Southern Ontario to A.D. 1650* (London: Ontario Archaeological Society, 1990), 177. Metropolitan Toronto Reference Library.

ethic associating generosity with health and peace, militated against sharp material differences in lifestyles. It is also possible that a semi-sedentary people like the Iroquois, who moved to more fertile lands every 20 or so years, worried less about acquiring personal property than some more sedentary peoples.

On balance, then, a simple desire for material aggrandizement is not enough to account for increases in warlike activity.

A more intriguing perspective focuses on the possibility that increased reliance on cultivated crops led to significant changes in gender roles, which in turn contributed to changes in other patterns of behaviour. Regional differences in ceramic production point to one of the ways agriculture affected gender roles. Before corn, women—the pottery makers—married outside their bands; after corn, women continued to make pottery but also cultivated crops, and therefore adopted a more sedentary life. Their role as the primary agents of interaction between villages was assumed by the men who (after clearing the fields) still left home regularly to hunt, fish, gather wild food, and make war. Whereas in the past a new wife would move to live with her husband's family, now the pattern was reversed. In the course of these changes, women came to oversee the use of space within the longhouse—an especially important task at a time of rising population. They also played significant roles in the (s)election of men to the village councils that oversaw the merging of different clans within each village.

The roles assigned to women resulted in a birth rate similar to that of the hunter-gatherer era: one child every fourth or fifth year. A mother with work to do could not carry more than one child at a time, but after age four or five, children could keep up on their own. Evidence from the immediate post-contact period also points to low birth rates: Iroquoian women nursed their children for two to three years, during which time they abstained from intercourse, and many rituals required sexual abstinence. Marriage appears to have been delayed as long as possible, perhaps in part because the families of young men wanted them to remain and participate economically in the household for as long as possible. Certainly premarital sex was common: it seems that many women may have married only when pregnancy obliged them to assume the more economically demanding and socially restricted roles of wife and mother. In an economy based exclusively on hunting and gathering, men had gained status and prestige by providing for their families, especially in winter. With the rise of agriculture, however, hunting became less essential for survival, and men's role was devalued accordingly. The new system of matrilocal residence must have posed many challenges for men; one archaeologist has even suggested that sweat lodges, which emerged in this era, helped young husbands to bond with other male members of their new households. Moreover, to achieve and maintain status in the larger society men needed opportunities to demonstrate individual daring, courage, and prowess—opportunities that warfare would have provided. Whatever the reasons, a pattern of conflict based on individual daring, revenge, and the pursuit of prestige, all of which could be satisfied by swift raids, the taking of captives, and ceremonial torture, emerged in the period following 1300 and extended into contact times.[6]

As persuasive as this theory may be, by the late fifteenth century intertribal conflict had escalated to such a point that the need for status alone seems inadequate to explain it. A more holistic perspective suggests that changing environmental conditions may have altered the very circumstances that had undermined men's status in the first place.

Iroquoian societies were farming in a fragile ecological zone at the northern edge of productive agriculture. A study of the location characteristics of over 300 Iroquoian villages settled between the years 900 and 1550 has revealed a strong preference for sandy, well-drained soils located on moderately sloping terrain in regions with more than 90 frost-free days. Such conditions were well suited to early horticultural techniques: sandy soils could be worked easily with digging sticks made of wood, bone, or stone and allowed good natural drainage, especially if they were located on moderate slopes.[7]

Ontario did not have many micro-environments with the right combination of soil, temperature, and slope for farming of this type. Nor was the climate predictable in this period. In fact, between roughly 1450 and 1850 much of the world was affected by the 'Little Ice Age'. In the Great Lakes region, temperatures were on average 1–2°C lower than they are at present. As small as this difference may seem, it could well have affected production of corn and beans, both of which are sensitive to cold and were already being grown at their northern limits.

The Neutral people significantly altered their diet during the Little Ice Age. Whereas in the fourteenth century corn and beans were the staples and deer meat only a relatively minor component, at village sites dated after 1500 deer bones are much more common. This suggests that a changing climate may have made it too risky to rely on agriculture as a major source of food. Valuable evidence for this argument has come from sediment layers preserved on lake bottoms. In the past, changes in vegetation were attributed to the impact of Native farming—for example, white pine, a shade-intolerant species, was thought to have spread widely between 1300 and 1500, when Iroquoian farmers were clearing fields that they later abandoned. Yet there is no significant correlation between the incidence of white pine and Iroquoian settlement. The sediments show that white pine declined north of Lake Nipissing and increased to the south as regions that had once been too warm cooled and became more hospitable, with the converse effect occurring in more northerly areas. This evidence is consistent with the idea that Iroquoian agriculture, already vulnerable at what botanists term the biotic margin, was also affected, in this case, negatively.

Jesuit missionaries in Huronia recorded hard winters, crop failures, droughts, and famines almost every year between 1628 and 1650; in the twentieth century, crops in the same region failed, on average, only one year in ten. Although (as we will see) much of the suffering inflicted on the Hurons in the early seventeenth century can be attributed directly to the European presence, climatic conditions contributed to the sad spectacle of what one Jesuit missionary described as 'dying skeletons eking out a miserable life, feeding even on the excrements and refuse of nature'.[8]

The early peoples of what are now southern and northern Ontario differed in a number of ways. Most northern bands spoke a language belonging to the Algonkian rather than the Iroquoian group. Environmental conditions differed considerably between south and north, and northern peoples continued to depend on hunting and gathering long after southern peoples had adopted the more

sedentary lifestyle of agriculturalists. Yet the divide was not as great as has often been imagined, on either count. For one thing, the transition from an environment that supported farming to one that did not was gradual; and some Algonkian peoples also grew crops. For another, despite their linguistic differences, northern bands did interact with the Iroquoian peoples to the south, and this interaction contributed to cultural complexity and change over time.

The northern peoples also differed among themselves. In the northwest of the province, where the boreal forest cover and harsh winters made for limited food resources, band numbers were smaller and subsistence strategies more varied than in the more central region. Some archaeologists have speculated that the migratory life necessitated by the sparse ecosystem worked against strong band organization and status distinctions, fostering instead a culture of overall economic homogeneity and social equality that remained largely unaltered from the late Archaic to the eve of contact. Perhaps so—but grave goods from the Woodland era suggest that bands in the northwest did have cultural links with the south, as well as a sense of band solidarity and a degree of social stratification.

Farther south, between Lake Abitibi and the northeastern shore of Lake Superior, a group of Algonkians who would come to be known as the Ojibwa developed a culture that reflected the influence both of southern Iroquoians and of northwestern Algonkian peoples, and a subsistence economy based heavily on fishing. In the late Archaic period, they gathered briefly in the spring to fish, using the mainly individual techniques of spearing and angling, but did not stay together long because the fishery they were sharing could not support large numbers. Over time, however, they began using seine nets. This technique was more labour-intensive, as nets had to be made, mended, and attended to by many more people, but it was also more productive, allowing larger groups to stay longer at the fishery site—and perhaps necessitating a chieftain system for social control and food distribution. By the late Woodland era, these Algonkians were also working a fall fishery, using gill nets and freezing large portions of the catch for future use and possible trade with the Iroquoians to the south.

Fluctuating labour requirements—more hands were needed in fall than spring—led to increased cooperation between bands. At the same time, preserving food for the winter promoted greater stability and eased the pressure to disperse into smaller groups for extended winter hunting. Artifacts found in the Lake Nipissing area suggest that at least one Algonkian ritual practised as late as the nineteenth century, the Midewiwin, or the Society of Good Hearted Ones, dated from the Late Woodland era. The movement towards group identification suggested by such cultural activity is reflected in the use of common pottery styles among various Algonkian bands. In fact, although it used to be thought that pottery was brought to the Algonkians via trade and inter-marriage with the southern Iroquoian peoples, it is now believed that Algonkians manufactured their own.

Trade between Iroquoian and Algonkian bands took place within a fairly structured set of relationships. The Hurons who traded corn and other foodstuffs for beaver and deer pelts appear to have considered themselves clearly superior to their northern trading allies. Huron, not Algonkian, was the language of trade; Huron men married Algonkian women, who had to relocate to Huron territory, but Huron women never married Algonkian men; Hurons did not eat Algonkian food. Nevertheless, the northeastern Algonkians, who also traded with bands farther west, were nicely situated to control the flow of goods both north and south. As in Huronia, certain families controlled these trading paths and bequeathed that control to their descendants.

Even before 1500, then, some of the northern hunter-gatherer societies were far from isolated, and their social structure was increasingly non-egalitarian. Cultural change was already well underway by the time the first Europeans landed on Canada's Atlantic coast.

CHAPTER TWO

Cultural Transformation: 1580–1653

*T*he Europeans who visited the eastern shores of North America in the sixteenth century did not find the gold, spices, or passage to Asia they were seeking, but they did discover something equally valuable: a rich new source of fish. Portuguese, Basque, and French cod fishermen frequented the Grand Banks in ever-increasing numbers, and trade goods brought by these fishermen began to trickle into the Great Lakes region as early as 1520. Verrazano, Cartier, and other explorers soon followed, their ships' holds stocked with metal goods, combs, mirrors, and glass beads for trade.

No one knows for certain why the peoples of the Americas found such trinkets desirable, but with their arrival the indigenous people in the Great Lakes area revived the long-dormant practice of depositing spiritual goods in graves. One suggestion is that they made sense of the newcomers by situating them in the context provided by their traditional culture. Perceiving Europeans as otherworldly creatures arriving from under the water or beyond the horizon (regions where such beings were traditionally believed to live), the First Peoples may have extended to the baubles these visi-

tors brought the same spiritual value formerly accorded to artifacts of native red copper, crystal, and shell.[1]

The absence of gold soon dampened European enthusiasm for trade and exploration. However, in 1580 consumer demand for felt hats made of beaver fur soared, just as fur supplies from Russia became scarce. The opportunities for trade in fur provided the spur for a renewed push into the interior regions of North America. Before long, the diseases, weaponry, and cultural influences introduced in the course of that push would prove catastrophic for many of the First Nations. Yet those factors had no bearing on either activities or perceptions at the time of first contact; accommodating change was a way of life for the peoples of North America. The significance of the Europeans' arrival can be fully understood only in the context of the long-established patterns of behaviour of the people who lived in and controlled access to the continent on the eve of contact.

By the end of the sixteenth century, three main nodes of Iroquoian settlement had emerged in and around what is now southern

Castor de 26 pouces de longueur entre teste et queue

A beaver—'26 inches from head to tail'—as depicted in *Voyages du Baron de Lahontan dans L'Amérique Septentrionale* (La Haye, 1706). A fashion for felt hats made of beaver fur spurred the development of the fur trade, but Europeans also prized beaver meat for its medicinal properties and as a source of food. The tail was especially sought after: according to Lahontan, its 'flavour and appearance resemble those of the choicest bacon'. National Library of Canada C-099255.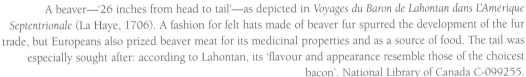

Ontario. At the head of Lake Ontario lived the Neutral people. In what is now northern New York State were the Five Nations Iroquois—a confederacy of the Mohawks, Oneida, Onondaga, Cayuga, and Seneca. Finally, in the region of Georgian Bay, local bands were joined by fellow Hurons, from the Humber and Trent Valley regions above Lake Ontario, whose conflict with Iroquoians from the St Lawrence region had escalated as the latter—now also under attack from Mohawk and Oneida warriors—fled their homes. Together, the formerly separate Huron groups created a community of 20,000 to 30,000 in perhaps 20

villages around the southern corner of Georgian Bay. In the midst of this turbulence, the French under Samuel de Champlain slipped quietly into the recently vacated territory of the St Lawrence Iroquoians and in 1608 established a settlement at Quebec.

When, seven years later, Champlain first travelled to Huronia, he saw a society in the making. After almost a century of upheaval, the Hurons were still struggling to incorporate new arrivals from the south, and political and economic control was highly decentralized. The powers of individual chiefs tended to be narrowly focused in specific military or civil

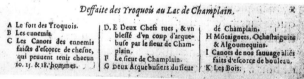

Deffaite des Yroquois au Lac de Champlain.

A Le fort des Yroquois.
B Les ennemis.
C Les Canots des ennemis faiĉts d'efcorce de chefne, qui peuuent tenir chacun 10. 15. & 18. hommes.

D.E Deux Chefs tues, & vn blefé d'vn coup d'arquebufe par le fieur de Champlain.
F Le fieur de Champlain.
G Deux Arquebufiers du fieur

de Champlain.
H Môtaignets, Ochaſtaiguins & Algoumequins.
I Canots de nos fauuage aliés faits d'efcorce de bouleau,
K Les Bois.

The Battle of Lake Champlain, July 1609, from Champlain's *Voyages* (1613). Like many European representations of life in the 'New World', this famous illustration of Iroquois warriors' first recorded encounter with firearms is quite inaccurate. The hammocks in the enclosed compound (not to mention the palm trees beyond) belong in Latin America—and Iroquois did not fight in the nude. Nor did they use what appear to be French river boats. CMC J10225.

functions. Because governance required consensus, and no single chief held suzerainty, the accord that Champlain offered had to be affirmed by every chief in the Confederacy.

As late as 1641, there were only 356 French in the area of Quebec, and in the early years they depended on the indigenous people's know-how, labour, and trading links to obtain furs.[2] Communication was facilitated by the practice of sending French traders to live with various bands, just as Algonkians such as the Nipissing and Ottawa had sent representatives to learn the language and customs of their Iroquoian trading partners. The first such intermediary, a young servant of Champlain's named Étienne Brûlé arrived in

Huronia in 1615. Like the Nipissing and Ottawa traders before him, Brûlé adopted his hosts' customs, including their language, thus acknowledging the Hurons' superiority in the relationship.

Traditionally, the Hurons had supplied more northern groups with corn and other crops in return for copper, fur, and fish. Well before the mid-1630s, however, they began trading directly with the French at Quebec—exchanging furs for goods such as cloth, knives, metal cooking utensils, and guns—and paying tolls to various Algonkian tribes, especially the Kichespirini of the Ottawa River. Like other Algonkians such as the Nipissing and Crees of the northwest, the Kichespirini did not deal directly with Europeans, but traded furs to the Hurons for corn and some European goods. Believing that dead animals, if treated properly, would return to life, the Nipissing and Ottawa inevitably depleted their local fur-bearing populations and as a result were forced to become intermediaries in the fur trade, drawn into the developing trade network of the more northerly Crees.

Occupying more than 4000 square kilometres around the western end of Lake Ontario, the Neutral people numbered roughly 40,000 and lived in perhaps 40 settlements of varying sizes. Their political system appears to have been more centralized than that of either the Hurons or the Five Nations, with civil and military affairs more completely in the hands of one leader, and grave goods from their burial sites suggest that specific individuals were particularly privileged. In fact, these sites are quite similar to the Rice Lake mounds, with sub-floor chambers and piles of disarticulated skeletons.

Like the Hurons, the Neutral controlled a strategic point along an axis of European-oriented trade. Among the many glass trade beads and assorted European metal goods found in Neutral burial grounds are some items that could only have come from the south.[3] This alternative to the usual east–west trade flow enabled the Neutral to keep both the Five Nations and the Hurons at arm's length in the early contact period. At the same time, their neutral position enabled them both to take advantage of trade from the east and to benefit from the Huron–Five Nations conflict.

Continual warfare with the Five Nations made it difficult for the Hurons to trade with any southerly tribes, while the Hurons' increasingly close alliance with the French made it difficult for the Five Nations to obtain French goods. Doubtless exacting some form of toll for the service, the Neutral granted both the Hurons and Five Nations asylum on Neutral territory, allowing them to conduct trade in a neutral zone. And, just as the Hurons linked the northern Nipissing and, through them, subarctic hunter-gatherers to European trading zones, the Neutral may have linked the Petun, the more northwesterly Ottawa tribes, and other subarctic hunter-gatherers.

Among the Five Nations, the Mohawks in particular made many attempts to wrest control of the French trade from the Hurons, but they were continually thwarted. When Dutch traders arrived in the upper Hudson River valley in 1614, the Mohawks moved quickly to establish a relationship with them; as a result, Mohawk pressure on French-Huron trading routes relaxed. However, the Dutch presence exacerbated rivalries within the Five Nations

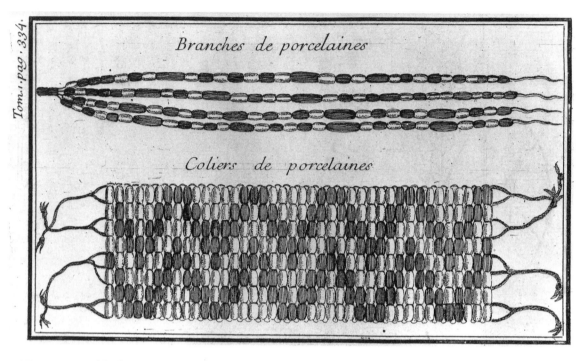

Wampum served both as a medium of exchange and as a record of transactions such as treaties. To the traditional seashells, Aboriginal peoples gradually added glass, tin, and lead beads acquired through trade. NAC C10891.

confederacy. Resenting the Mohawks' control of the new trade, the Onondaga attempted to bypass both the Mohawks and the Dutch and establish direct trade links with the French, but with little success.[4]

In effect, even though European trading posts were hemmed in, and European traders were able to operate only with the permission of Aboriginal groups, the European presence anchored the Native trading system[5] and led to a more focused, regularized, and dramatically increased distribution of goods—and to better-defined relationships, friendly and unfriendly alike. By the 1630s, many of the peoples situated along the corridors of trade had begun to appreciate European goods for utilitarian as

well as spiritual reasons. Desire for these goods encouraged the intensification of inter-tribal relations, increased pressure on local ecosystems, sparked the evolution of more sharply graded social structures, and in some cases promoted the gradual emergence of more centralized political systems.

Yet Europeans did not control the winds of change sweeping the Great Lakes region in these years. In the early contact era, the Europeans had yet to establish their hegemony, and Native societies dealt with European inputs on their own terms. The First Peoples were confronting 'a change in the processes of change, not the beginning of change'[6]—a change that came from the complex interplay of Native cultural traditions, inter-tribal rivalries, and the specific relations that each group developed with particular European powers.

There is heated debate as to when European-introduced disease first ravaged the peoples living around the Great Lakes. Archaeological evidence dates the first epidemics in the region to the mid-1630s, long after initial contacts had occurred. Why did infection take so long to arrive? One answer may be found in the fact that, before the 1630s, few children travelled to New France. Both smallpox and measles were more likely to be fatal to adults than to children. On a ship without many children to serve as carriers, therefore, such infection might well run its course during the Atlantic crossing. In June 1634, one of the first vessels carrying a large number of young families with children arrived in Quebec City; soon the Montagnais contracted measles and transmitted it to Huron traders in the vicinity. The disease raged through Huronia and was followed several years later by a series of virulent smallpox epidemics.[7]

The 'scythe of infectious disease' swept through the Five Nations, Hurons, Petun, Neutral, and Nipissing, with devastating effects. Experiencing a death rate possibly double that experienced by Europeans during the infamous Black Death of the fourteenth century, affected populations declined by up to 60 per cent and more in a period of five to eight years. These plagues knew no favourites. All peoples along the major trading corridors were affected relatively equally. Yet by 1653, the Neutral, Petun, and Huron populations had been largely wiped out, and their territories had been taken over not by the immune

About every 15 years, a Huron village would celebrate the Feast of the Dead. The bones of those who had died since the last feast were disinterred and, following a night of ceremonies and gift-giving, deposited in a common pit, probably symbolizing community solidarity. At the same time, the feast served to reinforce trading relationships with other groups (Algonkians and Europeans were often invited as guests) and to demonstrate, via gift-giving, status within Huronia. NAC C147966.

disease-carriers, the French and Dutch, but rather by the Five Nations from south of the lake. Disease alone cannot account for this radical change in inter-tribal affairs. Also instrumental was what the different European trading powers brought with them, in addition to disease: missionaries in the case of the

Huron converts at prayer; detail from a 1657 map of New France (see p. 22). Although the numbers of converts increased over time, the majority of Hurons never accepted Christianity. NAC C71502.

French, muskets in the case of the English and Dutch.

Récollet missionaries reached Huronia in 1615 and were followed by Jesuits, who arrived in New France in 1626. Both orders believed that the North American peoples could not be Christianized without a more general indoctrination into French culture. However, their approaches were radically different. The more dogmatic Récollets made no effort to learn the local languages and generally lived apart from the people they hoped to convert, whereas the Jesuits actively participated in community life. In general, the latter were more successful.

In 1634, a small group of Jesuits led by Jean de Brébeuf set up a permanent presence in Huronia. By 1639 they numbered 13, and under a new superior, Jérôme Lalemant, they began the construction of a large mission centre, Sainte-Marie-aux-Hurons. Lalemant also introduced *donnés,* men who gave their lives to the Church without taking its vows; these lay assistants soon outnumbered the missionaries.

Smaller missions of shorter duration were established among the Petun, Nipissing, and Chippewa, and in 1640 a brief visit was made to the Neutral.

Initially, the Hurons accepted the Jesuit presence as a reaffirmation of the French-Huron trading relationship. By 1646, the Jesuits counted as many as 500 converts; in 1648, with Huronia under increased siege from the Five Nations, 2,700 Hurons were baptized. But the Jesuits failed to appreciate the extent to which the Hurons' society was integrated with their traditional religion. Christianity challenged not only the Hurons' spiritual beliefs but their whole social and political order; to accept it, according to one Huron chief, would amount to 'overthrowing the country'.[8]

In the Huron universe, good and evil spirits were constants: neither would ever triumph, and humans did not expect to move towards a state of perfection. Balance with nature was the goal, and human regard for the spiritual well-being of animals, rocks, and trees was expressed in a complex system of taboos governing conduct vis-à-vis the natural world and designed to propitiate the good and evil spirits inherent in all matter.

The same cosmology underlay Huron social relationships. Children were not physically punished, scolded, or disciplined: they were indulged—or, from the Jesuit perspective, spoiled. 'The Savages love their children above all things,' one Jesuit reported; 'They are like the Monkeys—they choke them by embracing them too closely.' To foster 'self-reliance rather than obedience, the self-directed warrior rather than the other-directed soldier', Huron children were given the free-

dom to experiment. In the same way, they grew to appreciate the importance of cooperation and respect for others, and to see how balance and harmony were attained through generosity and sharing—and disrupted by personal acquisitiveness. The primacy of community over self also informed the Huron judicial system. Reparations for wrongdoing became the responsibility not simply of the individual but of his or her kin and clan.[9]

In the Jesuit cosmology, by contrast, balance had no part. Eradication of evil required total submission to God, and vigilant control of the natural world. Education must be formally structured and policed, justice strict, and punishment severe. Children had to learn to obey. The family should be a microcosm of the ideal hierarchical society. Like capitalism—the other ideology driving European expansion—Christianity stressed obedience and regimentation. And just as humans could manipulate and control other humans, so they could manipulate and control the natural world.

The social independence of Huron women astonished and dismayed the missionaries. 'The women have great power here,' one missionary noted. 'A man may promise you something, and, if he does not keep his promise, he thinks that he is sufficiently excused when he tells you his wife did not wish to do it. I told him then that he was the master, and that in France women do not rule their husbands.'[10] The Jesuits worked hard to strengthen family units by abolishing the Huron women's rights to premarital sex and easy access to divorce and remarriage. Even during the 1640s, however, when the conversion rate increased, women resisted, making life as miserable as they could for the men who did convert. As one Jesuit reported of a male convert:

> *They [the women] drove him away from their cabins, and refused to give him anything to eat; they reproached him with the death of one of his nieces, who had been baptized. He was left without the means of support, and was compelled to do what is usually the work of women. He was mocked at, and spurned from every company: and quarrels were picked with him. If at any time he was invited to a feast, some insolent persons present would call out that he should not have been invited, because he was a Christian, and because he brought misfortune where ever he went; then he might certainly make up his mind to die sooner than he expected; and that he would be clubbed to death as a Sorcerer.[11]*

If the Jesuits failed to subordinate Huron women, however, they succeeded in sowing discord throughout Huronia. Joseph Chihoatenhwa, an active proselytizer who was one of the first Hurons to be 'struck with water' (baptized), quite possibly became the first Christian martyr in Huronia when, in 1640, he was ambushed and murdered, most likely by fellow Hurons.[12]

Because traditional religion permeated all aspects of Huron society, Christian converts could no longer participate in the most important activities of community life: governmental affairs, fighting, hunting, and religious ceremonies such as the Feast of the Dead. All these, and many other functions, entailed observances deemed invalid and savage by Christian teaching. As converts were won, there emerged within Huronia a significant minority whose beliefs were at odds with those of the community at large.

The epidemics that crippled Huronia in the years after 1634 cut heavily into the very young (the warriors of the future) and the very old (the traditional leaders). By stripping Huronia of its leadership, they contributed to the erosion of religious, social, and political beliefs. Disease reinforced a widening split in Huronia between those who saw missionaries as agents of death—Why, many Hurons wondered, did so many people die so soon after being baptized?—and those who saw in the missionaries and their links to the French their best hope to continue trade and protect their homeland from the escalating attacks of the Five Nations. To encourage conversion, the French granted Christians preferential trading rights and withheld muskets from all non-Christians.

The Dutch were less interested than the French and British in colonization and evangelization: they viewed the New World as a business. Active, like the other imperial powers, in the Grand Banks fisheries, the Dutch explored more southerly routes to the interior and in 1614 set up a trading post on the Hudson River near what is now Albany. In the 1620s, the Dutch West India Company obtained a monopoly of the region's fur trade, and after the Mohawks pushed the Mohicans to the east of the Hudson River, the company obtained all its fur from the Mohawks. At first the Dutch were wary of trading arms, but by the late 1630s independent Dutch and English traders were supplying muskets to the Mohawks, and soon the Dutch West India Company itself began to sell guns. By 1648 the Mohawks had at least 800 guns, and the Seneca likely had several hundred. In contrast, the French were reluctant to sell guns, even to Christian converts, for fear of endangering Jesuit missionaries;[13] as a consequence, the Hurons had only 120 French guns, lighter than and inferior to those supplied to the Iroquois by the Dutch.

But guns did not cause the wars that the Iroquois won: depopulation did. In the 1640s and 1650s, the main objectives of Five Nations warfare were people, not pelts. Traditional Iroquoian warfare has been aptly described as 'mourning war': in order to avenge a death, enemy captives were required for ritual torture, regardless of whether that enemy had been responsible for the death. Not all captives were tortured and killed; some were adopted to fill the place of the deceased within the Iroquois family, clan, and tribe. In this way, the spiritual power of the deceased was replaced, and the nation maintained its collective strength while simultaneously weakening the collective spiritual and physical strength of its enemies.

As a result of the demographic crisis caused by the epidemics of the 1630s and 1640s, warfare escalated to levels unprecedented in the post-contact period. The first large raids undertaken by the Seneca against the Hurons were launched immediately following what appears to have been the first epidemic among the former. The Neutral also engaged in massive war after epidemics; one raid on the Fire Nation of northern Michigan resulted in the capture of between 800 and 1,000 women and warriors, most of whom were adopted by the disease-ravaged Neutral. Beginning in the late 1630s, the Five Nations Confederacy became the aggressor in these wars. In only five of 36 documented raids on Algonkian and Huron groups in the decade

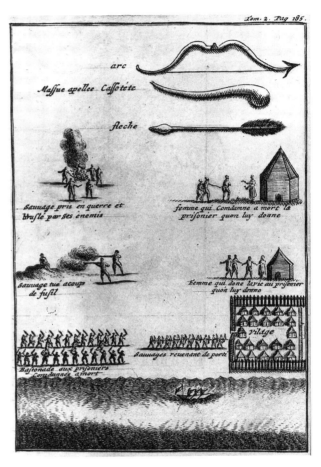

Aspects of Iroquois warfare, early eighteenth century. At the top, the weapon between the bow and arrow is a club called a cassetête. On the left are scenes from the battlefield, with warriors being burned and shot. On the right, women determine the fate of the prisoners given to them: the first is condemned to death, the second is spared (perhaps to be adopted). At the bottom, three condemned prisoners run the gauntlet, and members of a war party return to their village (note the regularity of the village layout depicted here, reflecting European notions of order). NAC C99243.

following 1639 did the Iroquois take fur and goods back to their homeland; instead, they returned home with captives.[14]

Hurons became increasingly reluctant to

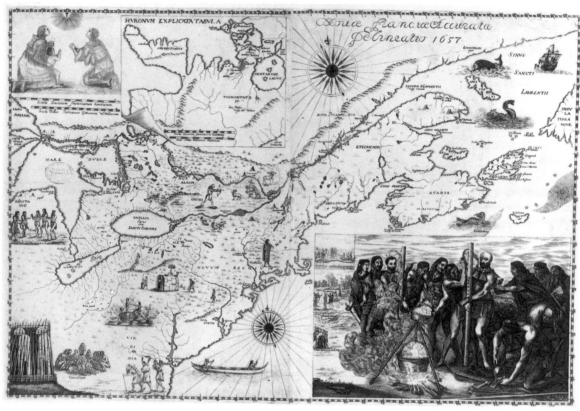

'Novae Franciae Accurata Delineatio', 1657. At the bottom right is an early depiction of the martyrdom of Fathers Jean de Brébeuf and Gabriel Lalemant, two of the five Jesuits based at the mission of Sainte-Marie-aux-Hurons who were killed in the course of the Iroquois invasion of Huronia, 1648–9. Although it was the Iroquois who captured the priests, adopted Hurons fighting on their side were the most active participants in the ensuing torture. All five priests were canonized in 1930. NAC C116786.

make the dangerous journey to the St Lawrence; the raids had effectively cut off the French from their allies in the fur trade. When the French moved inland, establishing Montreal and constructing a fort on the Richelieu River in 1642, the Mohawks escalated their attacks. In 1646, in an effort to mollify them, the French gave the Mohawks permission to hunt in new areas north of the St Lawrence, along with secret assurances that they would do nothing to protect non-

Christian Algonkians living or hunting in those areas. Meanwhile, within Huronia, traditionalists sensed the ambivalent nature of French support for their people; some defected to the Iroquois, but many more were captured by Iroquois warriors.

Strained to the breaking point by disease, social breakdown, cold winters, and poor harvests, Huronia collapsed in the face of a series of well-prepared Iroquoian attacks. In the spring of 1649, armed with muskets and iron hatchets, 1,200 Iroquois overwhelmed two central villages, killing or taking captive some 380 Hurons.[15] That summer, French traders swooped into Huronia and returned to the St Lawrence with some 5,000 pounds (well over 2000 kilograms) of beaver fur. By winter the remaining Hurons were disinterring their dead to strip them of the robes they had been buried in; but still many froze. Just before the final, devastating Iroquois attack, the Jesuit priest Bressani recorded this plea from one of the Huron chiefs:

Brother, thine eyes deceive thee when thou lookest at us; Thou thinkest that thou seest living men, and we are nothing but ghosts, and souls of the dead. This Land which Thou treadest is not solid; it will open very soon to swallow us. . . . Thou must save the remains of this ruined country. Take us into thy hands, thou who sayest that thou bearest us in thy heart. Thou hast seen more than 20 thousand of us dead at thy feet; if thou wait a little longer, not one of us will be left to thee; and vainly thou wilt grieve for not having saved at least what thou couldst. It is not necessary to deliberate longer; it is necessary to depart.[16]

The following spring, the surviving French missionaries appeared in Montreal with 300 'sad relics of a nation once so numerous'.[17] Other small groups of Hurons fled west, where they joined a multitude of refugees from other bands.

The Petun and Nipissing peoples suffered similar fates. Nor did Neutralia escape: weakened by disease and unpredictable growing seasons, and exhausted by a long military campaign against Algonkians in the northern

Mary McKee, Huron, Anderdon, Essex County, 1916. In the course of the Iroquois tribes' territorial expansion, the Neutral and Erie peoples were completely wiped out, but a small number of Hurons survived. Some regrouped at Lorette, Quebec; others joined Ojibwa in the upper country. Eventually some of their descendants made their way to southwestern Ontario, where Mary McKee was photographed. Others went as far as modern-day Oklahoma. CMC 19946.

Michigan region, the Neutrals possessed few firearms, and their central chief, Tsouharissen, had recently died with no succession arranged. In 1651, more than a thousand Iroquois razed a central Neutral village, killing young and old and taking women as captive adoptees.[18] By 1653, the Neutral people were no more. The land that would become south-central Ontario had become the preserve of the Five Nations Iroquois.

CHAPTER THREE

Contested Terrain and Cultural Mixing: 1653–1763

$\mathcal{T}$he mid-seventeenth century marks a turning point for the peoples north of the Great Lakes. Before then, they controlled events in the 'upper country'—the *pays d'en haut*. A century later they would have lost much—though not all—of their independence. Yet this period was not one simply of Native loss and European gain. 'Contact,' as historian Richard White has noted, 'was not a battle of primal forces in which only one could survive. Something new could appear.'[1]

By the early 1650s, the position of the Five Nations Iroquois seemed unassailable. The Hurons, Petun, Neutral, and Erie had all been forced from their homelands. Ten years later, the French explorer Pierre-Esprit Radisson encountered small, starving bands of Huron-Petun who had been driven to eat their children's beaver-skin diapers, which had been 'beshit above a hundred times'. As Five Nations raids continued, the desperate remnants of hitherto separate peoples clustered together, but longstanding rivalries, diverse traditions, and conflicting territorial claims impeded united action by the refugees.

Nevertheless, some durable new political alliances were forged. Among them was the union of some 20 bands from three Algonkian nations—the Mississauga, Saulteaux, and Chippewa. Pushed from their traditional lands between the north shore of Lake Huron and the eastern end of Lake Superior, they congregated in what is now northern Michigan, to become the people known in Canada as the Ojibwa, in the US as the Chippewa, and among themselves as the Anishnabe. The Ojibwa were members of the Algonkian confederacy known as the Three Fires, which also included the Ottawa and the Potawatomi (who inhabited what is now southwestern Michigan).

The scale of conquest stretched the fabric of Iroquois society. In the past, when the Iroquois had taken captives to replace lost warriors, these individuals had usually been assimilated quite successfully. By 1650, however, the Five Nations were capturing entire villages of Huron, Erie, and Neutral people. These groups of captives were required to assist the Five Nations in war and other external affairs, but they were often allowed to live apart from their 'hosts', maintaining their social and political distinctiveness. By 1657 the number of new-

Site of early Iroquois–Ojibwa warfare. This photograph, taken in northern Ontario in 1959, shows a depression in the soil believed to be a pit where Iroquois once hid to ambush Ojibwa. John MacFie photo. AO C330-6-0-0-30.

comers was so large that one Jesuit claimed 'more Foreigners than Natives of the country' lived within the Confederacy; a few years later, another characterized the Five Nations Iroquois as 'only aggregations of different tribes whom they have conquered'. Many of the adopted Hurons were Christians, and by the mid-1650s French missionaries began to direct their proselytizing at the Five Nations. As in Huronia 20 years earlier, the introduction of Christianity undermined traditional beliefs and political structures. Schisms developed in the Confederacy, and it grew difficult for the Five Nations to reach consensus.[2] Meanwhile, with the Hurons ousted, the Ottawa, Ojibwa, and Nipissing all vied with the Five Nations

Iroquois for the role of intermediary in trade with the French. In 1654, 120 Ottawa, Ojibwa, and expatriate Huron traders managed to evade the Iroquois and reach Quebec; two years later, double that number succeeded. Despite Iroquois harassment, Nipissing traders persisted in their arduous journeys to link the Crees in the north with the French in Montreal and Trois-Rivières.

The motivation of these traders was as much political as mercantile; at Montreal, trade fairs began with the traditional Algonkian ceremony celebrating alliances and reciprocity, symbolized by the exchange of goods. Thus, for the Five Nations Iroquois, direct contact between the emerging refugee nations and New France represented both an economic and military threat. The southern lands were conquered, but the land north of Huronia remained contested.

By the early 1660s, the Five Nations had been defeated more than once in fights with allied groups of Nipissing, Ottawa, and Ojibwa. Overshadowing these setbacks were more severe losses to the Susquehanna, long-time foes to the south, and the increasing aggression of the Mohicans and Algonkians to the east. The Five Nations were waging war on three fronts. They no longer enjoyed armament superiority over their southern and eastern foes and, thanks to French trade, were steadily losing that advantage in the northern arena as well; in 1662, Ojibwa armed with muskets wiped out a war party of a hundred Five Nations Iroquois near Lake Huron. Around the same time the new king of France, Louis XIV, dispatched a thousand well-trained troops with orders to subdue the Iroquois, who were already weakened by a series of

Pictograph at Agawa Rock, Lake Superior. The Ojibwa first acquired horses—some 400 to 500 of them—as part of the plunder at the battle of Fort Duquesne in 1755. Photo Andrew Leyerle.

Coke Smyth, 'Indians Bartering', *c.* 1840, lithograph. In the early and mid-1700s, European articles of clothing were the goods most in demand from French traders at Michilimackinac, far surpassing hunting equipment such as rifles and flints. This painting suggests that some First Nations women may have played an active role as traders themselves, perhaps exchanging food-stuffs for clothing. NGC 30197.12.

Canada Post stamp, 1986. Molly Brant, the sister of Joseph Brant, played an important role in the American Revolutionary War as a liaison between the British and the Mohawks. In her later years she lived in Kingston, in accommodations provided by the British in recognition of her assistance and in compensation for the loss of her palatial residence in New York, where she had lived as the consort of Sir William Johnson. Women made up a third of all Loyalists, but more than half of all Mohawk Loyalists, suggesting that many Mohawk men died in the war. Canada Post Corporation; reproduced with permission.

James Peachey, 'A View of the Ruins of the Fort at Cataraqui', 1783. Fort Frontenac was sacked by the British during the Seven Years War. In the summer of 1783, having decided to rebuild the fort and settle the area with Loyalists, Governor Haldimand acquired land from an aged Mississauga chief named Mynass in return for a promise that the chief's family would be clothed during his lifetime. Artist James Peachey was an officer in the 60th Regiment. NAC C2031.

James Peachey, 'Encampment of the Loyalists at Johnston. . .', 6 June 1784. In March 1784 Sir John Johnson, the son of Sir William Johnson, arrived at Johnstown (now Cornwall) seeking areas to settle. He was confronted by local Mississauga who claimed the land as theirs. Angered, Johnson nevertheless agreed to bargain. An amicable settlement was reached following the intercession of Joseph Brant, who cautioned Johnson 'to use those Indians in an easy manner . . . for many reasons, in the first place, it gives the dam rebels larger mouths for many things against us.' NAC C2001.

Elizabeth Hale, 'York, 1801'. Lots around the waterfront and larger, 100-acre park lots were reserved for the bureaucratic élite in Lieutenant-Governor Simcoe's plans for his newly designated capital. 'You will smile per-haps,' Richard Cartwright confided to a friend, 'when I tell you that even at York a Town Lot is to be granted in the Front Street only on condition that you build a house of not less than 47 Feet Front, two Stories High and after a certain Order of Architecture. . . . it is only in the back Streets and Allies that the Tinkers and Tailors will be allowed to consult their own Taste and Circumstances. . . .' 'Seriously,' he concluded, 'our good Governor is a little wild in his projects' (quoted in Edith Firth, ed., *The Town of York, 1793–1815* [Toronto, 1962], 22). NAC C40137.

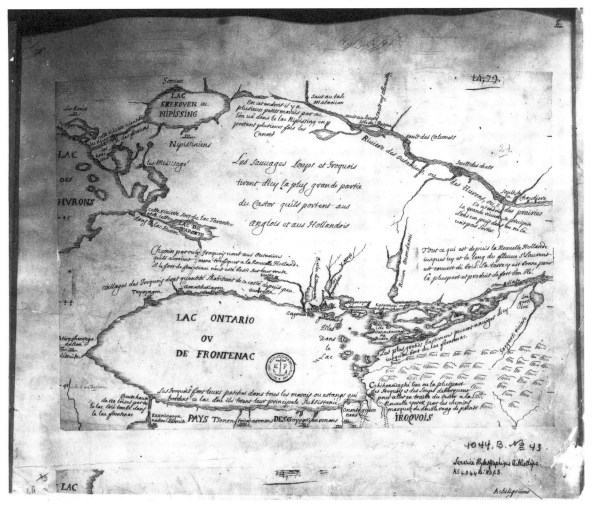

A French map of Iroquois villages north of Lake Ontario, *c.* 1680. As the Iroquois moved into the region, they established villages at the feet of major routes into the northwest fur region: on the portage between the Grand River and Lake Ontario's western end; near the mouths of the Humber, Rouge, Ganaraska, Trent, and Napanee rivers; and on Rice Lake. NAC National Map Collection 6409.

debilitating epidemics. In 1666, the French razed five Mohawk villages and destroyed their food supplies. The Five Nations agreed to a peace treaty.

The Treaty of 1666–7 has generally been seen as a great success for France. Certainly the St Lawrence heartland needed a breathing space. But the Five Nations also benefited by the treaty: it enabled them to concentrate their resources against the Susquehanna and Mohicans; and, because it did not curtail their right to hunt and settle in what is now southern and central Ontario, it gave their conquest de facto recognition, which the Five Nations

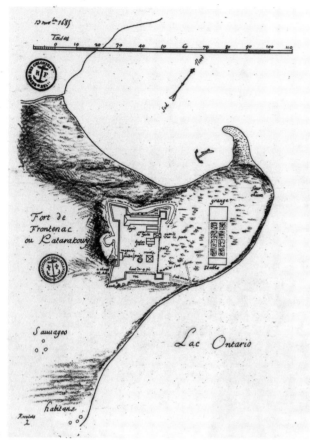

Fort Frontenac, 1685. French traders had great difficulty competing with the English, whose trade goods were of higher quality. Only a few people from the Iroquois Confederacy settled and traded at Fort Frontenac; most stayed closer to the other end of Lake Ontario, maintaining links with the British at Albany. NAC National Map Collection 4755.

were quick to act on. Seven Iroquois villages—bases and toll gates for the trade in furs acquired to the west and north—were soon established along the northern shore of Lake Ontario. By the early 1670s, the Five Nations were well poised to participate in and profit from both the southward flow of fur to Albany and the eastward flow to New France. At the same time, the possibility of establishing a trading relationship with the British, who in 1664 had ousted the Dutch from Albany, encouraged the Iroquois to seek their assistance. Until this time, the Five Nations had fought without allies. But that independence was forever gone: even as the treaty with the French was being finalized, other Iroquois were approaching the British—a people who, as one French observer put it, 'did grasp at all America'.[3]

Emboldened by the peace treaty, the French began planning their first interior trading post. In 1673, accompanied by 400 men, the newly appointed Governor of New France, Louis Buade, Comte de Frontenac, set off for the Cayuga village at the Bay of Quinte. Five Nations emissaries, however, asked to meet at the mouth of the Cataraqui River (the site of modern-day Kingston), where there was no Iroquois village and therefore, they told Frontenac, no risk of favouring any particular tribe within the Confederacy. They neglected to say why there was no settlement at a site that offered easy access to the Ottawa River and the interior: the land was too poor to sustain any sizeable population. Mistaking marsh reeds for meadows, Frontenac announced that a fort bearing his name would be constructed at that spot. Unimpressed, the Iroquois used the British as a bargaining chip and demanded better prices for fur than those offered by the British at Albany.[4] Despite their peace treaty, the French would not dominate events on Lake Ontario's north shore.

Events in the north bring into sharp focus two emerging themes in this period of Ontario's history: European expansion along the fur trade frontier had begun, slowly but inexorably, to limit certain kinds of Native participation in that trade; and French expansion, while still driven to some extent by economic motives, also reflected the political need to keep the British out. In 1670, the Hudson's Bay Company received its royal charter; nine years later it was operating three forts on lower James Bay. The French now faced competition from north and south, and they urgently needed to cultivate and retain Native allies. Keeping a close watch on British activities, they moved inland. As early as 1673, Jesuits at Sault Ste Marie warned that the English at Hudson's Bay were drawing trade away from Lake Superior. By the mid-1680s, English traders from Albany had started doing business close to the French post at Michilimackinac, at the junction of Lakes Michigan and Superior.[5] The French constructed a series of forts designed, as a 1685 map put it, to prevent 'les sauvages' from travelling to 'la Baye de Hudson'.[6]

Having resolved their conflicts with the Susquehanna and Mohicans to the south and east, in 1675 the Five Nations made a final effort to take control of the northern and western fur-bearing regions. Until at least the early 1680s, Iroquois bands roamed freely around southern James Bay. They may even have provided a direct link between the British there and at Albany; a 1699 French map describes a major river in the region as 'the River of the Iroquois', and northeastern oral histories speak of the peoples' great fear of the Iroquois presence. After 1680, French activity in the region became increasingly organized. Pressured by colonial merchants who argued that the economy of New France would be devastated should the British retain control of

'Expedition contre les Iroquois en 1695'. As this late seventeenth-century illustration suggests, most historians of New France accorded the First Nations allies of the French only a supporting role in the victory over the Iroquois. They recognized the allies' contributions as hunters and fur providers, but assumed that all the significant battles were waged by the French. Despite its ethnocentric bias, this perspective has been accepted by most historians of the Iroquois, perhaps because it elevates the Five Nations over other Native peoples: in the end, only the Europeans could subdue them. NAC C30926.

the northern trade, the French government chartered the Compagnie du Nord to trade in the James Bay area.

A series of raids and counter-raids ensued as the French and English fought for control of the forts dotting the lower coast of James Bay. To forestall Iroquois movement north, the French constructed a new fort at Niagara, in Seneca territory, and rebuilt and fortified Fort Frontenac. New France now mounted a series of massive attacks against the Five Nations.

But by the early 1680s, Governor La Barre, heading a flu-ridden fighting contingent of 1,100, accepted a humiliating peace treaty dictated by the Iroquois at Fort Frontenac. His successors Denonville and Frontenac mounted better-organized campaigns in 1687, 1693, and 1696, but the Five Nations were undaunted. Emboldened by the renewal of European hostilities between France and England in 1689, and believing they could now rely on British support and arms, they forced the French to abandon several western posts, including Fort Frontenac, and even attacked Lachine, near the heart of the colony.

Except in a 1693 attack against the Mohawks, the French had concentrated less on fighting than on burning cornfields and destroying villages. Denonville, however, was convinced that the Iroquois would simply regroup and resettle the vacated areas. He therefore encouraged the Ojibwa, some 400 of whom had participated in the 1687 campaign (and who ridiculed the notion of attacking cornfields rather than Iroquois), to stay in the south and keep up the military pressure on the Five Nations.

In this period, neither the Ojibwa nor the Ottawa were dependent on the French. They also fought against tribes, such as the Miami and Sioux, with whom the French wished closer relations. They entered into diplomatic negotiations with the Iroquois at various times. Whenever possible they traded with the British. They arranged tithes, marriages, gift exchanges, and war alliances without consulting the French. And both Ottawa and Ojibwa attempted to block other nations from direct contact with the post at Michilimackinac, where they supplied the French with food and canoes, continued to trade in furs, and, as the French complained, made 'a profit on everything'.[7]

Well before the 1680s, French traders, called *coureurs de bois*, had replaced the Ojibwa and Ottawa as intermediaries in the fur trade, but not all French traders did business with other interior peoples. Rather, many provided the Ojibwa and their allies with a form of home delivery, sparing them the long and often dangerous trip to Montreal. Even when the *coureurs de bois* bypassed the Ojibwa and dealt directly with the Crees, the Ojibwa profited, by charging tolls to traders who passed through their territory.

By the late 1680s, however, demand for fur was declining and there was a glut on the French market. In 1696, the French government ordered that the fur trade cease and all interior posts be abandoned. Although some *coureurs de bois* continued in the interior along with missionaries, and a trading depot remained at Fort Frontenac, the fur trade was severely curtailed. The western suppliers were not pleased. If 'the French come to visit us no more,' one angry Native leader warned, 'you shall never see us again.' One option was to accept Denonville's request to move south and fight the Iroquois.[8] Those who accepted the proposal were motivated in part by the desire for revenge and conquest. But they also had another reason. By now, the British-controlled fur trade operating out of Albany via the Five Nations looked more promising than the declining French trade out of Montreal. Anyone who hoped to benefit from it, however, would have to get the Iroquois out of the way. In effect, the Ojibwa and Ottawa accepted French musketry in order to facilitate a trading

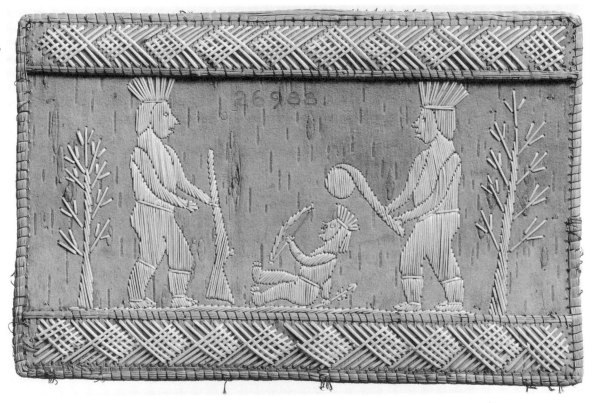

Around 1900, on a porcupine quillwork box, an Ojibwa artist re-created from memory a rock painting from Quarry Point, Lake Couchiching, depicting an Iroquois warrior surrounded by two victorious Ojibwa following the final battle that pushed the Iroquois invaders out of Ontario. Ojibwa oral history speaks of bloody and brutal battles with the Iroquois—one with the grisly name of Battle of Skull Mound—at times involving more than a thousand warriors on one side or the other. With permission of the Royal Ontario Museum © ROM 78ETH62 NS26988.

and diplomatic alliance with France's enemy. The Three Fires—a confederacy of the Ottawa, Ojibwa, and Potawatomi (who inhabited what is now southwestern Michigan)—and some Hurons massed in the Georgian Bay area. By the late 1690s, the Ojibwa had pushed the Five Nations completely south of Lake Ontario. Vanquished, the Iroquois sought peace.

In 1697, the Treaty of Ryswick ended French-English hostilities in Europe. In 1701, at Montreal, a colonial peace was concluded between the French, 200 representatives of the Five Nations, and more than 700 representatives of the Three Fires and other western nations.

Without the support of Kondiaronk, a widely respected Huron-Petun leader, this meeting would never have taken place; despite the outbreak of an epidemic that would soon take his own life, Kondiaronk persuaded many upper-country nations to travel to Montreal. But the negotiations had fallen into disarray,

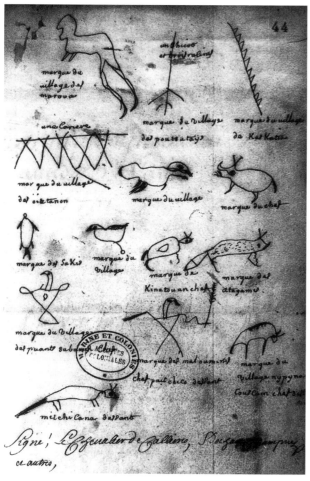

The Treaty of 1701. These are the totemic marks of some of the many chiefs—from the Five Nations, the Ottawa and Ojibwa, and other western nations—who signed the peace treaty with the French, ending the Iroquois wars. NAC C137798.

and Kondiaronk (who had been on the verge of leaving Montreal in disgust) lay dying. Seizing the moment, the French gave Kondiaronk the equivalent of a state funeral: a regal procession, including the Governor General, Ottawa and Huron-Petun chiefs, French soldiers and clergy, and Huron war-

riors, that seemed to symbolize both respect for Kondiaronk and the essential unity of the interests served by the French–Huron relationship—a relationship that the French hoped to extend to the peoples of the upper country. The peace negotiations continued.

Before the gathering, the Ojibwa and Iroquois had agreed to cease fighting, in return for which the victorious Ojibwa were awarded an open path to trade at Albany and control of the hunting territory north of Lake Ontario. But the Iroquois painted the agreement as a victory for themselves. Even as members of the Five Nations negotiated at Montreal, other Iroquois were conferring with the British at Albany. There, in return for British protection, they ceded to the British land north and west of Lake Ontario—land they did not and could not possess. This arrangement enabled the British to maintain two legal fictions: that the Iroquois controlled the northern hunting region, and that the British too enjoyed some sort of proprietary rights there.

The French were unaware of these other agreements. Although they were, thanks to the Ojibwa, in a position to dictate to the Five Nations, the French did not want a draconian peace. They wanted Iroquois–Three Fires enmity to continue, and by elevating themselves to the role of guarantor of peace and mediator of last resort (their fortunes had always rested less on military might than ability to conciliate), they hoped to kindle the fire while preventing a conflagration.[9]

Within a year, however, as the War of the Spanish Succession began in Europe, French hopes for the Great Lakes region were rapidly fading. Of course, France had never controlled the area. Her small trading posts had been allowed on Native land only in return for presents—a form of rent payable annually—and traders regularly paid for permission to traverse the territory. The closure of the fur trade, withdrawal from interior posts, and end of present-giving, along with the cessation of the brandy trade in 1702, stripped from the French the tools they required to mediate in the interior.

The establishment of a post at Detroit in 1701 succeeded only in bringing more Ottawa and Ojibwa farther south and thus within closer reach of British trade. Plots between the British and Iroquois and the Iroquois and Ottawa to attack the French became commonplace.[10] The Treaty of Utrecht, which ended the European war in 1713, made matters worse for France. Not only did it appear to cede Hudson's Bay to the British, but Clause 15 recognized British suzerainty over the Five Nations and forbade French 'Hindrance or Molestation' of them or any of their friends. The treaty also gave the region's First Peoples freedom to trade with whomever they wished—as the Ojibwa and Ottawa were doing in any case—even as it opened the interior to British expansion. And expand the British did.

The Iroquois were the first casualties of the new European rapprochement. In 1714 and 1715, British traders trekked through Five Nations territory and made direct contact with western tribes. New France responded swiftly. With the market for fur once again on the rise and Louis XIV's colonial policy on the verge of collapse, France reopened many of its interior posts. Yet Albany continued to command a major share of the trade. In 1720, working through a French trader who had been adopted by the Seneca, Governor Vaudreuil craftily gained permission to build a 'manor house'—in reality a French post—at Niagara, a strategic point on the route between the west and Albany. Smaller posts were erected at the location of modern-day Toronto (the terminus of a well-travelled route into the interior), and at Quinte, to the east. The Iroquois could only stand by and watch their role as middlemen disappear when, in 1726, the British responded by building a trading fort at Oswego, on the south shore of Lake Ontario opposite Fort Frontenac.

Desperate, the French resumed the brandy trade, abolished open bidding for monopolies at the forts (a system that had encouraged high prices and sharp trading practices), and allowed trade to be conducted at a loss in order to undercut British competition. The effect was immediate. Montreal merchants hired some 500 *engagés* (*habitants* from New France) to travel and trade in the interior in the 1730s— roughly double the number hired in the 1720s.[11] Population movement, cultural interaction, and fur-trade competition increased, as did Native dependence on European goods.

In response to British competition, a number of Ottawa and Ojibwa moved north and west, displacing some Crees. Encouraged by British traders, coastal Crees began to camp for extended periods near British posts. Known as 'homeguards', they became general provisioners for the British traders. But unlike the French—unlike even the British in the south—the British in the north did not ally with the local people. Nor was an alliance desired by the Crees. The Crees of the interior, called 'uplanders' by the British, maintained a more traditional lifestyle than the homeguards

John Elliott Woolford (1778–1866), 'Point Thessalon, Lake Ontario', 1821, watercolour over graphite. While this image was the work of a later era, it shows the great size of the canoes used by the Ojibwa and, eventually, the voyageurs. In 1725, to enable British traders to reach the north shore of Lake Ontario, the Ojibwa sold them 200 canoes—each 10 metres long and capable of carrying 3 tonnes of trade goods. NGC 23431.

and whenever possible played off not just the French and British but different British traders against one another. The uplanders were primarily hunters; they may also have been intermediaries between the British and bands in the western and southwestern interior. Hudson's Bay men distrusted them, denying them entry to their forts and forcing them to trade through narrow openings in the palisades.

Yet the British traders realized they could not hope to turn a profit without the uplanders' participation. Accordingly, in the customary ceremonies—gift-giving, pipe-smoking, speech-making—conducted prior to trading, the British plied the uplanders with virtually undiluted brandy and enticing gifts. At times, they traded goods at a loss in an attempt to keep the uplanders within the British trading network. The uplanders had long understood the practical value of European trade goods;

more than 60 years earlier, 300 Crees who traded 3,000 pounds of beaver pelts to the British at James Bay had preferred axes, knives, and kettles over beads and trinkets. To the British, the Crees now gave gifts of low-quality furs and other local products, rather than traditional symbolic items. Even as, in the south, trade with the French became more and more a matter of diplomacy, trade in the north took on a more purely commercial character.

The central unit of exchange was the 'Made Beaver' (MB)—one prime beaver pelt—and all other goods, including furs, were assigned a value in MB. Gift-giving, brandy sales, measuring and weighing items, assessment of quality, and translation of value in terms of MB all created opportunities for bargaining and profit-taking. Yet British traders had little room to manoeuvre in trading with uplanders. The Crees had fixed needs. Their society abhorred hoarding. And the carrying capacity of their canoes was limited. Together, these factors worked against the sort of strategies typical of purely market-based exchange systems. Reducing the prices charged for goods would not attract more people bringing more furs. Instead, those coming to trade would bring fewer furs, since their needs could be more easily met—and without straining their carrying capacity. Gifts that could be consumed on the spot, such as alcohol and tobacco, were much more effective in attracting Cree traders.

Nor could the British trade low-quality items or charge higher-than-normal prices. It mattered little to the Crees if the costs of producing goods in England rose or the market for furs declined. If the British traders attempted to adjust prices or quality to reflect market pressures back home or increase overall profits, the uplanders would simply leave and trade with the ever-hovering *coureurs de bois* instead. In the fierce competition for furs in the hinterland, the French had more than held their own, and the Crees remained in close contact with French soldiers and traders at such northern posts as Témiscaming, Abitibi, Michipocoton, and Nipigon, or farther west at Fort St-Charles and a series of smaller tributary posts. They manipulated the French-British competition to their own benefit, extracting higher prices and better trade goods. So did their trading partners.

Trading posts were prime sites for cultural exchange. Relations between the homeguards and British traders were as much social as economic. Although the Hudson's Bay Company officially forbade sexual relations and illicit trade between their employees and the local people, its regulations were widely ignored. After the 1680s, company employees were not allowed to bring European women to the Bay. As a result, the chief trader often took a Cree woman into the post to live as his 'bedfellow'. Lesser traders could entertain Cree women in their quarters during the day, but not overnight. Officially, company servants were denied any contact with women. The incidence of venereal disease suggests that this edict was widely ignored.

The birth of mixed-blood children to women living near the forts was a sign of a more general intermingling and merging of cultures. Fur traders began to use snowshoes and moccasins, and some local people adopted less practical items of European dress; a man named Sakie, at Moose Factory, wore a captain's coat 'laced hat . . . stockings [and] a white shirt'. Hudson's Bay traders conformed to Cree marriage formalities, seeking the permission of the bride's family and presenting them with gifts. On retirement, some traders even took their Cree wives back to Britain with them, and many traders made provisions for their 'country wives' in their wills. As early as 1721, Miscamote, a homeguard leader at Fort Albany, expressed his wish to 'be buried nigh the British', and in 1745, when Sakie died, he was buried 'after the English fashion'.[12] Such willing renunciation of sacred traditional burial practices is testimony to the depth of cultural interaction at the Bay.

Not all Crees worked so closely with the British. A case in point was Esquawenoe, an uplander leader who frequented Moose Factory for two decades. Described as 'the grand politician of all' and a 'sly cunning fox', Esquawenoe was known to trade with the French and had a son who was a prominent trader at French posts. In the late 1750s he was a very old man, but the British authorities' distrust of anyone with French connections had grown to the point where they determined 'to take him into custody'. After four days of incarceration, Esquawenoe hanged himself in his cell.[13] He would not be the last of his people to do so. Intercultural exchange also took place at French posts in the central Great Lakes region. At Michilimackinac, as we have seen, the French depended on the Ojibwa and Ottawa for food, and most who wintered over were engaged in the fur trade. Like the British at the Bay, French fur-trade employees commonly married or lived with Native women. Although missionaries tended to see them as prostitutes who had 'found out that their bodies might serve in lieu of merchandise and

would be still better received than beaver skins', the women were considerably more than sexual objects to their French partners.[14] Some became active traders on their own account. By the 1780s Sarah Ainse, an Oneida who had traded on the north shore of Lake Erie and at Michilimackinac in the mid-1760s, owned two houses in Detroit, as well as four slaves, and had accounts with two Detroit-area merchants totalling more than £5000.[15]

Like the Crees in the north, the Ojibwa and Ottawa women and their Métis offspring (children with European fathers) provided merchants with potentially lucrative links to Native fur traders, while kinship ties enabled French traders to cultivate markets and influence in Native society. Native women helped European traders adapt to life in the interior, teaching them essential skills (such as snowshoeing) and acting as guides and general labourers. Through such liaisons, the women gained access to powerful European traders and prized European goods and increased status within their own societies. Small wonder, then, that between 1698 and 1765 almost half of the marriages recorded at Michilimackinac were between French employees and Native or Métis women. During the same period, roughly 40 per cent of all the children born there had French fathers; the garrison had to expand its walls at least three times before 1763, so quickly did the Métis population grow.[16]

In the first half of the eighteenth century, several hundred Métis plied an unlicensed trade in furs throughout the *pays d'en haut*. Travelling extensively, they aided in exploration: Joseph La France, born in 1707 at Michilimackinac to an Ojibwa mother, jour-

Trading in the upper country, 1673. Despite the fanciful palm tree and exotic marine life, this Dutch illustration depicts an increasingly common occurrence. By 1684, as many as 800 *coureurs de bois* were trading in the interior. NAC C127428.

neyed more than 17,000 miles by foot and canoe between 1723 and 1742, to trade with both the French at Quebec City and the English at Albany.[17]

The peace between the French, Five Nations, and Three Fires in 1701 had ushered in a 'golden age' for the Ojibwa who, by 1736, had established at least five settlements on the north shore of Lake Ontario and numbered some 1,500 people. But the competitive nature of the interior fur trade made common action on the part of the Three Fires Confederacy increasingly difficult. For these people, the war that erupted between France and England in 1744, as part of a general European confrontation over the Austrian Succession, was merely a more violent extension of ongoing trade battles.

As early as 1738, La France had noted that the 'avarice and injustice' of the French had 'disgusted the Natives',[18] and when the British

FORT ROUILLE—1749

French trading post at Fort Rouillé, 1749. Although they had been allied with the French in the wars against the Iroquois, the Ojibwa traded with the British virtually within sight of French posts such as Fort Rouillé, towards the western end of Lake Ontario, at the site of modern-day Toronto. *Canadiana Views*, vol. 1 (n.d.); NAC C14253.

began to block supply shipments from France after 1745, many Ojibwa were quick to transfer their trade. Although the French ultimately prevailed in the colonial theatre of the Succession war, which ended in 1748, many Ojibwa and Ottawa remained with the British. In 1751, some Mississauga reaffirmed an alliance with the Iroquois and thus, symbolically at least, asserted their independence from both European powers. By 1755 the French had effectively recognized Ojibwa independence by marking southern Ontario on their maps as the 'Country of the Missesagues'.

In the struggle between France and England for colonial supremacy, the *pays d'en haut* was only one front. Throughout the late 1740s and early 1750s, British colonists pushed westward, threatening to snap the thin band connecting French Louisiana to French Quebec. Now, for the first time, the English-speaking colonists began to receive significant support from their mother country. Weak in the Atlantic region, France responded as best she could. Europe had come to fight in America: the War of the Conquest had begun.

Both the British and French courted the Ojibwa on the eve of the Seven Years War (1756–63). The French ordered commandants at Niagara, Frontenac, Detroit, and the newly reopened Fort Rouillé to sell goods at British prices, no matter how heavy the loss. Brandy flowed, for as one Ottawa chief acknowledged, the warriors 'love[d] their drink'.[19] Through the Iroquois, the British sent wampum belts to the Ojibwa at Niagara and Fort Rouillé, inviting them to join the war against the French, but for many, an impressive French victory at Fort Duquesne in July 1755 tipped the scales in favour of New France. The plunder taken by the Ojibwa exceeded any they had known: 1,000 rifles, as well as gold, silver, and cloth. Anticipating even more, most Ojibwa sided with the French.

From the French perspective, however, the necessity of providing presents, plunder, food, and drink made the alliance uneasy.[20] Several times the French had to send reinforcements to protect the small Fort Rouillé from pillage at the hands of their presumed allies, the Mississauga. Nor were material goods always enough. As one Ojibwa warrior put it, 'I make war for plunder, scalps, and prisoners.' Following successful battles at Oswego in 1756 and Fort William Henry in 1757, Governor Montcalm of New France was unable to back up his guarantees of safety for British survivors: his Ojibwa allies scalped as many as they could, starting with the wounded in the infirmaries.[21]

For the Ojibwa who fought at Oswego, the victory was pyrrhic. The destruction of the trading post removed a major source of British goods at a time when the flow of French goods had been cut off by a British naval blockade. Far worse, starting in 1755, smallpox spread throughout the Ojibwa peoples. By the time of the victory at William Henry, the disease had

begun to take its toll, and two years later the Ojibwa were too weak to give any support to the French.[22]

At Fort Frontenac, the loss of a huge cache of supplies destined for First Nations allies broke the back of France's accord with the Three Fires. By the time the British moved against Fort Niagara later that year, neither the Ojibwa nor the Iroquois believed it would make any difference to them whether the French or English prevailed; they agreed to stand aside and let the Europeans determine the outcome. France lost the Niagara battle and the next year lost the war. The response of Minevana, an Ojibwa chief, made his people's position clear: 'Englishmen, although you have conquered the French, you have not yet conquered us! We are not your slaves.' Claiming they had been 'wheedled and led on', the Ojibwa sought a working relationship with the British.[23]

But General Jeffrey Amherst, the British commander-in-chief, had no interest in rapprochement. Whereas France had seen the fur trade more as a means of maintaining First Nations support than of making profits, and therefore permitted a decentralized trade with free flows of rum, weapons, and presents, Amherst insisted on rationalizing the enterprise. Against the advice of Sir William Johnson, the Superintendent of Northern Indians, he restricted general trade to garrisoned posts, limited the availability of ammunition, ordered an end to the rum trade, and banned the giving of presents.

The latter in particular was a fateful decision. Presents were payment for the right to cross, camp in, and construct forts on First Nations territory. Presents meant peaceful rela-

General Jeffrey Amherst. Amherst justified the use of brutal means against Native people, including biological warfare, on the grounds that 'Total Extirpation is scarce sufficient Atonement for the Bloody and Inhuman deeds they have Committed.' NAC C117699.

attacks on British forts. Amherst responded brutally. 'Could it not be contrived,' he wrote to his second-in-command in July of that year, 'to Send the *Small Pox* among those Disaffected Tribes of Indians?' In fact, his men anticipated him; they had already broken the siege of Fort Pitt by giving the insurgents 'two Blankets and a Handkerchief out of the Small Pox Hospital'. The district was ravaged by smallpox throughout the spring and summer of 1763.[24]

It is tempting to see Pontiac's campaign as part of an organized war for national self-preservation waged by a unified cultural group. For some participants, especially the southern tribes directly affected by British settlement, it may indeed have been so. For the Ottawa and Ojibwa of the north and northwest, whose homelands were not threatened, plunder and resumption of present-giving were more important. Moreover, some southern Ojibwa, led by a Mississauga named Wabbicommicot, self-styled 'Chief Man North and West upon Lake Ontario and so far upon Lake Erie as ye big [Grand] River', refused to take up arms. Wabbicommicot desired freer trade but counselled peace, and ultimately it was he who in 1765 persuaded Pontiac to lay down his weapons.[25]

For people like Wabbicommicot, Pontiac's war was not one of national significance. What they sought was a fair working relationship. Increasingly desirous of—and, in some cases, dependent on—European goods, they sought rapprochement, not revenge. And in the end, when the British promised to reinstitute trade and present-giving, the Aboriginal people thought that that was what they had won. The British had admitted blame and accepted the consequences. A middle ground could be re-

tions. Presents signified respect between allies. Presents were recompense for past wrongs. An alliance without presents could not be. Already suspicious of British motives and fearing the advance of European settlement on their hunting territories, the western tribes smouldered under Amherst's unaccustomed restraints. After several false starts, Pontiac, an Ottawa chief from the Detroit area, massed support from four different tribes and, in the spring of 1763, launched the first in a series of established. In this sense, the Ojibwa, although weakened, could continue to see themselves, if not as victors, then at least as a proud and unconquered people.

But in fact Pontiac's uprising and its aftermath represented the beginning of the end to peaceful coexistence. No longer could the British take the western Aboriginal peoples, including those north of Lake Ontario, lightly. Now it was imperative that they deal more systematically with the inhabitants of the *pays d'en haut*. In order to maintain control of both the conquered habitants of New France and a restless Aboriginal population, the British devised a policy that laid the foundations for the settlement by Europeans of the region north of the Great Lakes. If Wabbicommicot envisioned a country within which First Peoples and Europeans could coexist, the British envisioned a colony increasingly fixed by finite borders and exclusionist notions of belonging.

CHAPTER FOUR

The 'Men with Hats': 1763–1791

*I*n February 1763 the Treaty of Paris ended the Seven Years War and Britain was able to add New France to the list of its North American holdings: Nova Scotia, Newfoundland, the vast expanse of Hudson's Bay Company land in the northern interior, and the 13 American colonies to the south.

One of Britain's first acts with respect to its new territory was to issue a Royal Proclamation. To forestall the formation of any alliance between the French in Quebec and the First Peoples to the west and south, Britain hived off Quebec by prohibiting any European settlement in the newly delimited 'Indian Territory' and stipulating that Aboriginal land could be sold only to the British government. This gave the Crown firm control over future land and settlement policy while appearing to guarantee the region's First Peoples their independence and traditional rights to land (to this day, the Royal Proclamation of 1763 remains one of the most important bases of Aboriginal title in Canadian law). In addition, imperial administrators hoped that if the growing numbers of American colonists could be prevented from expanding to the west, they could be funnelled

directly into Quebec, whose 75,000 French-speaking inhabitants they would surely outnumber before long.

Except for 25 to 30 farms along the Detroit River, established under the French regime in 1749, the upper country was virtually without European inhabitants. Those who traversed it—usually fur traders—did so with care; to cross Seneca land near Niagara in 1764, the British had to swear that no farming or permanent settlement would take place. However, especially south of the Great Lakes, where agricultural land was richer and more accessible, the Proclamation Line was largely ignored. Tensions mounted between the colonists to the south and the imperial authorities, but the British were prepared to dedicate neither the money nor the troops necessary to prevent westward movement. Rather, they allowed their security in the Great Lakes area to depend on the goodwill of the local First Peoples.

The passage of the Quebec Act in 1774 exacerbated these tensions. Territorially, New France was restored; the new Quebec incorporated the former French lands to the east and the Indian Territory as defined in 1763. This change meant little to the First Peoples of the *pays d'en haut,* who continued under the 'protection' of the British superintendent of Northern Indians. But the southern colonists recognized the Quebec Act as a stratagem for keeping the west out of their control, and they considered it 'intolerable'. A year later, rebellion erupted in Massachusetts. Because Quebec administered the western lands, the Rebels invaded the upper country, only to be repulsed late in 1775. In July 1776, the 13 colonies declared independence.

North of the Great Lakes, the American Revolution represented the first major test of British Native policy since the Pontiac uprising. Retaining control of the military posts in First Nations territory at Carleton Island (off Cataraqui), Niagara, Detroit, and Michilimackinac was crucial. From these posts, garrisons to the west and south could be provisioned, and offensives into New York, Pennsylvania, and the Ohio and Illinois territories could be launched; to them, First Nations allies and British supporters from both the northern and southern regions could be attracted.

Aware that success depended largely on the attitudes of the local peoples, British Commander-in-Chief Guy Carleton and, after 1778, his successor Frederick Haldimand redoubled efforts to provision and offer presents to tribes on the north shore of Lake Ontario and the upper St Lawrence. Similarly, through the Northern Indian Department administered by Sir William Johnson (whose wife Molly Brant was an influential Mohawk), every attempt was made first to guarantee the neutrality and ultimately to win the active support of the Six Nations Iroquois in northern New York (the Tuscarora tribe had joined the

Confederacy in 1722). Although Mississauga at Niagara aided the British in battles to the south, the evidence available suggests that most Mississauga remained aloof from the fray, on occasion even flaunting their independence; in 1780, the 'insolent' Mississauga at Cataraqui forced the military to huddle in their blockaded fort at night.[1]

After the defeat of General Burgoyne and his force of 7,000 regulars at Saratoga, New York, in October 1777, the British shifted their strategy. Henceforth they would rely on guerrilla activity by United Empire Loyalists (around one out of six Americans supported the British—or at least did not support the Rebels) and, whenever possible, Native allies. A corps of Loyalists and Seneca of the Six Nations, raised and commanded by John Butler, staged a series of devastating guerrilla raids out of Niagara. These successes attracted more support for the Loyalists' cause—as did the retaliation they provoked. After an American force of 5,000 swept through the Six Nations territory late in 1779, an equal number of Iroquois retreated to Niagara, swelling the ranks of the 'loyal'.

The offensives waged from the northern posts, although successful, were not sufficient to alter the war's overall course. When the French entered the war on the side of the Americans in 1778, the line of battle was greatly extended, and British resources became correspondingly stretched. Gains made could not be held. To the chagrin of the northern Loyalists, who had won their battles, the British called a halt in April 1782. Fearing retribution from the victors, many Americans who had supported the British trekked north in search of a safe haven.

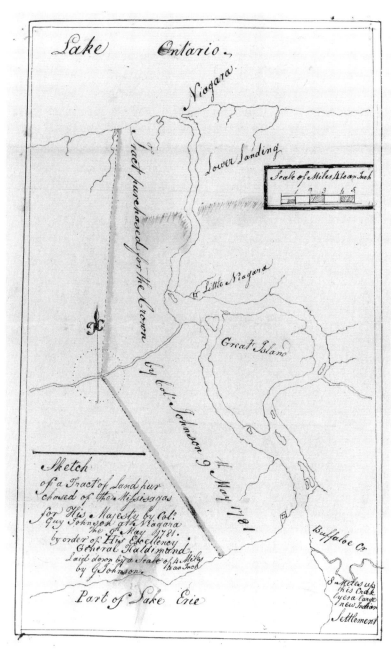

Map of the First Mississauga Land Surrender, 9 May 1781. The British were hard pressed to provision the thousands of Loyalists who had fled north after the American Revolution. Accordingly, Commander-in-Chief Frederick Haldimand ordered the Lake Ontario garrisons to begin growing their own food. Advised that the best agricultural land lay on the west side of the Niagara River, under Mississauga control, in May 1781 the British appropriated 3 million acres of Mississauga land, in exchange for just 300 suits of clothing. AO RG 1-A-1-1, vol. 1, 67.

By the end of the conflict, as many as 100,000 Loyalists had left. Most travelled on to Britain, but some 7,500—of diverse classes, cultures, ethnic backgrounds, and motivations—had settled in the country of the Mississauga, mainly in the Bay of Quinte area. Seen in the context of the region's early history, this forced mingling of people from widely varied backgrounds represented simply one more in a long line of refugee movements in the *pays d'en haut*. 'Strange is the collection of people here,' one visitor observed in 1784.There were farmers from northern New York State, often of German, Irish, or Scots backgrounds; African-American slaves of elite Loyalists; and Iroquois and other Native people who had supported the British. Most Loyalists possessed little wealth or education. Many had arrived in America no more than a decade before. As immigrants, these Loyalists had already been uprooted: what they wanted now was stability and continuity, not rebellion and change.

Under the smokescreen of war the foundations of a colonial society were being laid. Contracts for provisioning and supplying the army and its Native allies offered considerable opportunities for merchants aspiring to better their economic and social positions. But not all candidates had the necessary qualifications. John Butler, for example, was extremely successful in attracting Iroquois support and engineering guerrilla raids, and in 1786 Haldimand considered appointing him superintendent of the Northern Indian Department. In the end, though, he decided that Butler was 'deficient in Education and liberal sentiments'. Several years later John Graves Simcoe, Upper Canada's first lieutenant-governor, would make much the same point, declaring that his administrators should not be of the type 'who kept but one table, that is who dined in Common with their Servants'.[2] The rules were clear for those who knew how to read them. To join the ranks of the elite, whether as a merchant or as a bureaucrat, breeding, respectability, and the proper social bearing were fundamental requirements.

Such requirements excluded most Loyalists and all Native people. In the negotiations leading to the peace settlement of April 1783, Britain's First Nations allies had been completely ignored; in fact, the British had allowed the Americans to take possession of Six Nations lands that the British had never owned. Joseph Brant, the Mohawk spokesman for thousands of Native people stranded near Niagara, was outraged. To show that the British would continue to protect First Nations land (in return for the support of the First Nations in war and trade), Haldimand, now commander-in-chief and governor of Quebec, quickly took control of several western posts in American territory, initiating a dispute with the United States that would continue to simmer until 1794, when Jay's Treaty finally settled it.

Realizing that these forts could not be retained for long, Haldimand offered to find land for all First Nations allies dispossessed of their traditional territories during the Revolutionary War—even though his government had no such land to give. And when many of the Loyalists clustered at makeshift refugee centres in Quebec asked to stay in the upper country rather than move to Cape Breton or Nova Scotia, Haldimand acquiesced.

It remained to find the land. Between 1783

Mary Ann Burges, 'Lt General Simcoe'. John Graves Simcoe was Upper Canada's first lieutenant-governor, from 1791 to 1799, although he spent only four years (1792–6) in the colony. MTRL JRR T34632.

and 1790 Haldimand engineered nine agreements with the Mississauga, Iroquois, and other nations, acquiring for the British state territory spanning from the Upper St Lawrence to Detroit. In 1790 a treaty was signed at Detroit that ceded to Britain a huge tract of land along the north shore of Lake Erie.

In violation of the 1763 Proclamation, which allowed only the state to purchase First Nations land, several military officers and prominent local merchants had already acquired some of the Lake Erie territory from local tribes. The Proclamation had offered protection from 'great frauds and abuses . . . committed in the purchasing of lands of the Indians', and the local chiefs may have understood the new treaty as a similar way of protecting their land from squatting settlers. From the British perspective, however, the treaty extinguished all rights of the First Peoples to the land. The Crown could sell or grant it to whomever it wished, and on all subsequent deeds the totemic symbols of First Nations chiefs were replaced by stamps of British approval. 'The Men with Hats who have come to reside [here],' said one chief, 'always asked for leave to build a House and for a little piece of ground for a garden—But Father, after they had got up their house, they took and fenced in large tracts of Land, contrary to our wishes and intentions.'[3]

Injustice became the trademark of British land deals with the First Nations. Sarah Ainse, the Oneida trader, was one of those who had purchased land on the north shore of Lake Erie, and she had moved there in 1787. When she claimed that the Crown's 1790 purchase did not include her large, well-situated property, almost two dozen local chiefs testified on her behalf. But in 1798, Upper Canada's executive council, influenced by non-Native speculators, denied her claim. She was stripped of all land and received no compensation. Although she persisted as a trader, her fortunes took a downturn thereafter. Local merchants occasionally forgave her accounts, and the Moravian Mission at Fairfield offered her charity at least once. An entry in the Mission's diary for 1803, noting that 'Sally . . . was here this week trading wares for corn,' remarked that she was 'very old'. Nevertheless, she continued to petition for her rights for another 20 years, until her death in 1823. All her efforts were in vain. Merchants, missionaries, and settlers would grant Native people charity but rarely justice, and never equality.[4]

The treaties made with First Nations peoples at this time share several features. The land involved was often defined only in the vaguest of terms. Northern boundaries were determined to be either as far as a person could walk in a day, or as far north as one could hear the sound of a gun fired from the lakeshore. In one case a blank deed was all that 'testified' to the nature of the transaction. In another there was no formal documentary evidence at all, and in still others the evidence was contradictory. When Lieutenant-Governor John Graves Simcoe arrived on the scene in the 1790s and reported this sloppy documentation, in particular the blank deed, his superior (the Governor General at Quebec) cautioned him 'not to press that matter or shew any anxiety about it' since it 'throws us entirely on the good faith of the Indians for just so much land as they are willing to allow.'[5] A corollary to a subsequent agreement seems to have papered over the blank-deed problem. In other cases, however—including one involving the site of Ottawa, Canada's capital—the legal title to the land remains in dispute today.

A second common characteristic of these treaties is that the First Nations received very little for the immense expanses of land they ceded. The Mississauga, for example, in 1784 exchanged 3 million acres of land along the Niagara Peninsula and inland for less than £1,200 worth of gifts. As Haldimand had

Mary Ann Burges, 'Mrs Elizabeth Simcoe'. Elizabeth Posthuma Gwillim, the wife of John Graves Simcoe, was a capable artist herself. Along with her diary, her sketches are a rich source of information about life in the colony. MTRL T31494.

instructed, the British negotiators paid 'the utmost attention to Economy'.

In effect, the Mississauga and eastern Iroquois, rather than the British, paid the costs of rewarding the Loyalists. But why did the Mississauga, who less than a century before had shed blood to acquire this territory (and whose oral tradition exalted those battles), suddenly give it away for so little? A number of explanations have been suggested: the slow and unthreatening rate of European settlement; a lack of unity among the Mississauga compared to 90 years earlier; increasing dependence on and desire for European trade goods; and the fact that negotiations were conducted by military agents from the Indian Department, who were experienced in dealing with Native people and often trusted by them.

None of these factors can be completely discounted. Yet perhaps the best explanation is that the Mississauga and Iroquois did not think that they were giving away their land rights forever. The surviving documents are vague or contradictory even in English; the translations were likely far worse. In the case of the appalling Niagara Peninsula treaty, the interpreters apparently did 'an atrocious job'.[6] Mississauga oral history relating to the Gun Shot Treaty of 1792 is evocative in this regard: '. . . I am astonished. Disappointed. When I remember the promise made by the Govmt. His [Gov. Simcoe's] words were very sweet. At that time he did not give me any writing to hold in my hands but I know all. [Hunting, fishing and trapping rights, were guaranteed to us by treaty], and I never realized anything for it.'[7]

British and Native concepts of ownership were fundamentally at odds. The Mississauga 'owned' land in a communal sense; no particular individual or group could lay exclusive claim to any of it. Although they had had contact with individual European settlers and were aware of the fences around particular properties, any notion of private, freehold tenure was entirely foreign to them. In return for presents, the Mississauga were willing to allow the British a share in the use of the land; by the time they realized what 'ownership'

meant to Europeans, which was not until the 1790s, a great deal of their prime land had already been taken from them—at least as far as the British were concerned.

The British divided even as they conquered. Haldimand had planned for the Six Nations Iroquois to settle near the Bay of Quinte, but the local Mississauga worried about the influx of so many Iroquois, and Joseph Brant, their liaison with the Indian department, wanted to be closer to the Seneca and other western members of the Six Nations. Accordingly, Haldimand granted them a 675,000-acre tract along the Grand River. Unlike their counterparts at Quinte, the Grand River Mississauga had fought with the Iroquois in the Revolutionary War, and—perhaps for that reason—they welcomed the new arrivals. Brant drew his influence from the power of his sister Molly and from his ability to deal with the British Indian department, and not all Iroquois acknowledged him as the sachem of the Mohawk tribe. At least in part because they resented Brant's leadership pretensions, a smaller group of Mohawks under John Deseronto decided to stay at the Bay of Quinte.

It became clear almost immediately that British and Iroquois understandings of the Six Nations land grant diverged widely. As far as the British were concerned, under the provisions of the Royal Proclamation they, not the Six Nations, still controlled all sales, rentals, or other land transactions. Brant disagreed, and within several years he had sold or leased much of the land to non-Native settlers. At issue was whether the Six Nations, by accepting the grant, had become subjects of the Crown, or whether they retained their sovereign independence as allies and were thus free

Elizabeth Simcoe, 'Mohawk Village', 1793. This sketch by Mrs Simcoe gives pride of place to two outposts of civilization: the church on the right and the agent's house on the left. AO F47-11-1-0-109.

to dispose of the land as they wished. This dispute would not be finally decided in law until 1959, when the Six Nations peoples were declared 'loyal subjects.' As one historian put it: 'The first Americans received the dubious distinction of being very belatedly recognized as the last Loyalists.'[8]

It is often assumed that the Loyalists who moved north were a fairly quiescent, apolitical lot. Such was not the view of Governor Haldimand, who was beseiged with petitions for land, construction materials, food, clothing, horses, cows, sheep, arms, and ammunition, on top of the hoes, axes, ploughs, seeds, and clothes provided free of charge. In addition, the British government set up a claims commission through which Loyalists could

seek compensation for goods confiscated by the Rebels. Although only 13 per cent of Loyalists settled in Quebec and the future Ontario, 52 per cent of the claims heard originated from there. Payments of claims, plus half-pay pensions for all officers of Loyalist regiments or their widows, plus the cost of provisions totalled £1 million for the upper country alone.

In addition, of course, the Loyalists received free grants of land. In the spring of 1784, Haldimand opened 13 townships—eight on the St Lawrence River and five west of Kingston—laid out on the strip, or seigneurial, landholding model. Settlers drew lots for the land within each township, with the size of each grant determined by military rank and social position. Unmarried civilians received 50 acres; married enlisted men received 100 acres plus 50 for each family member; field officers received 1,000 acres plus 50 for each family member. Some, like Sir John Johnson, refused to choose by lot and instead appropriated the choicest acreages for themselves and their friends. Generally, however, the lottery principle was honoured—if only because most Loyalists would not have tolerated too blatant a subversion of it.

Distinct religious and ethnic groups—Roman Catholic Highlanders, Scottish Presbyterians, German Calvinists, German Lutherans, and British Anglicans—settled in their own townships. Not all, however, stayed on the land they were allotted; in some townships, as many as two-thirds of the landholders either failed to take up their land or moved within a year. Townships with higher proportions of American-born residents had higher rates of transiency, suggesting that some Loyalists may have moved back to the United States. Nor did all Loyalists conform to Captain Thomas Gummersal Anderson's nostalgic image—'honest, attend[ing] to their own business, . . . kind'. In 1787 Hugh Gallagher, married with a young son, lost his allotment in the Niagara District because he was 'disapproved of' as '[a] man of infamous character; frequently suspected of robbing Indians of their silver works and a common disturber of the peace, . . . known to fire at his neighbours' Cattle in the night time, and worry them with Dogs, through much Malice.'9

By 1790, the 'Loyalist' population in what had been Mississauga territory had swollen to between 14,000 and 20,000. Simply by swearing an oath of allegiance, the so-called late Loyalists (arriving after about 1783, probably motivated less by loyalty than by free land) became eligible for a grant of 200 acres each—more than some of the first-comers had received. In response to their vigorous protests, the Upper Canadian government ensured that all original Loyalists would receive at least 300 acres, and each of their children, sons and daughters, 200 acres when they came of age.

As the population grew, demands increased for freehold land tenure and an elected assembly located in the upper country itself. Like their counterparts in Nova Scotia and New Brunswick, upper-country Loyalists couched their demands in the 'country party' rhetoric that, in England, had developed in response to excessive centralization of power and the corrupt exercise of such power by cliques and oligarchies protected by appointed governors and their councils. In short, most Loyalists opposed the power structures set in place by imperial administrators acting on behalf of the Crown.

Far from wishing to overturn authority, the Loyalists simply wanted to achieve a place of respect and power within the hierarchical structure of their new society. Even when petitioning for changes in the way they were governed, they routinely stressed their devotion to 'His Majesty's Interest' and their willingness 'to sacrifice their Lives and their Properties in defence of his Crown'. What they desired, they claimed, was only the re-establishment of past prerogatives and institutions—prerogatives that, in fact, many of them had never before enjoyed. By couching their demands in terms of restoration, they presented a conservative face and thus contributed to the Loyalist myth so celebrated by an older historiography. In their fundamental objective, they stood as one with imperial administrators: all they wanted was a larger piece of the pie.

During the Revolution, many Loyalist women had shown exceptional courage. Left behind with their families while their husbands went to fight, some acted as British spies. Others sheltered and provisioned Loyalist raiding parties. Almost all had to fill the traditionally male roles of providing for the family and making decisions on its behalf. Those who resolved to leave the sphere of conflict often had to negotiate with the Rebels for permission to go. Then, accompanied in many cases by young children, they travelled through enemy territory to find asylum either in New York refugee camps or in the British-held territory to the north.

When the dust settled, however, the new society these women helped to establish was no less patriarchal than the one they had left. Men were the decision-makers, women and children the followers. A married woman became a 'femme covert', a person with no legal identity separate from her husband. As historian Janice Potter-MacKinnon points out, when a Loyalist widow petitioned for compensation, no matter how heroic her accomplishments had been, in her plea for support she would invariably cite her status as 'a poor helpless woman', 'a Feeble Woman', a woman without a man to protect her. Even so, the all-male adjudicators of Loyalist claims awarded, proportionally, much more to men than to women.[10]

The subordination of women was not the only inequality built into the structure of life in the *pays d'en haut*. Far from encouraging the

assimilation of French-speaking Quebecers, the Loyalist migration in many ways accentuated the reality of social diversity in Britain's northern colonies. The Quebec Act had been a sign of Britain's recognition that this cultural divide could not be eradicated, and the American Revolution had underlined the importance of acknowledging colonial needs and sensibilities. With a possible war with the United States brewing over the western forts still held by Britain, imperial administrators realized that they would have to tolerate a certain amount of diversity, but keep it constrained within strict bounds. Thus land grants and compensation payments were designed to preserve and enhance social differentiation. Compensation to Loyalists for losses incurred during the Revolution reflected each individual's social and economic standing prior to the conflict. The highest-ranking British officers received the most land, and efforts were made to settle enlisted men in the same townships as their commanding officers (though these efforts did not always succeed).

A similar concern with containment influenced the design of new political structures in this period. Administration of the upper country was now costing Britain more than £100,000 per year, and the passage of the Self-Denying Ordinance of 1778 had made it illegal for Britain to tax her colonies unless they had representatives in the British parliament—an unthinkable prospect. When the Loyalists demanded an elected assembly, the imperial authorities willingly acceded. Together, the Constitutional Act of 1791 and further legislation the following year created Upper and Lower Canada. Each of the new colonies would have a locally elected assembly with the

Elizabeth Simcoe, 'Cartwright Mill', 1795. Mills were among the earliest and most expensive buildings erected on the Loyalist frontier. The first was built at Cataraqui (later Kingston) in 1783. At Niagara in the early 1780s, the sawmill was 'to be built first to get boards and small timber for the grist mill'. AO F47-11-1-0-160.

right to impose taxation and the responsibility to meet fiscal needs.

The Constitutional Act laid the legislative foundations for the first 50 years of Upper Canada's political and social development. Reflecting the vision shared by a ruling elite composed primarily of British landed aristocrats, it gave Upper Canada a lieutenant-governor who, as the Crown's representative, could grant or withhold or reserve royal assent to any legislation. The lieutenant-governor was also to appoint both an executive council to

offer him advice and serve as the final legal court of appeal in the colony, and a legislative council, the 'upper' section of the bicameral legislature. Legislative members were to number at least seven and, like members of the British House of Lords, to hold their seats for life. The assembly, the 'lower' section of the legislature, was to consist of no more than 16 representatives elected for terms of no longer than four years. To become law, proposed legislation had first to pass both the elected assembly and the appointed legislative council, then receive the lieutenant-governor's assent, to be followed by the Crown's confirmation within two years. Finally, matters of local and regional concern were to be handled by district councils appointed by the central government; by the 1820s there were 11 such bodies. This complex structure left considerable control in the hands of imperial administrators, and the powers of the two councils, especially their control of patronage, generated much dissatisfaction in both the Canadas.

The Constitutional Act also contained significant implications for Upper Canada's economic and financial future. Lacking direct access to the sea, Upper Canada had to depend on Lower Canada to handle trade to and from Great Britain. In this situation, Upper Canadian merchants were generally the junior partners. Because the Upper Canadian commercial class had no say in the development of ports, canals, or general commercial infrastructures in Lower Canada, its ability to promote local commercial growth was limited. Moreover, at a time when customs duties were the major source of revenue for almost all British colonies, the Constitutional Act made Upper Canada reliant on Lower Canada for its share of the duties collected. This fiscal dependence would become increasingly intolerable for Upper Canada.

On a broader level, Britain retained control of the colony's commerce by means of the Navigation Laws. Restricting foreign participation in colonial trade and requiring colonies to ship raw material to the motherland in return for manufactured goods, these laws spawned a particular type of business elite. Within the British Empire's protected free trade zone, colonial merchants shipped whatever they could and imported as much as possible. Up to now, strong military contacts plus an upper crust background had been the *sine qua non* of social advancement in the *pays d'en haut*. Now, these new 'co-ordinators of colonial commerce' would begin to challenge commissioned officers and the colony's nascent landed aristocracy for positions of power and prominence in Upper Canada.

CHAPTER FIVE

Rural Life: 1791–1871

*I*n the 1860s John Kilborn, a Loyalist's son, looked back on his 70 years in Upper Canada. In the pioneer period, he thought, the 'State of Society, however humble was in many respects superior to the present. All the parties then were more or less dependent on each other for favours and occasional assistance, and all felt more or less interested in each others condition and prosperity. . . . All were acquainted and were friends, entirely unlike our present position.' Loyalist Captain James Dittrick agreed: 'We visited one another, and all appeared like one family. There was no distinction, as is the case now days—all were on an equality and willing to do any kind acts and services for one another.'[1]

Nostalgia for a kinder, gentler past is, of course, not uncommon. Nor is the tendency to ignore less attractive aspects of times past—especially where other people's experience is concerned. Just as Kilborn and Dittrick looked back with selective fondness on the days of Upper Canada's earliest pioneers, so might we in the twenty-first century be tempted to think of the entire period of Ontario's rural beginnings—from the Constitutional Act of 1791 to

Confederation—as a simpler, cleaner, safer, more stable and family-oriented time than our complex urban present. But, in fact, many rural Upper Canadians endured very harsh conditions. To a large extent, birthplace, ethnicity, gender, colour, and class determined individual expectations, behaviours, and rewards. And for the First Nations peoples, there was little room in the colony that European settlers began to build in the 'Country of the Missesagues'.

On 20 August 1796, a group of Mississauga led by Chief Wabakinine travelled from their village at the mouth of the Credit River to Upper Canada's newly designated capital at York.[2] The fishing had been good that day, and they had caught enough fresh salmon to offer some for sale. Mississauga at Upper Canada's other emerging urban centres, Kingston and Niagara, were starting up similar commercial ventures. But competition from white fishermen was increasing so swiftly that the very next year the colonial government would take measures to protect Native fisheries—though these laws were never enforced. In 1790, the Mississauga had warned that none but the

First Nations would be permitted to fish the Credit, to no avail; by 1804, whites were catching so many salmon, especially those travelling upstream to spawn—and the pollution caused 'by washing with soap and other dirt' was discouraging other fish even from entering the river—that the Mississauga complained, 'our families [are] in great distress for want of food.'[3]

Wabakinine himself did not live to see that distress. In the 1770s, he had organized Ojibwa to fight with the British against the Americans, and in the 1780s, he had helped to negotiate three treaties giving the British immense tracts of land north of Lake Ontario. Like many other Mississauga, he had thought his people were merely renting out the land and that, in return, they would 'always be taken care of' and permitted to 'encamp and fish where we pleased'.[4]

By the 1790s, however, First Nations people throughout the area realized how misplaced their trust in the British had been. In 1784, there were only 6,000 non-Native people in Upper Canada; by 1791, that number had tripled, and by 1812, it would triple again. By then, a majority of Upper Canada's non-Native population was immigrants from the United States who came in search of cheap land, and many brought with them strong antipathies towards Native people. These feelings were often reciprocated: when approached by 'a Yankee stranger' who wished to purchase land, one Mississauga chief refused to sell: '[the Yankee's] mouth is all sugar and his words very sweet, but I do not know what is in his heart.'[5] In 1792, a Mississauga chief named Snake was murdered by British soldiers in Kingston and no one was punished for the

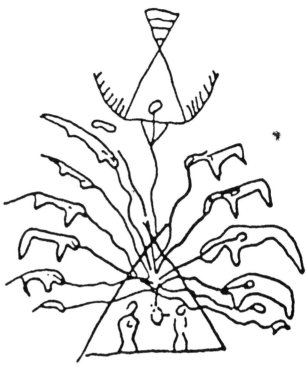

Turtle and shaking tent ceremony. The turtle was a central deity, or *manitou*, in the Mississauga cosmology. Each *manitou* spoke a different language, and Mikinak, or Great Turtle, acted as their translator. This sketch (from a depiction on birchbark of a shaking tent ceremony) shows Turtle, at the centre, translating as various other animal *manitous* enter the tent. From *Reading Rock Art* (1994). Image by Wayne Yerxa, courtesy of Grace Rajnovich and Natural Heritage Books.

crime. This was not unusual. As early as 1773, the superintendent of Northern Indians counted 18 such cases and concluded that colonists could kill Native people with virtual 'impunity'. Scarcely a week after Snake's murder, Elizabeth Simcoe, the wife of Upper Canada's first lieutenant-governor, visited Kingston and in a diary entry remarked on the 'unwarlike, idle, drunken, dirty tribe' of Mississauga who 'saunter up and down the

Rock art at Burntside Lake, on the Ontario-Minnesota border, watercolour sketch by Selwyn Dewdney. Mikinak, or Great Turtle, is standing guard over the combatants on the left. The Ojibwa believed that Mikinak was powerful in war both because of his protective shell and because, unlike his earthly counterparts, he possessed great speed. With permission of the Royal Ontario Museum © ROM 995.64.7 (18III GI).

Town all day.'[6] Such views were commonplace among the elite of Upper Canadian society.

Numbering about a thousand in the early 1780s, the Credit River band had dropped to 330 by 1798. The survivors still faced the threat of disease, which continued to spread as white settlers moved north. As early as 1793, a Mississauga family named Different stated in a petition that 'when white people sees anything that they like they never quit us untill they have it. . . . The taking or stealing from us is nothing for we are only Massessagoes.' Some Mississauga adopted a belligerent stance,

accosting surveyors, threatening settlers, burning mills, and hunting cattle. But the several bands in the lower Great Lakes region seldom acted in concert. In May 1796, in a rare attempt at united action, Wabakinine, believing that the British were about to form an alliance with the Six Nations people at the Grand River against the Mississauga and Ojibwa, sent warnings to his fellow chiefs. The British were compelled to assure six Ojibwa chiefs that no such plan existed.[7]

A month later, at the southern end of Burlington Bay, John Graves Simcoe was preparing to return to Britain after five years as lieutenant-governor. At a gathering held 'to compliment the Gov.' on the eve of his departure, Mrs Simcoe recorded in her diary, 'Wabekanine and a number of his tribe . . . gave us the largest Land Tortoise I ever saw.' The next evening, the Simcoe entourage enjoyed a fine dish of 'Tortoise ready dressed'.[8]

The tortoise played a crucial role among the numerous *manitou* (deities) that, for the Mississauga, represented 'the ultimate sources of existence'. Some of these spirits, like the Great Lynx and the Large Snake, were evil; others, such as the Thunderbird, were powerful guardians. None, however, spoke the same language, and only Mikinak, the Great Turtle, possessed the power to translate—both between individual *manitou* and between *manitou* and humans. Who better to present to the chief of a troublesome alien culture? Surely Mikinak could translate more effectively than any human. Perhaps he would also report back to Wabakinine on the intentions of the interlopers; he had performed a similar service in 1764 when, after visiting the British at Niagara and Montreal, he advised the Ojibwa at Sault

Ste Marie to seek peace because the British had superior arms.[9]

The Turtle was also a powerful protector in war.[10] That Wabakinine looked to Mikinak for assistance suggests that he did not accept at face value the assurances of the British. With good reason: Upper Canada's administrators were indeed looking to isolate the Mississauga from potential allies. They also had their eyes on the vast stretch of Mississauga land between Burlington Bay and the Etobicoke Creek, land that could constitute the final link between Niagara and York, if only it could be obtained cheaply. However, the Mississauga had seen Joseph Brant get a good price from the British for land the Mississauga had relinquished to other tribes following the American Revolution. As one government official put it, '[the Mississauga] are perfectly apprised of the value of money, and of its use.'[11]

We cannot know how these matters weighed with Wabakinine as he made camp on the waterfront opposite Berry's tavern in York on the night of 20 August 1796. At midnight, three white men dragged Wabakinine's sister away from the camp (they would later claim that they had paid her money to sleep with them). Frightened, Wabakinine's wife shook Wabakinine awake and—half drunk, half asleep—he staggered after his sister's abductors. The men made short work of the chief, repeatedly kicking him and striking him with a rock as he lay on the ground. They also severely wounded his wife. Wabakinine died at his village on the Credit River the following day, the second Mississauga chief to be murdered by whites in four years, and his wife died several days later. Their murderers went unpunished.

As the government sent to Quebec for some

4,000 guns to protect the colony in the event of an uprising, the Mississauga looked to Brant for help. Promised by the government that all his land sales, although illegal under the Proclamation Act of 1763 (because made directly to settlers and white speculators), would be sanctioned if he counselled moderation, Brant urged the Mississauga to lay down their arms.[12] Nor could the Mississauga find allies south of the border, where several recent battles with the American army had left the local people in no position to provide assistance. Alone, the Mississauga were too weak to resist.

The government's divide-and-conquer policy culminated in a land agreement in 1805. The Mississauga, weakened by disease, alcohol, and the loss of traditional leadership, ceded 80,000 acres—a tract of land 10 kilometres deep between Burlington and Etobicoke Creek—for a tiny fraction of its market value. The remaining local Mississauga clustered at the mouth of the Credit, the site of Wabakinine's old village, but the proliferation of mills and dams weakened the fishery. Finally, in 1847, the Mississauga would cede that land, too, to the state. Meanwhile, to the east, Mississauga in the Kingston area ceded 3 million acres of land to the Upper Canadian government in the early 1820s.[13] In a brief 25 years, the Mississauga had gone from being the state's landlords to being its clients.

The same process would be repeated as colonial settlement edged north. Close to 140,000 immigrants arrived from the British Isles between 1815 and 1835; by 1842, Upper Canada's non-Native population numbered about 450,000. By contrast, between 1770 and 1835 the Native population dropped from 14,000 to 9,300. After the War of 1812, the British military believed that they no longer

Newly built Mississauga homes at the Credit River, 1827. Each of these two-room log cabins housed two families. Homes were inspected by Methodist missionaries and assessed for cleanliness and organization. Kahkewaquonaby, the Mississauga chief and Methodist minister also known as Peter Jones, took part in such inspections and reported his findings in his journal: 'Bro Hurlbert's—All neat, like a white squaw's house, except the tea kettle which was out of place.' 'Jacob Snowstorm's—Floor and cupboard poor—bed tolerably good … one woman making baskets—one sewing—one idle.' 'Passed by one Indian Camp, a specimen of old times.' 'John Pigeon's—floor good but dirty—good tables but dusty … a Bible and Hymn Book etc on the shelf—everything looks like industry, and improvement in the house' (in B. Osborne and M. Ripmeester, 'The Mississauga between Two Worlds', *Canadian Journal of Native Studies* 17 [1997], 259–91). Many Native leaders believed that preservation of their traditional culture depended on their cooperation in such activities. By 1847, the Mississauga had ceded to the state the land on which these houses stood. Image from Egerton Ryerson, *The Story of My Life* (Toronto, 1883), 59. Thomas Fisher Rare Book Library, University of Toronto.

needed First Nations assistance in war; thereafter, the practice of giving presents to Native people declined—causing the need for assistance to increase. Responsibility for Native issues in Upper Canada then shifted from the military to the civil sector. In 1830, the state attempted to move a large number of Native people to a model agricultural settlement at Coldwater, between Lake Simcoe and Georgian Bay. Methodist, Catholic, and Anglican churches assisted the state in what would become an ongoing attempt to 'civilize' Native people.

But not everyone saw assimilation as the appropriate goal. In 1836 Sir Francis Bond

Head, Lieutenant Governor of Upper Canada, concluded that Native people would never be able to adapt to white culture: the only realistic solution was to let them die out in peace. Accordingly, he negotiated a treaty with the Ojibwa of the Saugeen region, acquiring 1.5 million acres of land for the state and relocating the band to Manitoulin Island in Georgian Bay, where, he assured them, they would never be bothered by whites. Protests from various missionary societies led the Colonial Office to overrule Bond Head's decision, but segregation, rather than assimilation, remained the approach of choice for most Upper Canadians, regardless of the policies and programs espoused by the state and religious groups.

Some 1,200 Ojibwa did settle on Manitoulin Island, where the Roman Catholic and Anglican churches vied for their souls. Farther south, the Methodists converted many of the Credit River Mississauga, including a chief named Kahkewaquonaby, who would become better known as Peter Jones. Influenced, in part, by Jones, the Mississauga of the Kingston area settled on Grape Island in the Bay of Quinte. Here they were beset by Methodist missionaries who believed that to be 'civilized', a society must be based on agriculture and the raising of livestock. But Grape Island was too small to provide adequate forage, hence the animals had to be kept on another island, and the women had to row for two hours a day in order to care for them.

Still, for some of the Mississauga, even Grape Island offered a better life than the one they had known in the 1820s; as one recalled: 'they were all happy drunkards . . . dying very fast. . . . Some of them were stabbed, some were drowned, some were burned, and some were frozen to death. And thus we were going to destruction at a great rate.'[14] Others quit the island for the backcountry north of Kingston. Petitioning for land, they were granted a 2,680-acre reserve; but, to the consternation of the white authorities, instead of using the land for farming, the Mississauga resumed their traditional hunting and foraging culture. Eventually the remaining Grape Island Mississauga were moved to another reserve. Yet throughout the nineteenth century, the Mississauga never abandoned their tradition of communal ownership for the European model of individualized private property; nor did many other Native bands. Similarly, attempts by Peter Jones to enforce British criminal law among the Port Credit Mississauga were resisted; instead, they followed 'a code of several Rules and regulations among themselves.'[15]

Nevertheless, Native leaders often welcomed and even petitioned for residential schools, or 'teaching wigwams', to help them learn European ways. In the 1870s, at the northern frontier town of Fort William, Native and Métis children had significantly higher rates of school enrolment than the rest of the population. Peter Jones became an extremely effective proselytizer for residential schooling as a vehicle for teaching the Methodist faith. Shingwaukonse, a chief of the Garden River Ojibwa near the Sault, took a more pragmatic approach, looking to missionary schools not for spiritual instruction but for the education his people needed to adapt to broad economic and social change. Both, however, believed that the schools should at the earliest possible time be run not just for Native people but by them.[16]

For all societies, 'culture' is a protean term. Different bands and different groups within

Ojibwa fishing at the Sault, by William Armstrong, 1869. According to Ojibwa creation mythology, a deity named Michabous invented the fishing net after watching a spider build a web to catch flies. NAC C114501.

bands took firm positions on different issues, each attempting to protect those parts of their culture that they considered most essential. Indeed, many of the most prominent Native leaders believed that participation in the new economic and social reality offered the only hope for preservation of their traditional culture. What from a distance may look like a uniform retreat in the face of an overwhelming foe was actually a complex process of accommodation, compromise, and calculated response aimed at protecting what each group deemed most central to its cultural identity. In this sense, Native peoples continued to exercise an agency, however limited, that white society never succeeded in appropriating.

Ultimately, however, efforts to promote assimilation in Upper Canada were not about providing the wherewithal to participate constructively in white society; Native people remained decidedly second-class. In the residential schools, bureaucrats allowed Native people to play no significant role. This was not Peter Jones's vision, and not one of his children went to a residential school. For those children who did, such schooling did not lead to acceptance in the dominant white community. At Fort William, residential school enrolment had been high, yet in 1871, Native and Métis men were significantly over-represented in the lowest-paid occupational groups. In short, European immigrants were not prepared to suffer the competition that a more constructive approach would produce. The real purposes behind 'Indian policy' were displacement and containment.

Nor did the white population wish the Native people to enjoy the benefits of development. Conflicts arose over the state's right to build roads versus the Native peoples' rights to reservation lands. Local municipal councils wanted unfettered access to Native lands for road-building. For the first half of the nineteenth century, such ambitions were largely kept in check by the various superintendents of Indian Affairs, whose duties included protection of Native rights to unceded and reservation land as set out in the Proclamation of 1763. In 1851 the Western District superintendent berated Lambton County councillors for their refusal to allow 'the poor Indians the enjoyment of a small remnant of their once rich domain' and accused them of wishing 'to see these unoffending people driven beyond the Rocky Mountains'. When individual bands were consulted about road-building through their reserves, after a period of bargaining they invariably agreed, yet the colonial state and local municipal organizations often preferred to dispense with such niceties, arguing that rights of public access superseded rights of Native ownership. Officers in the Indian department acted as arbitrators when bargaining did take place, thus providing some degree of protection. But in 1853 and again in 1860 (when the colony took over formal control of Indian Affairs from the imperial government), the Upper Canada legislature merged the departments of Indian Affairs and Crown Lands, making conflicts of interest inevitable. From that time forward, the province's govern-

ments evinced little or no sympathy for Native people's right to control road development on their reserves—and this is still a contentious issue in Ontario.[17]

In farming, fishing, and mining—key 'frontiers' of contact in nineteenth-century northern Ontario—white immigrants denied Native people the right to participate as equals. For the first three-quarters of the nineteenth century, Ojibwa in the Rainy Lake region, an area in the northwest most noted for its hunting, trapping, and fishing potential, successfully pursued commercial farming. Their crop was wild rice, or *Manito Gitigaan*, which they had been cultivating for centuries before European contact. Hardly 'wild', this grain requires annual seeding, weeding, protection against predators (muskrats and blackbirds), and water control, as well as careful processing after harvesting. In the early 1800s, the Ojibwa sold their wild rice and other produce to both the Hudson's Bay Company and its Montreal-based rival, the North West Company.

As cultivation increased, so did population: the Rainy River Ojibwa grew from 455 in 1822 to 1,800 in 1875. By the 1880s, resource and railway companies provided ready markets for their produce. Farming was deemed a priority in Treaty Three, signed by the Ojibwa in 1873; yet in 1881 the federal government passed a law requiring Indian agent approval of all the Ojibwa's commercial transactions, lest, in the words of Prime Minister John A. Macdonald, the 'wild nomad[s] of the North-West' waste their earnings on liquor. Anyone who bought from the Ojibwa without such approval risked summary conviction—but the Indian agent could be hard to find. As a result,

Cultivating wild rice at Rice Lake, 1921. As much as hunting and foraging, farming was a traditional part of many Native cultures. People in the Rice Lake area had been growing wild rice for several millennia before the arrival of Europeans. Legislation that discouraged purchase of their farm produce, and the loss of much of their land, curtailed such pursuits in Northern Ontario. NAC, PA 84653.

customers soon found other suppliers. The Ojibwa's troubles were compounded when, to facilitate logging, the Ontario government permitted the damming of a large river, and the ensuing floods swamped much of the Ojibwa's farmland. By the 1890s, many Ojibwa had abandoned farming altogether. Now white settlers could complain that many reserves were not being used in a 'productive' way—for farming, that is—thus providing the justification the government would use to appropriate them a few years later.[18]

Many of those forced out of farming turned to hunting and trapping. A century earlier and for centuries before contact, fish had been the foundation of the diet of the peoples of the central and northern Great Lakes and their primary trade item. But by the late 1800s, Ojibwa could no longer make a living by fishing—a direct consequence of the incursions made by non-Native commercial fishing companies, incursions actively supported by the state.

The first comprehensive legislation concerning fishing on inland waters, passed in 1857, had facilitated the leasing of Native fishing grounds to non-Native companies. William Gibbard, the first Fishery Overseer appointed under the Act, believed that 'the Indians would be far better off if they attended

The troubles on Manitoulin Island, *Canadian Illustrated News*, 8 August 1863. Despite treaty guarantees of their rights, Native people were regularly fined and jailed for 'illegal' fishing. In 1863, Fishery Overseer William Gibbard led a party of armed deputies in an unsuccessful raid on Manitoulin Island. He died not long after, in mysterious circumstances. NAC 134371.

to their farms instead of dabbling in fisheries.' Accordingly, of the 97 licences he issued in 1859, 85 went to white applicants and only 12 to Native groups.

In effect, Native people were now required to compete for the opportunity to exercise their never-ceded right to fish, and to do so within a system heavily biased against them. They fought back, destroying the nets and other equipment of the white fishermen. But by the 1880s, the Great Lakes fisheries were dominated by non-Native commercial companies, the largest of which were American-owned. Even Gibbard admitted that the Americans operated 'in a manner incredibly reckless, and altogether regardless of the most ruinous consequences', leaving 'old nets upon the ground to rot . . . with putrefying masses of fish entangled amongst them'. Meanwhile, Native people were regularly fined and jailed for 'illegally' fishing in waters to which treaties guaranteed them free access. Plainly, as an Indian agent in Grey County acknowledged in 1896, Native fishing would not be tolerated if it involved competition with whites.[19]

By the mid-1840s, the mineral resources of the north had attracted interest in the south. Accordingly, in 1845 the colony extended its jurisdiction to Sault Ste Marie and began to survey the land on which Ojibwa had lived

Shingwaukonse, *c*. 1849. 'Drive us not to the madness of despair,' the Ojibwa chief urged Governor General Elgin in 1849. 'We are told that you have laws which guard and protect the property of your white children, but you have made none to protect the rights of your red children. Perhaps you expected that the red skin could protect himself from the rapacity of his pale faced bad brother?' In nineteenth-century Ontario, the rapacity of white settlers, speculators, and government administrators prevailed, but Shingwaukonse's Garden Island descendants kept pressing for equal rights in economic and educational development. Today, on a local level, they have achieved some success. Shingwauk Project, Algoma University.

and farmed for generations. Mining companies were granted leases and commenced operations despite impassioned protests from local leaders such as Shingwaukonse, who in 1849 wrote to the governor general:

> . . . *you have hunted us from every place as with a wand, you have swept away all our pleasant land, and like some giant foe you tell us 'willing or unwilling, you must now go from amid these rocks and wastes, I want them now! I want them to make rich my white children, whilst you may shrink away to holes and caves like starving dogs to die.'*[20]

Shingwaukonse refused to shrink away. Later the same year, with some 25 Native comrades and several sympathetic whites, he seized a copper mine at Mica Bay from the Quebec and Montreal Mining Association and occupied it until the spring of 1850.

The Ojibwa believed that copper had great spiritual power, but the mining clash was less about preservation of a spiritual resource than about access to a saleable commodity. As Peau de Chat, an Ojibwa chief from Fort William, put it, 'A great deal of our mineral has been taken away and I must have something for it.' Shingwaukonse agreed: 'We want pay for every pound of mineral that has been taken off our lands, as well as for that which may hereafter be carried away.'[21] These chiefs did not oppose resource development in itself (although many whites, then and later, chose to explain the conflict in those terms): what they wanted was a fair chance to participate in it. For Shingwaukonse, it was just one aspect of a multi-faceted approach to development, one that would include Native-managed schooling and allow for reciprocity and cultural exchange. For the state, however, resource development was a one-way street.

Finance minister Francis Hincks, who had profited from northern mining speculation, consistently ignored or denied the petitions of Native leaders to set up lumber mills and mining operations. The Robinson Treaties of 1850, which acquired for the Crown 52,700 square miles (140,000 km²) of land in the Georgian Bay–Lake Superior region, signalled the future direction of the state's Native policy. Whereas earlier treaties had left it to individual bands to decide how they would distribute the annual payments they received, the Robinson Treaties stipulated that a portion of each payment was to be distributed to individuals within each band, effectively undermining the collective property ownership so central to traditional Native cultures.

The thrust of these initiatives was extended in 1857 when—without consulting any Native chief—the Upper Canadian government passed the Gradual Civilization Act. Under this coercive legislation, voting rights would be granted to any Native man, literate in either English or French, who could answer a skill-testing question (naming the world's continents) and was willing to renounce the principle of collective ownership in favour of individual property rights. Those who accepted enfranchisement, however, would lose their legal status as Indians. Intended, as one chief put it, 'to break them to pieces', the Gradual Civilization Act created two categories of subjects in Upper Canada: Indians and citizens. This particular initiative, however, failed. More than two decades later, in 1880, barely 50 men had been enfranchised. 'At this rate,' remarked one MP, 'it would take 36,000 years to enfranchise the Indian population of Canada.'²²

The name 'Gradual Civilization Act' re-flected white society's common view of the new land and its peoples: both were wild and forbidding. Europeans often experienced a kind of disorientation when confronted with the 'almost impenetrable and exceedingly dreary' bush. '[T]he landscape,' one recent arrival complained in 1831, 'is unvaried and exceedingly confined—nothing but trees, trees, trees continually.' One gentlewoman from England described the forest as a 'rural prison house'. 'The communication with York,' a British soldier posted at Amherstburg, opposite Detroit, wrote in 1804, 'is through pathless woods that extend to the Pacific.'²³ Still, many Upper Canadian writers looked on the forest with wonder and interest, responding romantically with stylized depictions of the sylvan sublime.

Those willing to learn from the local Native people would discover that the forest was neither pathless nor unbroken. A network of trails facilitated movement north of the lakes, and for centuries Aboriginal farmers had been maintaining cleared land (often by means of fire) for planting their crops—on a reconnoitering trip in 1799, one settler came upon a cleared area, in what is now Waterloo Township, planted with 'spuds and pumpkins'. The Native peoples were managers of their forest environment; cleared plains abutting dense forest provided environments attractive to many species they hunted. Some astute settlers looked to Native examples for guidance in selecting choice farmland and appropriate crops. Others looked to the trees themselves. 'The nature of the soil may be invariably discovered by the description of the timber it bears,' noted a guidebook published in 1831; 'on what is called hard timbered land,' for example, 'where the maple, beach, black birch,

Daniel Smith, herbalist, Six Nations Reserve, 1949. Herbal remedies were the norm in the nineteenth century, in the old world as well as the new. Early settlers benefited from Native knowledge of the medicinal value of local plants. CMC J3107.

ash, cherry, lime, oak, black walnut, butternut, hickory, plane and tuliptree etc. are found, the soil consists of deep black loam.'[24]

Once they had decided where to homestead, however, the settlers declared war on the trees. As Anna Jameson, visiting from Britain, reported in the 1830s, a 'Canadian settler hates a tree, regards it as his natural enemy, as something to be destroyed, eradicated, annihilated by all and any means.' Thirty years later, the president of the Agricultural Association of Upper Canada was still urging his members to apply themselves to 'the subjugation of the forest'. By the next decade the 'ecological revolution' was largely complete.[25] With as much as 80 per cent of southern Ontario's original forest cover gone, the government passed legislation (widely ignored) aimed at persuading farmers to plant trees on their property near roadways. Some of the more farsighted lumberers—forced to look ever farther afield for good stands of pine—even began to argue for limited conservation measures. But they were a minority. In addition to stripping Ontario of its pine stands, lumberers polluted its rivers with sawdust, beached logs, and eroding soil. Farmers, in importing crop seeds, also introduced numerous less desirable plants, including thistles, wild mustard, burdock, and a fast-spreading species called Ambrosia—more commonly known as ragweed.[26]

As for animal life, the variety and the abundance must have astonished the first newcomers from Europe. Charles Fothergill, who arrived from Yorkshire in 1816, described 186 bird species, 105 mammals, 27 fishes, and 15 reptiles. A devoted naturalist who tried to establish a natural history museum, Fothergill believed that humankind 'has no right to injure or wantonly destroy any animal'. But such sentiments were rare. Even a man like Elkanah Billings, the founder of Upper Canada's first natural history journal, *The Canadian Naturalist and Geologist*, in recording his admiration for the pileated woodpecker in

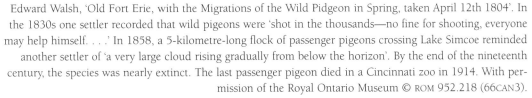

Edward Walsh, 'Old Fort Erie, with the Migrations of the Wild Pidgeon in Spring, taken April 12th 1804'. In the 1830s one settler recorded that wild pigeons were 'shot in the thousands—no fine for shooting, everyone may help himself. . . .' In 1858, a 5-kilometre-long flock of passenger pigeons crossing Lake Simcoe reminded another settler of 'a very large cloud rising gradually from below the horizon'. By the end of the nineteenth century, the species was nearly extinct. The last passenger pigeon died in a Cincinnati zoo in 1914. With permission of the Royal Ontario Museum © ROM 952.218 (66CAN3).

the mid-1800s complacently noted that he 'shot several of them on the Bonnechere River in the County of Renfrew'. For most Upper Canadians, wild animals were either pests or they were game, to be hunted and killed, either way. By 1892, a Royal Commission on Fish and Game would report a 'sickening tale of merciless, ruthless, and remorseless slaughter'. Its conclusion was only too predictable: 'Where but a few years ago game was plentiful,

it is hardly now to be found.'[27]

Conservation was not much on the minds of settlers struggling to make a better life for themselves and their families. The story of Wilson Benson is representative of his time and class. Born in Belfast in 1821, Benson had worked as a linen weaver, agricultural labourer, and peddler before embarking for Upper Canada with his 14-year-old wife, Jemima, in 1841. Over the next eight years, he

Hunters, Cobourg, Upper Canada, *c.* 1860. A series of laws passed in the nineteenth century to protect various game species had little impact. Here, carcasses hang from a tree and several slain deer lie on the ground await-ing 'processing'. Isabella Valancy Crawford's poem 'Malcolm's Katie', about life in the backwoods of Upper Canada, evokes a lust for the kill: 'They hung the slaughtered fish like swords / On saplings slender; like scim-itars, / Bright, and ruddied from new-dead wars, / Blazed in the light the scaly hordes'. NAC PA 125812.

worked at 20 different occupations and moved more than a dozen times; Jemima worked as a domestic and dressmaker and bore at least two sons. Following the loss of their home and store to a fire in 1849, Jemima's brother suggested that they take up farming close to his own operation near Orillia. After sending Jemima there 'to ascer-tain from her how she liked the place', Benson moved his family north and became a farmer at age 28. He would move only twice more: first to a bigger farm in Artemesia Township in Grey County and finally, after suffering a crip-pling accident on the farm in the early 1870s, to the village of Markdale, a few miles away. There, with the help of his second wife, he became a respected merchant and lived until his death in 1911.[28]

With many occupational and geographic moves in the early years, followed by relative stability and moderate success in farming and storekeeping, Benson was typical of thousands of immigrants in the early nineteenth century. Upper Canada was known as a place where a struggling fellow arriving with a little cash could work for a while to save a down payment; purchase (often on time) a parcel of farm land; after years of intensive labour, own and operate his own rural enterprise; and eventually bequeath to his children a small stake for the future. These prospects attracted particular attention in Britain following the Napoleonic Wars, when land enclosure and, in many regions, sluggish industrial growth made employment difficult to find. Between 1815 and 1865, well over a million Scots, Irish, and English people left their homes for British North America. As it had for almost every decade since 1791, Upper Canada's population doubled in the 1840s, reaching 952,000 in 1850, and the Irish potato famine of the mid-1840s contributed the greatest single influx of migrants in this period. Unlike those who came before and after, these migrants often arrived in broken health—17 per cent of those who left Liverpool died on board or in quarantine at Quebec, and most were virtually penniless.

Not all the new arrivals came from the British Isles: some 12,000 Germans settled in Upper Canada after 1850, and by 1860 a sizeable number of African-Americans were living in the colony. Although kin groups often settled in the same general area, rural society in Upper Canada typically consisted of what a Scots farmer in Huron County in 1846 called a 'mixty moxty Quire hotch potch of high and low country scotch, English, welch, irish, dutch, french, Yankees of the states, new brunswick, and novacosea with native born canadians'.[29]

In 1860, only one out of five Upper Canadians of African-American descent was an escaped slave; two out of five had been born in Upper Canada. While some lived in separate enclaves, the 1860 census found the Black population dispersed across 312 county and city wards, and mixed marriages were fairly common. Black people suffered significant discrimination in Upper Canada at this time.[30] The writer Susanna Moodie, whose legendary journals recount her journey from England to Upper Canada in 1832 and her settlement in the backwoods, reports a Black man, married to a white women, killed by a white mob. More representative was the experience of a Black community in the southwest of the province. In 1829, the Cincinnati Colonization Society had arranged with Lieutenant Governor Colborne to send a sizeable group of African-Americans from Cincinnati to settle in Upper Canada. Of the approximately 200 men, women, and children who made the move to Wilberforce, most left again within a few years. The Canada Company, which owned much of the land in the area, had refused to sell to the new arrivals on the grounds that their concentration 'alarm[ed] the present inhabitants, who appear to have a repugnance to [Black people] forming communities near them.' Scattered instances of violence further 'encouraged' dispersal. 'The truth of the matter', as one informed observer reported in 1863, seemed to be that

as long as the coloured people form a very small proportion of the population, and are dependent, they receive protection and favours; but when they increase and compete with the labouring class for a living, and espe-

Canada, Settlers house in the forest, on the Thames nr London CW April 1842

Henry Francis Ainslie (1803–79), 'Canada, Settler's house in the forest, on the Thames, nr London CW, April 1842', watercolour and ink. Axes, even more than railways, transformed the Upper Canadian landscape. For settlers, trees were the enemy. Most farmers managed to clear fewer than 1.5 acres per year, and clearing and planting went on simultaneously. Crops grew up amidst the stumps, which were easier to pull out once they had rotted. NAC C 000544.

cially when they begin to aspire to social equality, they cease to be 'interesting negroes', and become 'niggers'.[31]

In Upper Canada, as in most frontier communities, supplies of cash were limited Merchants would calculate the amount owed in cash and then collect the equivalent in goods. Nobody owed a literal bushel of wheat; rather, one owed a sum of money that might be paid off in wheat. This barter system shocked many recent arrivals. 'Ministers in the Townships or Country circuits,' the Reverend John McLaurin told a correspondent in Scotland, 'are paid their stipends, nearly, if not altogether in produce! . . . at the then market rates; or as may otherwise be agreed apon. This appears hard to such as never have tried it; and indeed it is so, if not reduced to some System.'[32]

Exports were important to Upper Canada's settler economy, and Great Britain provided a protected market for Upper Canadian grain and forest products for much of the first half of the century: natural products from the colonies were shipped to Britain and manufactured goods from Britain sent to the colonies. But that protection varied from year to year, and in the 1840s the system was largely dismantled with the ending of timber protection and the repeal of the Corn Laws and the Navigation Acts—changes that provoked violent protest from some local merchants and led to suggestions that Upper Canada should join the United States.

Most farms produced many things besides wheat—barley, tobacco, rye, pork, ashes, lumber. One farm produced 39 different crops in a single four-year period. In 1803, only half the land under tillage produced wheat, and only 20 per cent of that wheat was exported. Even at the height of wheat production in the 1850s, when the export market was buoyant, wheat took up less than a quarter of the average farmer's cultivated land, and at least half of Upper Canadian wheat exports went not to Britain itself but to its other North American colonies. A Reciprocity Treaty with the United States (1854–66) facilitated the existing trade flow in a wide range of natural products. Agricultural diversification intensified after 1850: by 1871, wheat, although still central to Upper Canada's rural domain, accounted for less than one-quarter of tilled land, and mixed farming, dairy, and livestock production assumed increased importance.[33]

In 1814, speculator Thomas Smith probably looked to the export market to sell his 'copse' of 34,603 oak trees; between 1815 and 1870, exports of timber and wood products brought in almost as much as exports of flour and wheat. In the mid-1830s, some 3,500 men worked—wielding saw, axe, cant hook, pike pole, and oar—in commercial logging ventures. Many came from Lower Canada to the Ottawa Valley as seasonal workers, and clashes between French Canadian and Irish Catholic loggers sometimes occurred. Commercial logging was soon also underway in the Georgian Bay region. By the 1870s, the value of sawn lumber exports to the US surpassed the traditional trade in square timber to England. By the turn of the century, logging would employ 20,000.

A good portion of the output of the colony's sawmills—425 of them, as early as 1826—was destined for local building construction (farmers could have their own logs milled in exchange for half the lumber), and distilleries and steamboats also used large quantities of local wood. Probably as much wood went to heat settlers' homes as went to external markets. In the 1830s, John Dunbar Moodie estimated that 'a house with only two or three fires' would burn about one acre of timber in a year. Just to heat their homes, Upper Canadians in the 1840s consumed a million acres of woodland.[34]

In this general economic environment, many settlers managed to eke out a modestly comfortable living. With the help of neighbours, a rough log cabin could be built in two or three days for less than £10. The design and construction of such structures owed a good deal to government legislation. After 1811 all buildings in Upper Canada were taxed according to the material used and the numbers of storeys and fireplaces. Therefore the astute

George Harlow White, 'A Woodcutter, Gravenhurst, 1873'. Most small farmers managed to produce only enough for their own needs. Many made extra money from the trees they cleared from their land, selling either the timber itself or the potash produced from the ashes left over after the felled trees were burned. Such income probably facilitated a great deal of Upper Canada's agricultural expansion. Note the fire at the back left, perhaps burning wood for potash. The farmer's home is at the back right. MTRL JRR T30547.

rate and needing only one fireplace, the one-and-a-half-storey log cabin became the most popular dwelling in rural Upper Canada, outnumbering any other type by roughly two to one in the first half of the 1800s. On average, it would take 30 to 40 years before a farm family could afford to build a frame or brick house.[35]

While some farms produced less than they consumed and others a healthy surplus, most produced just about enough for their own needs. A farmer starting out at a young age could reasonably expect to achieve modest prosperity over the course of a lifetime, and many a son was given a farm by his father. Still, it was a slow, arduous climb even to the middle of the ladder. Well before any major influx of settlers, much of southern Ontario's best farmland had been appropriated by a few speculators, and the government controlled almost a quarter of the land in each township through Crown and 'clergy' reserves (initially only the Anglican church was given reserves, a situation deeply resented by other denominations).

As early as 1800, up to two-thirds of the land in the Home District—the site of the colony's capital, York—belonged to speculators. By 1815, in the Western District, members of two fur-trading families, the Babys and the Askins, owned a third of the best patented agricultural land—land registered as belonging to a particular individual—and between 1820 and 1840, up to one-third of all patented land in Peel County was in the hands of speculators. By the mid-1850s, good land was no longer available for purchase from the government, but some 2 million acres were in private hands, ready for sale.

Some settlers simply squatted, often on

farmer would build a one-and-a-half-storey log cabin, generally about 8 by 5.5 metres, with a full attic for sleeping. Taxed at the one-storey land in the legal possession of Native people. By 1840, about one-fifth of the Six Nations reserve along the Grand River was occupied by non-Native people whose numbers—about 2,000 individuals, or 400 families—rivalled those of the Six Nations themselves. For 40 years the Six Nations protested, but political considerations always outweighed their legal rights. Although anyone convicted of squatting faced a jail sentence and became ineligible for grants of Crown land, on the Upper Canadian frontier law and order were often no more than romantic notions. Settlers squatted on the Iroquois lands with impunity, gaining a cheap entry to a farming future. Other settlers leased land, especially in the richer and longer-settled agricultural districts—the districts where speculators had been most active in the early years.[36]

By the 1840s, the bushland of Grey County, where Wilson Benson and his family finally settled, was Upper Canada's last best west. It was still largely undeveloped; we know that in 1852 Benson had to transport his wheat 70 kilometres for milling (the miller would likely have received a share of the produce for his services). Even in Peel County, one of the richer farming areas in the colony, many of the farmers had not, by 1861, 'moved beyond the primitive amenities of a pioneer society'. The many challenges faced by Wilson Benson and his family were common for people of his class in rural Upper Canada. Not only was land increasingly difficult to acquire, many farm families earned too little to support their farms and, falling into arrears with their taxes, were forced to forfeit their land. Untold numbers simply abandoned their plots or were evicted by creditors, 'picked,' as one farmer put it in

the 1860s, 'as bare as a bird's ass'.[37] Most settlers would live in at least two or three locations—and often many more—tending to settle for longer when there were more dependents or children of working age. Even in rich agricultural regions, movement was pronounced. Those who arrived first and commandeered the best land tended to be the most successful; later arrivals predominated amongst those who yet again pulled up stakes, often, in the 1860s, moving with family and other kin as far west as Manitoba in search of a secure farming future.

To make ends meet, some farmers also kept stores or taverns, or worked as timber contractors and put their earnings towards the purchase of more land in order to provide adequately for their sons. Frederick William Richardson, a shoemaker from Ireland who arrived in the Ottawa Valley in 1819, was one. Supplementing farming with timber contracting, he amassed enough acreage to set up six sons and two grandsons on their own farms.[38] The sale of forestry products probably tided many families over the land-clearing phase, when returns from the farm itself would have been minimal. In some cases the connection was even more intimate. Under the *agro-forestier* system, a lumber company such as the Hamilton Brothers of the Ottawa Valley would own farms and lease them to tenants whose produce would help to feed the company's employees. Wood workers themselves often farmed part-time to supplement their wages—a practice that the Hamilton Brothers exploited to justify reducing salaries and hiring only on a seasonal basis. As the lumbering industry spread north, so, too, did the *agro-forestier* system: 'On the first approach of cold

William Eliot, 'Spectacle in a Tavern at Mosa, 1845'. Drinking was commonplace in nineteenth-century Upper Canada. In the 1830s, William 'Tiger' Dunlop observed—ironically, no doubt—that Upper Canada 'may be pronounced the most healthy country under the sun, considering that whiskey can be procured for about one shilling sterling per gallon.' In 1817, the Yorkshire naturalist Charles Fothergill remarked on the 'indelicacy' that prevailed in the colony's taverns: 'decent and even pretty girls hawking and spitting about the room, occasionally scratching and rubbing themselves and lounging in attitudes in their chairs in a way that in Britain would be unpardonable.' J.J. Talman Regional Collection, University of Western Ontario.

weather,' a Muskoka farm wife commented in 1878, 'he starts for the lumber shanties, and engages himself to work there. . . . It is certainly a very hard and anxious life for the wife and children, left to shift for themselves throughout the long dreary winter, too often on a very slender provision of flour and potatoes and little else.'[39]

In 1836, John Dunbar Moodie, who had a few years earlier settled north of Peterborough with his wife, Susanna, wrote to a brother-in-law in Britain who was contemplating emigra-

Eliza Harris, 'Moving Day', watercolour, *c.* 1848. In this humorous sketch Eliza Harris (b. 1825), a member of a well-to-do London family, pokes fun at the gendered division of work. J.J. Talman Regional Collection, D.B. Weldon Library, University of Western Ontario.

tion that 'Canada has often been called the country for the poor man,' however 'the poor man here without industry, or who from habit or weakness is unable to endure hard labour is indeed in a deplorable condition,—and meets with no compassion.' Moreover, Moodie warned, 'Farmers only profit from the labour of their own families.' Like most farms, most families were still just resources in the making. The average rural home in 1850 held 6.4 people, but half of the rural population was children. Few families had sufficient labour power—specifically, grown sons. As early as age eight, children were expected to assist in

planting and burning. For most rural children, seasonal farm work continued to take precedence over school attendance. Rural schools developed haphazardly until, in 1846, legislation was passed instituting a more formal, centralized system extending throughout rural Upper Canada. Of his boyhood on his brother's farm north of York in the early 1820s, John Carroll, a Methodist preacher, recalled, 'it was . . . frugal fare and work, work, work.'[40]

Women were essential members of the rural workforce. Upper Canadian women were more likely to marry—and marry earlier—than their European counterparts. In 1791,

Julian Ruggles Seavey, 'In the Doctor's Study', 1890, oil on canvas. Doctors were rare in early Upper Canada, and not widely trusted. High infant mortality rates attest to the limits of their abilities and resources. This darkly ominous painting suggests that, even by the end of the century, doctors were not always warmly regarded. London Regional Art and Historical Museums, Gift of the Estate of Dr Fred Luney, London, Ont., 1987, 87.A.52.

William Chewett, a land surveyor, announced that after 'mature and deliberate consideration . . . [I] found a girl whom I mean to make a partner for life, and without which it is impossible to exist in this settlement.' One male settler noted that 'a capital help-mate . . . can do the work of a man, as well as her own domestic duties.' A Black settler recalled of his wife: '[she] worked right along with me . . . for we were raised slaves, the women accustomed to work . . . I did not realize it then; but now I see she was a brave woman.'[41]

Even those raised for a gentler life did much more than clean house. Anne Langton, who confessed to being 'somewhat too tenderly bred for a backwoodswoman', made candles, butchered and cured meat, baked, sewed, washed, gardened, cooked, and glazed windows.[42] In Langton's view, the economic importance of a wife in rural Upper Canada put her on a more equal footing with her husband—unlike a woman in 'the state of semicivilization' where she must 'be contented to be looked upon as belonging merely to the decorative department of the establishment and valued accordingly'. The doctrine of 'separate spheres' for men and women might have been gaining ground in the cities, but on the frontier all members of the household had to be prepared to make full use of all their abilities. Many rural wives not only worked alongside their husbands on the farm but managed the family's financial affairs as well. 'My wife always has the charge of the money,' one man testified in court. Another witness told the court that the wife 'does all the business most trading and bargaining, she generally makes the bargains and the husband signs.'[43]

Illness and injury were omnipresent features of rural life. In his first year at Orangeville, Wilson Benson cut his foot and was unable to walk for six weeks. In the early 1860s, his wife and youngest daughter died (he remarried soon after); in the 10 years between 1863 and 1873, he nearly died in an incident with a runaway horse, broke his ribs in a fall from a hay loft, and crushed his arm, leg, and head in a threshing-machine accident, after which he never regained the strength to continue farming.

Horse-related injuries were especially

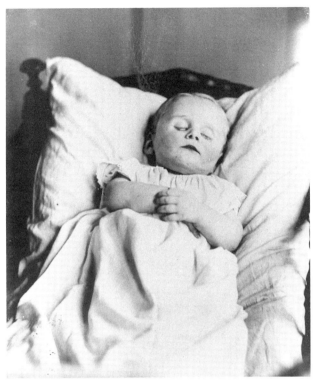

Anonymous child, *c.* 1870. A posthumous portrait was a fairly common way for bereaved parents to remember their lost children. In rural Upper Canada, children were far less likely than adults to survive illness or injury. The records of James Langstaff, a rural doctor in Richmond Hill, show that in the 1860s, one of every 40 children he visited died; the rate for adults was only one in 100; over the four decades between 1850 and 1890, one in every six or seven babies did not live through childhood. Nor were the odds necessarily better for the children of doctors themselves: eight of the Langstaffs' own 11 children did not survive infancy. Photographic Collection, University of Waterloo Library.

common—perhaps not surprising, given the state of the roads. Some roads were constructed and maintained by private companies that charged tolls for their use. Yet even as late as 1893, two-thirds of all expenditures on township roads and bridges came from statute

Sir James Alexander, 'Finish of the Party to the Falls, January, 1843'. Even in winter, road travel could be eventful. When Charlotte Harris of London went out 'driving' in December 1848, she encountered friends 'standing over a wreck of what had once been a beautiful sleigh. They had had a smack!' A little farther on, Charlotte and her friends 'met Dr Combe pulling his horse out of the ditch, and asked him what was the matter. "Oh! Nothing, the horse only went into the Ditch, it is no matter. Never mind!" So we left him. Driving through the town [London] Mr. Lutyens drove over a small boy—but, fortunately for him, he was not . . . hurt.' Small wonder that Dr Langstaff became an active advocate for government road maintenance. NAC C98771.

places the mud is from three to five feet deep. In passing horses are generally breast high, sometimes almost covered in it.' According to the Reverend Daniel Allan, of London, roads were 'more properly speaking mud canals'. City-dwellers might complain, but farmers—by far the majority of the population—made do. In any case, most farm produce was sent to market during the winter months, when cart wheels were replaced by runners that slipped easily over snow-covered roads. No doubt, as another farmer noted in 1817, the fact that 'business is mostly contrived to be done by sleighing' contributed to 'the neglect of the roads'.[44]

For many farm households, the challenges of frontier life were eased by proximity to family—relatives often lived only a few kilometres apart. Land was kept within cultural and kin groups, and families often wrote back to their home country to encourage other family members to emigrate. Many farmers also hired seasonal help, took in boarders, and invited friends and relations to work bees, where they would help out with some large job in return for generous quantities of food and drink.

Susanna and John Moodie were typical in many respects. At times the Moodies hired occasional help—which they could not afford to pay—and leased some of their land to tenants on a share-crop basis. Susanna's sister Catharine Parr Traill and brother-in-law for a time lived close by and helped when they could, but they too were struggling to manage a farm with a young family and insufficient cash. Susanna had just given birth at the commencement of the arduous year that she managed the farm in the absence of her husband, who, like many farmers, had been forced to

labour (labour that residents of the district were required by law to perform) or money paid in lieu thereof, and as a consequence the work was often badly done. Moreover, supervision was left to local residents, usually prominent farmers, and these 'pathmasters' tended to ensure the maintenance of sections near their properties at others' expense. 'In the spring, and fall of the year,' complained a resident of Lanark County, 'it is scarcely possible to pass where the road has a descent. In these

In the April 1854 issue of the *Cottager's Friend,* Mrs L.H. Sigourney commended 'that almost forgotten utensil, the large spinning wheel. From the universal yet gentle exercise it affords the limbs, the chest and the whole frame, it is altogether the best mode of domestic calisthenics which has hitherto been devised.' Image from Haight, *Country Life in Canada,* Belleville, 1971 (1885), 80–1.

seek work off the farm in order to make ends meet. She already had several children under the age of eight: truly a family in the making. During this time, Susanna found the greatest support, especially during periods of sickness, from 'the disinterested kindness of my female neighbours.'[45]

Many people on the rural frontier had supportive links with a broader community. Agricultural societies, designed to assist inexperienced farmers, held regular meetings where farmers could display their produce and livestock and share information. The Orange Order, a fraternal order originally formed to support Protestantism in Ireland, proliferated throughout Upper Canada in the 1830s and 1840s and offered not only social activities, some poor assistance, and funeral support, but—as we shall see—considerable political clout. Yet there was also a much harsher reality.

When the Presbyterian minister Daniel Allan set out on foot to visit his rural flock, he was subjected 'to the taunts and insolence and scorn of every vulgar waggoner and Sleigh-driver . . . merely because I couldn't afford to gratify his thirst for gold by an extravagant fee for hurling me a few miles thro the wilderness.' Wilson Benson lost a house and an acre of land to a sharp speculator, and he once had eight bushels of his grain stolen from the local mill, very likely by a fellow Irishman. Work bees were not always occasions for the expression of brotherly love: one rural magistrate 'used to go away to the woods when [he] heard there was a fight at a bee, and keep away until the blood had cooled down.' Formal law enforcement was chancy at best. Even Susanna Moodie sheltered a man for whom 'a warrant was out' from the local sheriff, and communities often took matters into their own hands.

One way of encouraging compliance with community norms was to stage a charivari—a raucous concert, typically performed on pots and pans, in which citizens would express their opinion of some dubious person or behaviour. An unusual wedding—say, between partners of widely differing ages— was a classic occasion for a charivari. In 1857, in the village of Tavistock (near Stratford), an angry crowd chased a prostitute and her client away from a hotel and continued to pursue them until they handed over an acceptable sum of cash. And in 1872 residents of Sand Point, in southeastern Ontario, disciplined a labourer caught stealing a coat by painting him with tar and parading him around the hamlet on a pump.

Less dramatic but probably more effective at setting standards were the church committees that sat in judgment on members accused of transgressions in any number of areas: behaviour within the family, business practice, sexual conduct, leisure activities. Without confession and repentance, the person 'found stirring up strife' would often be expelled from the congregation. Like the more secular charivari, the disciplinary activities of the local church reflected both the absence of boundaries between public and private spaces and the primacy of community values over what we now regard as individual rights. At a time when the police and judicial systems were only beginning to develop, these were important ways to enforce compliance with community norms.

The ability to define those norms was often simply a matter of power. Especially before the mid-1800s, rural magistrates and constables rarely acted against the wishes of influential citizens; in the Northumberland– Durham County region alone, we know of 50 cases of assault on constables and magistrates between 1813 and 1840. In the Brantford area, two gangs 'often join[ed] forces to club quiet citizens left and right'. The 'swamp angels' terrorized residents in Grey County. In Durham Township a group of self-appointed 'social regulators' called themselves the 'Cavan Blazers'. An overtly criminal organization known as the Markham Gang operated with impunity northeast of Toronto in the 1830s and early 1840s, as did the Ribble family in Elgin county in the early 1830s.[46]

Individuals without family support were especially at risk. In 1859, in a small village near Guelph, a destitute mother and child sought assistance at the home of two bachelors; when the men refused to help, the woman collapsed and died. In 1839, a girl named Julia Higgins, working for the Cruden family near Brantford, was found 'in the most wretched condition literally naked filthy and full of bruises so much so one would hardly suppose her a human being'. It appeared that Mrs Cruden had been the worst abuser. The local

John Langton's house, Sturgeon Lake, 1838. This sketch of a room in Langton's eight-room log house suggests a more comfortable life than most Upper Canadians likely enjoyed. Langton went on to become an influential civil servant specializing in financial matters. AO 719.

magistrate judged the case to involve merely a 'petty assault' and the Crudens got off with a fine. This was not the only violent incident in which the Crudens were implicated. Almost as soon as John Thompson, a newly arrived settler, purchased a farm from them, the Crudens began vandalizing his property and physically harassing him in an effort to drive him away and enable them to reclaim the farm. Thompson received only reluctant support from the magistrate, who was loath to confront a powerful local family on behalf of a stranger.[47]

Some settlers found it impossible to sustain a life on the farm. Near the end of her year alone, Susanna Moodie wrote to her husband:

I know not what to do about the farm, and I am so dispirited that I care nothing about it. I have no money to hire labour to cut the grain and the crop is but indifferent. I fear I cannot even let it on shares . . . Jorys and Garbut [labourers they had previously hired] dun me constantly. Oh heaven keep me from being in these miserable circumstances another year.

Eliza Harris, 'Col. Talbot's Den'. Thomas Talbot was an eccentric, autocratic, and wealthy land speculator who, between 1814 and 1837, settled 50,000 people on 650,000 acres of land in the Thames River area of south-western Ontario. Harris Family Papers, University of Western Ontario.

Such another winter as the last will pile the turf over my head.[48]

In 1840, the Moodies abandoned the struggle. He became sheriff for Hastings County, while she continued to write and publish; her best-known work, the classic *Roughing It in the Bush*, appeared in 1852. Simply in quitting the farm, let alone in their later employment, the Moodies were exceptional. Between 1851 and 1871, the number of industrial workers in the province doubled; but as a proportion of the total workforce, they increased by only 1 per cent. In fact, during the 1860s, when many Ontario farm families were moving west to Manitoba, their places were quickly filled by urban labourers: in central Ontario, of the labourers listed in the 1861 census who could be traced to 1871, almost four in ten had become farmers.[49]

For many in the backwoods of Upper Canada, achieving any degree of economic security was at best a long and difficult process. 'Affairs along the lake,' a Georgina Township resident lamented in November, 1830, 'show very much the same, misery and poverty being the usual habitans.' As late as 1914, most Ontario farm women would still be lugging water to the house from more than 15 metres away, and only one farm in ten would have indoor plumbing.[50] Assessment evidence dating from the 1840s points to the beginning of the regional differentiation that would characterize southern Ontario in the late twentieth century. A band of wealth stretched along the north shore of Lake Ontario from the Bay of Quinte to the head of the lake and into the Niagara peninsula and London area. Farther east, per capita assessment returns fell by nearly half.

Even for those who, like Benson, did succeed in establishing a measure of stability in their lives, the process was fraught with pitfalls beyond their control. Rural Upper Canada did not provide equal opportunities for all. Rampant land speculation gave enormous advantages to those who arrived first. Family connections and cultural background could as easily lead to exclusion and misery as to acceptance and success. In order to find a congenial place, many had to move more than once. As on other colonial frontiers, progress was measured in acres cleared, wetlands drained, and bushels harvested. In the process, Native people were displaced and Nature despoiled. In the typical parlance of the time, the white man's conquest of the wilderness was all but complete.

CHAPTER SIX

Towards a Canadian Polity: 1791–1867

*I*n the nineteenth century, differences between rural and urban life were not clear-cut: the distinctions that we see today emerged only gradually. In Upper Canada, cities developed slowly even by North American standards. On the eve of the War of 1812, Kingston was the only settlement of more than 1,000. York's population soon rivalled Kingston's, but these were small communities: there were scarcely 300 men over the age of 20 in York in the mid-1820s. For decades to come, the great majority of the colony's people—not just farmers but also industrial workers—would live in the country. By the time of Confederation, the largest manufacturers were located in the cities, but many of the smaller firms were still craft-based and rural. In the United States, most Irish immigrants found industrial work in the cities, but in Upper Canada, urban and rural areas showed little difference in ethnic composition, and the Irish—such as Wilson Benson—were as likely as any other colonists to live in the countryside.

Urban settlements came into being largely to serve the needs of rural people. Nevertheless, as those who aspired to power gravi-

tated to them, cities quickly became hubs of activity—political, administrative, commercial, legal, religious, educational, cultural—out of all proportion to their size.

'Every establishment of Church and State that upholds the distinction of ranks and lessens the undue weight of the democratic influence, ought to be introduced,' declared John Graves Simcoe in 1792.[1] In his wilderness domain, Upper Canada's first lieutenant-governor hoped to create a society mirroring the English one he had left behind—a society ruled by a landed aristocracy (through the appointed executive and legislative councils), a state church (the Church of England), and a small bureaucratic elite (at York). Simcoe and his bureaucrats disdained all things American, but many Upper Canadians were of American origin themselves. Some were already renewing ties with family and friends they had left a few years before, and merchants like the Loyalist Richard Cartwright and the Scottish-born Robert Hamilton regularly traded and otherwise communicated with their neighbours to the south.

A powerful commercial elite had established itself in the region a few years before

Simcoe's arrival in 1792. Merchant families such as the Cartwrights of Kingston, the Hamiltons of Niagara, and the Askins of Detroit—all of whom had connections with the Todds and McGills, the fur-trading families of Montreal—exercised significant economic, administrative, and legal power. Unable to dislodge this elite, the lieutenant-governor and his staff allied themselves with it. Merchants sat on the legislative and executive councils originally intended as the preserves of the gentry. Simcoe was pleased to be entertained at the homes of wealthy merchants such as Robert Hamilton—and social life in tiny York was an incestuous round of balls and suppers as wives vied to advance their husbands' fortunes. Who dined, danced, and dallied with whom was a serious matter, as Anne Powell, wife of the chief justice, underlined in anticipating a forthcoming ball to honour the Queen in 1806: 'rank will be settled and I fear some who claim precedence, will find themselves of less importance than they expect.' Social connections, especially those that might lead to marriage, were all the more significant given that offices could be owned and bequeathed to one's heirs: 60 per cent of the major appointments made at York between 1803 and 1812 went to members of established families.[2] But the emerging commercial/bureaucratic elite did not exercise absolute control.

Although merchants controlled the offices of the justices of the peace, settlers were sometimes able to use the courts to protect their own interests. In the early 1800s, district juries composed of small landowners occasionally overturned judicial decisions or handed down lenient sentences in matters of debt repayment, despite the risk of being fined by the

THE TIME HAS COME,
In Erin Village,
Where you can get
DRY GOODS

Suitable for the Season; GOOD ENOUGH for Lords and Queens; and

STRONG ENOUGH

For honest MEN and WOMEN at a

SHADE OVER HALF PRICE.

GROCERIES, at Prices LOW ENOUGH to astonish CREATION.

JUST LOOK!

HYSON TEA	1 10½d per lb.	TOBACCO, Good	1 3d per lb.
Good do	2 6d lb.	SOAP	3½d lb.
SPLENDID do	3s lb.	CANDLES	10d lb.
Very best GUNPOWDER 3	3d lb.	Very best CURRANTS 7½d	lb·
GROUND COFFEE	1s lb.	No. 1 HERRINGS	2 6d lb.

The Subscriber would take the privilege of returning his sincere thanks to the People of

ERIN, CALEDON, AND GARAFRAXA,

For the very LIBERAL PATRONAGE extended towards him since his commencement in business; and he hopes, still further, that by keeping

GOOD GOODS

and selling GOOD GOODS at very LOW PRICES, he may maintain their custom for the future.

Produce taken in exchange for goods.

Hugh McMillan.

ERIN VILLAGE, Nov. 21, 1859.

W   Mackenzie, Printer—Weekly Message Office, Toronto

Merchant's advertisement, 1859. By 1846, at least 160 villages in Upper Canada supported two or more stores, and itinerant hawkers and peddlers fanned out across the colony. The last line of this jaunty ad indicates that the barter economy was alive and well in the late 1850s. AO Mackenzie-Lindsey Collection F37, #32, 5254.

court for unpalatable decisions. As early as the 1790s, elitist political leaders like D.W. Smith—the acting deputy surveyor general, who consistently referred to the electors as 'peasants'—expressed concern about the 'violent levelling principles' held by some rural members of the assembly. Smith was particularly upset by a move to hold town meetings, a form of American political activity that he saw as usurping the functions of the elected assembly.[3] Perhaps even more disturbing was the fact that such activities were independent of the lieutenant-governor's patronage, of which Smith himself was a recipient. Grievances escalated as settlers saw their taxes used to build schools located too far away for their own children to attend and imperial administrators raised land settlement fees, padding their own pockets in the process.

Robert Thorpe, an Anglo-Irish judge of the Court of King's Bench, became a spokesman for some of the discontented. Frustrated when he was not appointed chief justice in 1806, Thorpe began to criticize what he considered the oppressive actions of the clique at the centre of power. While on his judicial rounds in the central and western regions, he also encouraged jurors to express their opinions on civil affairs. Their comments reflected the frustration felt by small farmers, many of them Loyalists, with respect to land settlement fees and the perceived Scots hegemony both locally (the Hamilton family at Niagara) and at York. Despite his position on the court, Thorpe successfully ran for election to the assembly in 1807. Then in June 1807 Joseph Willcocks—a fellow Irishman, allied to Thorpe, who had been dismissed from his position as sheriff of the Home District for 'general and notorious bad conduct'—moved to Niagara and set up the young colony's first opposition newspaper, the *Upper Canadian Guardian*.

Even though Thorpe had always stopped well short of promoting rebellion, York's bureaucrats and Niagara's 'shopkeepers' alike saw him as a troublemaker. Willcocks's new publication was the last straw. Closing ranks against the 'desperados', they enlisted William Allan, a Scots merchant and the postmaster at York, to open Thorpe's mail, and Lieutenant-Governor Francis Gore arranged to bribe American postmasters in order to 'procure a sight of the letters address'd to the [opposition] parties'. When the *Guardian* printed a petition signed by 350 Thorpe supporters, mostly small landowners, the executive council compiled a 'blacklist' of 64 names sorted into five categories: 'ignorant, but may be trusted' (7); 'ignorant and not to be trusted' (1); 'a little of the rogue' (36); 'a very great rogue' (8); and 'a dangerous fellow' (12). Finally, suspended by the imperial government, Thorpe left Upper Canada in July 1807.

Petty jealousies certainly played a part, but the Thorpe affair was more than a falling-out among the bureaucratic elite. The discontent for which Thorpe served as a lightning rod did not disappear with his departure. Willcocks's *Guardian*, lamented one member of the elite, seemed to be in every household in the western district. Gradually, the composition of the assembly changed to reflect this dissatisfaction. By 1812, under the loose leadership of Willcocks, 11 broadly reform-oriented members (out of 23) were generally voting together, arguing for legislative control of money bills, lower salaries for bureaucrats, lower assessment rates, and a loosening of the regulations (such as a stringent definition of 'Loyalist') that made it difficult for settlers to obtain land grants and easy for administrators to pocket fees.[4]

Religion was another way for citizens to express dissent. Methodism, which had origi-

Methodist camp meeting, 1859. This sketch is the earliest known depiction of a Methodist camp meeting. It took place at Grimsby, Upper Canada. Women and men lined the benches. Archives of the United Church of Canada/Victoria University Archives, Toronto, 90.162P/2019 N.

nated in England as an evangelical movement within the established church, came to Upper Canada, in an American-influenced form, with the Loyalists. Whereas the Anglicans stressed acceptance of the social hierarchy and deference to one's 'betters', the Methodists, the colony's largest religious group, emphasized fellowship, free choice, and individual salvation. Since most Methodists—indeed, most settlers—were of American background, their

religion also represented at least the potential for a sense of community with the republic south of the border.

Methodist practice was rarely overtly political. Nevertheless, it served to undermine the Tory values at the centre of Anglicanism. Methodist clergy generally came from the lower ranks of society themselves and preached in a forthright, energetic, even boisterous fashion. All classes were welcome to

Bishop John Strachan of Toronto, 1847. Strachan taught many of Upper Canada's future elite at his school at Cornwall before becoming rector of York in 1812. He viewed human nature as innately corrupt and believed that church and state had to work together to keep it under firm control. MTRL JRR T15000.

mingle on the fields where Methodist camp meetings were held, and Methodism played an important social role in bringing rural people together. In 1805, for example, some 2,500 worshippers attended a camp meeting at Hay Bay extending over several days. Many experienced what the itinerant preacher Nathan Bangs called the 'jerks': 'a spark of Divine power' that shocked worshippers, causing them to lose control and twitch, roll, sing, and fall to the ground. This, Bangs said, was God

relating directly to the individual, delivering the people 'from bondage' and bringing them 'into liberty'. Such communal religious experiences enhanced the people's sense of self-worth and helped to create an identity separate from that of the merchant-bureaucratic elite at Kingston, York, and Niagara. How long could the social order survive if such behaviour were tolerated? Men and women, boys and girls, could as individuals experience God's will. A woman who felt the call of God at Hay Bay left her husband to continue her spiritual journey alone, and exulted in the freedom she found, becoming a 'new creature in Christ'. How long could the patriarchal family order survive if such independence were permitted? Small wonder the Anglican elite forbade Methodist ministers to conduct marriages.

John Strachan, a prominent Anglican minister and school teacher, dismissed the Methodists' 'irrational' outpourings, but he saw the links between Methodism and Reformism and recognized the danger that the Methodists' 'republican ideas of independence and individual freedom' represented. Strachan urged the Anglican clergy to 'outpreach and outpractice our opponents'. But the Methodist clergy outnumbered their Anglican counterparts by two to one and enjoyed a virtual monopoly on the rural circuits, which they travelled on horseback while the Anglicans stayed put in their urban parishes. Additional tactics were required. Thus Anglicans frequently questioned the moral character of Methodist preachers, and when Methodist ministers were elected to the assembly, they were forbidden to take their seats, simply on the basis of their religion. Willcocks and his supporters, some of whom were themselves Methodist, deplored such tactics and did their best to fight back.[5] In 1812, however, the emerging Reform movement suffered a serious blow.

Relations with the republic to the south had stabilized after 1794, when Britain ceded her western forts to the United States, but the situation changed with the renewal of French-British conflict in the first decade of the nineteenth century. Believing that the Americans supported France, Britain attacked an American frigate, the *Chesapeake*, in 1807. Around the same time, the British also began to arm and supply various Native groups on the western frontier whose lands were being taken over by the expanding American nation. Harassed on the seas, frustrated on the frontier, and convinced that most of the American-born Upper Canadians were secretly awaiting deliverance, the US declared war on Britain in June 1812.

Senior Upper Canadian civil and military personnel also doubted the people's loyalty—not without reason. When General Isaac Brock attempted to impose a form of military rule, the assembly refused to comply. At least half of the Upper Canadian men called out for militia duty between 1812 and 1814 failed to appear, and those who did rarely stayed for the duration. Some deserted; others solicited from the Americans a 'parole of honour' promising, in return for their freedom, to refrain from fighting for the rest of the war.

Dramatic early victories at Detroit and Queenston Heights, where Brock lost his life, only temporarily eased local dissent. Indeed, militia participation peaked before Brock's death and declined dramatically thereafter. Although the sacking of York, in April 1813, led to criticism of the British regulars, the real-

ity was that the local inhabitants had virtually refused to assist in the battle. During the Americans' three-day occupation of the town, nearly every militiaman in the Home District (the administrative district within which York was situated) negotiated a parole. Governor General Sir George Prevost responded by appointing agents to root out traitors. Fearing that appointed government agencies would be strengthened at the expense of the elected assembly, many Reform leaders, including Willcocks, left the colony, some to fight on the American side.[6] Finally, in December 1814, the Treaty of Ghent brought an official end to a war that had come to a standoff.

The consequences of the war varied for different segments of the population. Iroquois fighters had been instrumental in achieving an early victory at Detroit in 1812 and, under the leadership of Tecumseh, Native allies from the US had fought valiantly in the Lake Erie region in the fall of 1813, only to be abandoned by the British at Morristown, where some 500 perished before an onslaught of roughly 3,000 Americans. Iroquois had been active as scouts, ambushers, light infantry, and flanking units in the Niagara region.[7] Yet the treaty gave them nothing, and later, when Upper Canadians filed claims for 'war losses', more than a quarter of those claims accused Native persons of theft.

The war was particularly hard on the Niagara area, severing the link to the old western fur-trading region and ending the already declining trade along the Detroit-Niagara-Montreal route. The York region, on the other hand, profited nicely from a growing trade in wheat and foodstuffs that was a result of the war. As early as 1812, some farmers could afford to pay the £20 charged in lieu of militia

'Surviving warriors of the Six Nations Indians', Brantford, July 1882. These veterans of the War of 1812 are, from the left, Jacob Warner, 92; John Turttle, 91; and John Smoke Johnson, 93. Johnson said he did not scalp anyone in the war; he thought the practice was brutal. NAC C85127.

service, and merchants like William Allan enjoyed a 100 per cent mark-up on goods sold to the military. Many local merchants benefited in similar ways, and the £350,000 spent by the military on supplies in York was doubtless responsible for much joy in the region. As important, the increased civil-military presence strengthened the position of York's bureaucratic-merchant elite as men like Allan rooted out dissenters and kept alert for treasonous activity. Although the Kingston area was largely untouched by the war, merchants there also made money, from both a legal trade with Lower Canadian suppliers and an illicit trade with American merchants, largely of the conservative Federalist persuasion. Aware that the Federalists were in decline as a political force in the US, the elites in Kingston, as in York, were determined that Upper Canada's Tories should not suffer the same fate.

Coming on the heels of the American and French Revolutions and the Irish Rebellion of 1798, the War of 1812 hardened conservative attitudes in Upper Canada and stiffened the

The house in Queenston where William Lyon Mackenzie founded *The Colonial Advocate* in 1824. Photo Peter Fowler.

William Eliot, 'Entertainment', 1845. Eliot stayed in this log house for a night in 1845, while on his rounds as a school superintendent. Its sparse furnishings were probably typical of most early nineteenth-century residences in Upper Canada. McIntosh Gallery, University of Western Ontario.

Entertainment.

George T. Berthon, 'The Three Robinson Sisters', 1846, oil on canvas. Trained in Europe, Berthon painted members of Upper Canada's élite the way they saw themselves: as stately aristocrats in the classical mode. This portrait is modelled on the fashion plates typical of *Godey's Lady Book*, an American magazine that flourished in the mid-1800s. Art Gallery of Ontario, Toronto. Lent by Mr and Mrs J.B. Robinson, 1944.

RIDEAU FALLS NEAR OTTAWA

A timber raft at Rideau Falls, near Ottawa, 1856. As early as 1840, more than 200 vessels a year were unloading timber at Garden Island, just south of Kingston at the entrance to the St Lawrence. There, at peak times, some 700 men worked for Dileno Dexter Calvin, one of the largest timber dealers in the Canadas, constructing timber rafts—some as wide as 40 metres and almost half a kilometre long—to send to Quebec City. Lumbering and land-clearing for farming had a dramatic impact on the forest; in 1832, a British traveller lamented the 'nakedness' of much of southern Upper Canada. NAC C 000482.

Stoneware crock, Franklin P. Goold and Company, Brantford, Canada West, *c.* 1859–67. With permission of the Royal Ontario Museum © ROM.

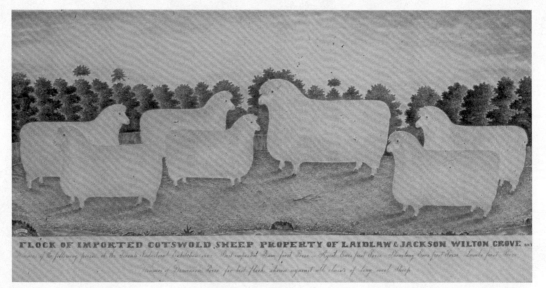

Joseph Smith, 'Flock of Imported Cotswold Sheep', 1887. Proud owners would often commission paintings of their prize-winning livestock. With permission of the Royal Ontario Museum © ROM.

In 1867 Captain Alexander McNeilledge of Port Dover transformed a candle box into a whimsical tribute to Confederation. Some of the inscriptions offer a brief self-portrait: '76 years—Use no specks—Chew no tobacco—Take only a wee drop as required . . . Not bad for an old Scotchie'. Courtesy Michael S. Bird.

elite's resolve to create a conservative fortress on the British North American frontier that would be impervious to extreme democratic influences. 'Disloyal', 'seditious', 'democratic', and 'American' became synonymous as terms of opprobrium hurled by the Tories at any who dared oppose them.[8]

To further their conservative ends, members of the elite often sought appointments to both the legislative and executive councils, and many—including the Revd Strachan—received them. Such overlapping appointments testify not only to the closed nature of the group that Reformers in the 1820s would call the Family Compact, but—more important—to the closeness of the links between the colony's political/administrative structure and its judicial system. Of course, the connections between political and judicial structures always tend to be close: politicians make laws and judges enforce them. In Upper Canada, however, they were so intimate that the same executive council that advised the lieutenant-governor on the colony's administration also served as the final resident court of appeal. In short, it was very difficult to distinguish between those who made the law and those who enforced it.

In keeping with British tradition, Upper Canada's elite viewed the law as an ally in the effort to preserve the social hierarchy within which they enjoyed privileged positions. At the same time they realized that—given the colony's vulnerable position vis à vis the United States, and the discontent evident within the colony before and during the war—too zealous an application of existing law could be counterproductive. Like Britain's ruling class, therefore, they opted for more subtle

George T. Berthon, 'Sir John Beverley Robinson', *c.* 1846, oil on canvas. Robinson, a student of Bishop Strachan's, personified the intimate connections between law and politics within the Family Compact. Appointed acting attorney general at the age of 21, before he had even been called to the bar, in 1818 he became attorney general and in 1820 he joined the legislative assembly, where he became the primary spokesman for the province's elite. In 1829, Robinson was appointed chief justice, a position he held until 1863. NGC 15192.

displays of power—such as a show trial orchestrated by Attorney General John Beverley Robinson in May 1814 at Ancaster (near Niagara). Dressed in regal robes, judges indicted 71 traitors and sentenced 17 to be hanged, drawn, and quartered, before finally pardoning nine, hanging eight, and quartering none. By tempering harsh justice with mercy in a setting evocative of the Crown's majesty, the elite hoped to cultivate loyalty on the part of citizens. A similar strategy informed jurisprudence in lower courts as well. Although the death penalty existed and could be imposed for a wide range of crimes, executions were rare.

The elite also attempted to use religious institutions to conciliate and control the population. While maintaining their belief that the Constitutional Act had established the Church of England as the state church, with all the majesty that entailed, Anglicans recognized that they were in a weak position amidst a religiously diverse and pluralistic society, and they trod softly in the years before 1820. Seven denominations, all predating 1812, competed with the Church of England for Upper Canadian souls. By 1817, Scots Roman Catholics boasted seven priests and 17,000 parishioners. Although their numbers were reduced during the war, Methodists numbered over 5,000 in 1820, with 24 preachers travelling 19 separate circuits. By comparison, in 1819 the Church of England had only nine resident clergy—and it was underfunded; in this period it actually received very little income from the Clergy Reserves, but Anglican parishioners believed that it was amply provided for, and were reluctant to contribute themselves. It was a time for the church to lie low and hope that administrative efforts to attract appropriate immigrants would tip the religious balance in its favour.

Majesty and mercy soon proved insufficient to paper over the essentially self-interested nature of the elite's program. In the

1820s, political, administrative, and legal decisions were having an increasingly oppressive effect on growing numbers of Upper Canadians. By the end of the decade, some assembly members began to coalesce as 'His Majesty's faithful opposition' (a term that had just become current in Westminster).

Several issues prompted the re-emergence of a Reform movement. In 1817, Upper Canadians who had been born in the US after 1783 were stripped of the vote and the right to own land. The so-called Alien Question continued to simmer through 1822, when—at the instigation of Robinson—one American-born representative was denied the right to sit in the assembly. Enraged, opponents of the Tories bypassed the lieutenant-governor and petitioned directly to England for justice. Petitioning had a long history in Britain as a way for common people to make their views known to authorities in an era of limited franchise (in Upper Canada, fewer than half the men were qualified to vote). Lieutenant-Governor Sir Peregrine Maitland nevertheless felt that petitions sent directly to the Colonial Office constituted a 'remarkable' departure: an understandable reaction, since the tactic undercut the executive's control of communications with imperial authorities. Even more remarkably, from Robinson and Maitland's perspective, the Colonial Office responded by requiring that American-born Upper Canadians be granted equal civil rights.

A series of other 'outrages' further escalated passions. In 1817 a fiery Scots Reformer, Robert Gourlay, canvassed citizens for their grievances and encouraged them to speak out. When Strachan attempted to silence him, Gourlay called the vicar a 'monstrous little fool of a parson' and organized a public convention, in July 1818, to discuss problems. Increasingly under siege, the elite abandoned any pretence of mercy. Robinson had Gourlay's mail intercepted. The assembly passed a Seditious Meetings Act—drafted with the assistance of the justices of the Court of the King's Bench, thus making any subsequent appeal to that body of dubious worth—banning public conventions. Gourlayites were dismissed from military and civil positions. Bartemous Ferguson, editor of a Niagara newspaper supportive of Gourlay, was fined £50, jailed for 18 months, and was not released until he posted the huge sum of £500 in sureties to ensure good behaviour for the next seven years. Under an 1804 law allowing the banishment of any recent arrival who disturbed the 'tranquillity' of the colony, Gourlay was arrested, put in solitary confinement for nearly eight months—during which his mental health deteriorated—and finally convicted and banished. Between 1804 and 1828 the state instituted 34 similar prosecutions—conceivably more, in proportional terms, than all the prosecutions undertaken in England to repress dissent during the period of the French Revolution.

Buoyed by increasing Anglican immigration from the British Isles, Strachan began to push the prerogatives of the Anglican church. Already in control of school textbook selections, he lobbied for an Anglican-controlled university. Reformers countered his blatantly false statistics on the relative numbers of Anglicans and Methodists by circulating another petition (this one with 8,000 signatures) decrying the 'clerico-political aristocracy'.[9]

Unruly social behaviour was common at this time. John Carroll, a Methodist preacher who had lived in the colony's capital in his youth, recalled that 'York boys' were very warlike: gangs were 'pelting one another with stones and clods almost everywhere, insomuch that it was dangerous to walk the streets'; gang members were 'expected loyally to bear fealty to [their] military commanders', many of whom were 'respectably connected' boys; and even girls took part in school brawls.[10] Now a series of violent incidents perpetrated by Tory supporters added to the rage engendered by the Alien Question, the Gourlay affair, and religious disputes. In 1826 the printing press of the Reform newspaper editor William Lyon Mackenzie was smashed in what became known as the Types riot, and parts of the press were dumped into Lake Ontario. George Rolph, a long-time Reformer, was stripped, tarred, and feathered by a band of sheet-covered men in blackface that included two magistrates, one of whom was also the local sheriff. In 1828 a vindictive series of libel charges initiated by Robinson against Francis Collins, another reforming editor, put Collins in prison for a year before the Crown halved the sentence.

The repression reached a climax of sorts in the case of Judge John Walpole Willis, who arrived from Britain in 1827 as a junior judge on the Court of the King's Bench. He quickly rendered himself suspect in the eyes of the elite by listening to Reform as well as Tory opinion. On several issues related to the tar-and-feather case he disagreed with his fellow judges. Finally he questioned whether the Court was empowered to sit without at least three judges present (legally it was not, but in practice it had done so countless times). The fact that he

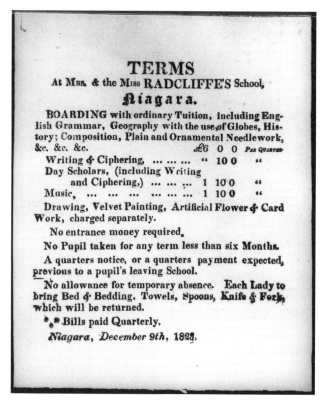

TERMS
At Mrs. & the Miss RADCLIFFE'S School, Niagara.

BOARDING with ordinary Tuition, including English Grammar, Geography with the use of Globes, History; Composition, Plain and Ornamental Needlework, &c. &c. &c.   £6 0 0 *Per Quarter*

Writing & Ciphering, ... " 10 0 "

Day Scholars, (including Writing
   and Ciphering,) ... ... 1 10 0 "

Music, ... 1 10 0 "

Drawing, Velvet Painting, Artificial Flower & Card Work, charged separately.

No entrance money required.

No Pupil taken for any term less than six Months.

A quarters notice, or a quarters payment expected, previous to a pupil's leaving School.

No allowance for temporary absence. Each Lady to bring Bed & Bedding. Towels, Spoons, Knife & Fork, which will be returned.

** Bills paid Quarterly,

Niagara, December 9th, 1828.

Advertisement for Radcliffe's School, Niagara, 1828. In the early nineteenth century, few schools taught anything more than rudimentary reading and writing. Many children learned to read either at home or at Sunday school. Some schools began to receive public funding in 1816. MTRL Broadside Collection BDS1520; 1828 Radcliffe.

raised these issues in public court further undermined public confidence in the judicial system. Far from supporting the political status quo, Willis argued that loyalty was not God-given, but must be earned: 'Statutes have not given to the People their Liberties; their Liberties have produced them.' The lieutenant-governor and his friends on the executive council ordered Willis's immediate dismissal.

The elite itself seemed impervious to prosecution. The ringleaders of the tar and feather incident evaded prosecution not only in that case but also on separate charges in a brutal rape. The two magistrates were even appointed to higher office by the lieutenant-governor, as were some participants in the Types riot. A York magistrate arranged for the civil damages charged against the Types rioters to be paid by public subscription, and several of the rioters retained Robinson and his close associate, the solicitor general, as counsel. Not only were law officers not obliged to initiate criminal proceedings against the alleged perpetrators of criminal acts, but they could even defend them in court. On the Alien Question, Robinson demanded a strict interpretation of the law and was quite willing to ignore the tradition of permitting American-born settlers to vote; however, on the issue of allowing the court to sit with fewer than three judges, he supported traditional practice despite its illegality. As John Willson, an independent Tory and speaker of the Assembly, noted in 1828, 'it had been difficult to awaken the people from their slumber but they had at last been roused to save their liberties; their complaints were now heard.' For many, the legal system had shown itself to be merely an extension of an arbitrary, devious, and repressive political system. Far from being above politics, law was its handmaiden.[11]

Reformers swept the 1828 election. Yet the Reform ranks lacked unity. Political parties in the modern sense of the term had yet to emerge. A new lieutenant-governor, Sir John Colborne, initiated some social and economic reforms and extended patronage beyond members of the Family Compact, and these moves helped to conciliate dissenters. Nevertheless, Colborne represented only the calm before the storm.

If violence simmered in the 1820s, it came

F.H. Consitt, 'The Rival Candidates', Perth, 1828. Early elections could be rowdy affairs: ballots were not secret, and whiskey, money, and force were regularly used to influence voters. Sometimes ethnicity also played a role: note the kilts among the supporters of the Scots-born Morris. Queen's University Archives, William Morris Collection, 2139; Box 3.

to a boil in the 1830s. Of the 51 riots recorded in Upper Canada before 1840, 44 took place in the 1830s. Indications of unrest elsewhere—the Decembrist uprising in Russia in 1825, the wave of revolution in central and western Europe in 1830, the Chartist movement and electoral reform in England, the rise of Jacksonian democracy in the US, and increasing conflict in Lower Canada—intensified anxiety among the elite, who increasingly

looked to the state and state-supported institutions to contain popular disaffection, imagined and real.

The 1830s marked the beginnings of the rise of the modern institutional state and, in its shadow, the emergence to power of a new ruling class. Now came state hospitals designed, as one doctor explained, to 'repress [the] vices' of the sick; 'houses of industry' charged with reforming their inmates to fit quietly into society; and the Kingston Penitentiary, the colony's largest public building—and an intimidating showpiece of elite power and morality.

At the same time the Tories worked to buttress their political position. Recourse to law was less and less an effective tactic, as juries increasingly failed to accept the Crown's evidence at face value. Their credibility undermined, Tories became more violent in their efforts to thwart the rising Reform movement through press attacks, strong-arm electoral tactics, disruption of political meetings, effigy-burning, and even personal assaults. Moderate Reform leaders like William Warren Baldwin and his son Robert could argue that 'every free Government [must] have two parties, a governing party and a party in check,' but for the Family Compact there were only loyal Tories or disloyal Reformers.

Meanwhile, under the leadership of the moderate Egerton Ryerson, Methodists edged closer to the Tory fold. By the 1830s, the tide of British immigration had radically altered the nature of Upper Canadian Methodism. As camp meetings and itinerant preachers were replaced by urban churches and educated, professionally trained clergymen, and public displays of emotion gave way to more rational principles, the gap between Methodists and Anglicans began to close. When, in 1831, access to the Clergy Reserves and the right to solemnize marriages were extended beyond the Church of England, Ryerson began to speak of Methodists as moderate Tories, loyal to the Crown and averse to radical political reform.

At that moment, it might be argued, a central component of Upper Canada's political and social culture hardened, perhaps permanently. Methodism of the American variety had

preached a voluntary, individual route to salvation, a route compatible with the notion of a society composed of autonomous individuals. For a religion to flourish in early Upper Canadian society, its adherents had continually to sell, cajole, and persuade—in more secular terms, it had to play an active part in the marketplace. Over time, under the pressures of anti-Americanism and British immigration, that aspect of Upper Canadian Methodism withered and its place was filled, at least in part, by a form of Christian loyalism. Although Upper Canadian Methodists continued to insist on the separation of church and state, they increasingly looked to the state for sustenance, stability, and protection. While their American counterparts marketed their beliefs, Upper Canadian religious groups lobbied their government.[12]

This shift was reflected in Ryerson's own life. Born in 1803 to a prominent Loyalist family and raised as an Anglican, as a young man Ryerson experienced an evangelical conversion and, over the objections of his father, left home to follow his calling. As a young man he strongly supported the colony's British ties, and in the 1840s and 1850s he became one of Upper Canada's most powerful bureaucrats, playing a central role in the creation of a state-sponsored school system and giving the Tories access, through the Methodists, to an organized religious body that proved invaluable in the management of local elections. 'Loyalty with us,' one Methodist noted, 'is an integral and essential part of religion.' After the 1830s, Methodists never again challenged the primacy of the state in Upper Canada.

If, to a degree, the Methodists served as a moderating influence within the Tory fold, the

Irish Protestants—many of them members of the Orange Order—played a very different role. Having lived as a loyalist minority in Ireland, they were easily enlisted in the service of the Upper Canadian elite's loyalism. Organized by unscrupulous Tory placemen and aspiring Tory leaders to intimidate dissenters, they provided the physical force that increasingly substituted for the rule of law. 'If you had been in London at the last election,' remarked a traveller named Richard Davis,

> you would have seen a set of government tools called Orange men, running up and down streets crying five pounds for a liberal; and if a man said a word contrary to their opinion he was knocked down . . . and all this in the presence of magistrates, Church of England ministers and judges, who made use of no means to prevent such outrages.[13]

Reformers kept the Colonial Office aware of events in Upper Canada through a series of petitions. They also became increasingly adept at local political organization. Township meetings and county conventions had been held throughout Upper Canada from the late 1820s onwards. Careful to avoid violence, the Reformers worked to extend political debate to a sector of society that the Tories had underestimated. Newspapers, which had multiplied from one in 1813 to 30 by 1833, with a total circulation of 20,000, had become especially effective vehicles for the Reform message. Nevertheless, the Reformers themselves were almost exclusively bourgeois, and they were far more interested in challenging the Tory establishment than in promoting any populist cause. The 40 per cent of males who lacked

the property qualifications to vote were not a part of the Reform movement, even if some of them did attend political meetings and use them, as many used petitions, to voice their needs and aspirations.[14]

Bourgeois Reformers organized and set the agenda for most petitions and all political meetings. And, since the Tories saw no need to dirty their hands cultivating grassroots support—few of their positions depended on elections—bourgeois Reformers dominated the assembly in 1836. In response, the Colonial Office appointed a new lieutenant-governor, Sir Francis Bond Head, hoping that he would promote conciliation. Unfortunately, Bond Head did not know the meaning of collaboration. The ensuing deadlock between the Reform assembly and the Tory governor resulted in the assembly's dissolution and a violent election in 1836 in which Bond Head led the Tories to an overwhelming victory and moderates like Robert Baldwin were entirely shut out of office. In despair, many moderate Reformers withdrew from politics, leaving the movement's leadership open to those of a more radical bent.

Advocates of rebellion were always a small minority in Upper Canada. Most Reformers saw little to be gained through physical confrontation with an established authority capable of calling in military support; they preferred to concentrate on holding the higher moral ground. William Lyon Mackenzie thought differently, however. Having survived more than one attack by Tory vigilantes, Mackenzie believed that anything less than the complete overthrow of the system would be a waste of time. 'To die fighting for freedom is truly glorious,' he wrote in November 1837. 'Who would

Adrian Sharp, 'Escape of Mr J. Powell'. On 4 December 1837 alderman John Powell and two others rode up Yonge Street to spy on rebel activity. They were intercepted by Mackenzie and three of his followers. Powell escaped and was the first to bring reliable information to the city. As he recalled later: 'Mackenzie rode after me and, presenting his pistol at my head, ordered me to stop. I turned on my horse and snapped my remaining pistol in his face; the pistol must have touched him, I was so near; . . . I drew up suddenly at Dr Baldwin's road, galloped up about twenty yards, and then jumped off my horse and ran through the woods. I heard them pursue me, lay down behind a log, for a few minutes, (a person on horseback was within ten yards of the place where I lay) . . . I went immediately to Government House. . . .' (*Christian Guardian,* 14 Feb. 1838, cited in *The Rebellion of 1837 in Upper Canada,* ed. Colin Read and Ronald Stagg [Toronto, 1985], 138.) NAC C4784.

live and die a slave? . . . Come if you dare! Here goes!' In December 1837, Mackenzie donned several overcoats (to ward off bullets) and led roughly a thousand ill-armed followers down Yonge Street from Montgomery's Tavern in an unsuccessful attempt to overthrow the government. A second uprising, near Brantford, failed as well: pursued by Loyalist militia, including 400 warriors from the Six Nations, the rebels fled to the US.[15]

Grievances had been intensified by an international financial crisis in late 1837, which was compounded when Bond Head refused to allow banking policy changes that might have eased the credit crunch. Yet the rebels cannot easily be distinguished from the loyal on economic grounds. Rebels did tend to be of American or Scottish rather than English background, and to be Presbyterian or Baptist rather than Anglican. They also tended to be concentrated in economically healthy areas of the colony, a group of townships north of the first areas of settlement but south of those most recently settled. The fact that only an ill-organized minority actually rebelled did not mean that dissent lacked wider support. When the government, having arrested over 800 alleged rebels, attempted to replicate the show trials of 1814, petitions for clemency with a total of more than 30,000 signatures flooded into Toronto. In this turbulent context, the Colonial Office took steps to repair the fractured Canadian political system.

John Lambton, Earl of Durham, was the British emissary charged with resolving the Canada problem. Durham disembarked at Quebec in June 1838, in full ceremonial dress, astride a white horse, and with an entourage that included an orchestra. Despite this display of majesty, Durham did not side with the Family Compact. Rather, he determined to end forever the elite's hold on local political power and preferment. After six months in the colony, he returned to Britain and prepared a report in which he recommended that, to promote the assimilation of the rebellious French, Lower Canada should join with English-speaking Upper Canada in a single united province. In addition, however, Durham offered a second recommendation: that the assembly should both initiate public policy and appoint 'the per-

EXECUTION OF LOUNT AND MATTHEWS.

TORONTO JAIL

The execution of Samuel Lount and Peter Matthews. Lount (a farmer, blacksmith, and rebel organizer living north of Toronto) and Matthews (a farmer from Pickering) were the only ones executed for their part in the 1837 rebellion. 'The general feeling,' the Reverend John Ryerson wrote, 'is in total opposition to the execution of those men. Sheriff Jarvis burst into tears when he entered the room to prepare them for execution. . . . They ascended the scaffold and knelt down at the drop. The ropes were adjusted while they were on their knees. [The Rev.] Richardson engaged in prayer; and when he came to that part of the Lord's Prayer, "forgive us our trespasses, as we forgive those that trespass against us," the drop fell!' (Quote from Egerton Ryerson, *The Story of My Life* [1883], cited in Read and Stagg, *The Rebellion*, 394–5.) NAC C1242.

sons by whom that policy was to be administered'. While the Tories went into shock, Reformers rejoiced at Durham's proposal for what they called 'responsible government'. In fact, though, Durham himself did not use that term. Nor—contrary to the Reformers' assumption—did he intend to strengthen the elected assembly at the expense of the appointed executive council, or to turn the latter into the equivalent of a modern-day cabinet. Indeed, he left a great deal of power with the lieutenant-governor, who was to govern in 'harmony' with the assembly. Political parties would not be encouraged: councillors would act as individuals, not as party representatives. In linking the executive council to the assembly, Durham actually hoped to strengthen the former by giving it the credibility necessary to administer a state that was becoming increasingly complex, economically and socially.

The Colonial Office shared Durham's short-sighted view of the way the colonies should be governed. Following Durham, it sent over a succession of governors to function according to the rules that Durham had sketched. Soon, however, a more comprehensive blueprint would emerge, devised by a set of moderate, business-oriented, urban-centred politicians, conservative and reform, from both parts of the new united province of Canada. Many of these men, like John A. Macdonald, a rising corporate lawyer in Kingston, and Francis Hincks, a banker and Reform politician, had honed their skills in the 1830s at the level of local commercial and political activity. The heirs to the Rebellion of 1837, they were the ones who would help to devise the new rules and then capitalize on them.

To understand how they managed to take the reins of power requires a closer look at the economic and social context from which this new bourgeois class emerged. By the 1830s, developing urban places such as Hamilton, Toronto, London, Cobourg, Port Hope, Kingston, and Port Stanley were vying for trade and economic power. Merchants and other urban landholders, anxious to modernize an increasingly inefficient system of civic rule by appointed magistrates, pushed for communities to incorporate, and by 1847, 13 towns in Upper Canada had done so. A desire for increased efficiency rather than increased democracy underlay this movement. High property qualifications both restricted the municipal franchise and kept the right to hold local office out of the reach of most urban dwellers: from the 1830s to 1860, between 60 and 80 per cent of elected councillors were businessmen, many of them merchants.[16] Paralleling a similar development in England, the municipal state offered local merchants opportunities to expand and consolidate economic power.

In cities like Hamilton and Toronto, members of the business class developed close social ties: they purchased pews together in the most respectable churches; their children married one another; they accepted, endorsed, and circulated each other's promissory notes. The fact that the Bank of Upper Canada—from 1821 to 1833 the colony's only chartered bank—was controlled by York's merchants gave them easier access to capital than their competitors in other cities had. In fact, this monopoly and the bank's closed-preserve mode of operations contributed as much to York's rise to dominance as did its rich hinterland and its position as capital. When Hamilton's businessmen finally chartered the Gore Bank in the early 1830s, they too treated it as their private preserve.[17]

Politics at the provincial level reflected the growth of regionally focused business elites. While most Upper Canadians continued to farm, the political leaders were becoming more

The steamer *Cobourg, c.* 1840. Cobourg was one of the larger urban communities in Upper Canada in the 1840s. This steamboat was built there but owned by a syndicate of Toronto entrepreneurs. NAC C11865.

representative of the business-minded, capitalistic society that was emerging in urban areas. Before 1830, about two-thirds of the assembly's members had been farmers. Of those elected in the 1830s, however, only a third had farmed, and half of those had also engaged in some other business pursuit.[18] These men wanted a stable political structure within which to pursue their economic ends.

In February 1841, the Act of Union joining Upper and Lower Canada in a single political body provided that structure. Lower Canadians, ruled since the rebellion by an appointed council, had no democratic say in

the Union's creation. In Upper Canada, however, the elected assembly had continued in existence, and for the union to become a reality, the assembly had to be conciliated. Public spending on roads and canals during the 1830s had increased Upper Canada's debt to a level that had become unsustainable. In addition to help with that debt, Upper Canada wanted new development projects in the St Lawrence commercial corridor—as did commercial interests in the lower province. In fact, the idea of union had been broached as early as 1822 by a group of Montreal merchants who understood how the existence of two

Four-dollar bill, Bank of Upper Canada, 1837. At this time banks printed their own notes and were expected to keep adequate reserves on hand to redeem them whenever a note-holder wished. By the early 1850s, bankers regarded Upper Canada as a banking paradise, with a population 'foolish enough and rich enough' to hoard their money 'in old chests, "holes in the wall" and other outlandish natural Banks of deposit' instead of returning it to the banks for redemption. National Currency Coll., Bank of Canada, James Zagon.

jurisdictions hampered development along their common commercial artery. Well aware of the Colonial Office's interest in promoting immigration and settlement, by 1839–40 Canadian businessmen and politicians in favour of union emphasized how helpful a system of canals along the St Lawrence would be. If the construction of those canals was beyond the financial capacity of either Upper or Lower Canada alone, a union of the two might solve the problem.

The promise of a £1.5 million loan from Great Britain did the trick. Debts were merged, even though Canada West (the new name for what most people still called Upper Canada) owed 13 times the amount that Canada East (Lower Canada) did. Consistent with Durham's plan to assimilate the French, Lower

Canada received the same number of seats (42) in the new assembly as its English-speaking counterpart, even though it had 200,000 more people. The official language was English and the capital was Kingston—a stronghold of Anglo-Saxon loyalism. The deck seemed stacked in favour of Upper Canada and British Canadians.

On economic matters most political leaders in the two sections agreed: development should be supported by active state investment in transportation improvements. Although views differed widely in the cultural sphere—both sides were equally committed to separate cultural development within their respective sections—there was also general agreement on the necessity of achieving true responsible government. For Lower Canadian leaders like Louis-

Hippolyte La Fontaine, a lawyer and former rebel, responsible government represented a way to defeat the assimilation project. For Upper Canadian leaders like the lawyer Robert Baldwin and the businessman Francis Hincks, it represented a way to pursue cultural and social as well as economic development in the rapidly maturing frontier society of Upper Canada. First La Fontaine and the Baldwin–Hincks team would collaborate to achieve true responsible government; then they (and their immediate successors) would set about implementing separate agendas for their respective sections.

In effect, then, the goal of assimilation was compromised from the start: a tendency towards dualism was already in place. Almost all contenders for political power agreed on the need for a strong central executive. Where Reformers and Tories disagreed was on which component of the executive branch should have primary authority: the executive council or the governor. Baldwin, Hincks, and La Fontaine all believed that executive councillors should be the central actors. The gulf between the governor and the Reformers was no less significant over the assimilation issue. Charles Poulett Thomson (Lord Sydenham), the first union governor, hoped that the union would serve as a container within which the French could be subdued and assimilated. Yet for the sake of their common goals as Reformers, Baldwin and Hincks were ready to stand by La Fontaine in his efforts to ensure 'la survivance': the retention and enrichment of 'our language, our laws and our religion' in Lower Canada.

Sydenham's conduct during the union's first general election left little doubt about his position on governance. 'In present day terms,' historian Irving Abella has remarked,

'[Sydenham] was at the same time governor general, prime minister, founder, organizer, leader and campaign chairman of his own party, chief electoral officer, commander-in-chief of the armed forces, chief crown lands agent, and head of the Civil Service Commission.' He selected his own candidates, cajoled voters with promises of jobs and government largesse, and took advantage of public balloting by threatening to fire public employees who failed to vote for his candidates. He gerrymandered political boundaries, hand-picked his own electoral officers, and located polls close to his areas of strength. Since elections were staggered over roughly three weeks, he arranged for them to be held in an order calculated to generate a bandwagon effect in favour of his candidates: sure winners were elected first, sure losers last. These tactics were successful, and aspiring local politicians like the young John A. Macdonald took careful note.[19]

In September 1841 Sydenham fell from his horse and died of tetanus. Although he had refused to recognize an alliance between Reformers, to govern effectively even he had to acknowledge that the union's two sections possessed separate languages, religions, civil law codes, judicial systems, and forms of land tenure. Before he died, therefore, Sydenham put in place a dual administrative structure. His successors as governor general (three in the space of only four years) all contributed further to the dualistic trend. As early as 1843, each section had its own law officer, Crown lands commissioner, provincial secretary, and superintendent of education. Far from moving towards a unitary system, then, the Colonial Office's representatives were setting the admin-

John Gillespie, 'View of King Street, Toronto, 1843–4'. In this proud depiction of the emerging bourgeois city, King Street is broader than it was in reality. Commercial buildings and a church steeple are shown in careful detail, and middle-class citizens stroll in the sunshine while workers and Native people are barely visible in the shadows at the left. With permission of the Royal Ontario Museum © ROM 955.175 85CAN128.

istrative foundations for the emergence of a dual—or federal—structure.

The Colonial Office was not pleased. Sir Charles Metcalfe arrived in April 1843 with orders to resist further erosion. Instead, recognizing that the assimilation project made harmony impossible to attain, Metcalfe repealed restrictions on the official use of French, approved Montreal as the new seat of government, and sponsored a general amnesty for most rebels. He stood firm, however, on the issue of executive control. So too did the Reformers, who had long since tired of trusting governors. In a bitter and violent election in 1843, the Reformers went down to defeat in Upper Canada, but their French-Canadian allies, under La Fontaine, swept the lower province. The determination of Hincks and Baldwin to ally themselves with La

Fontaine had paid dividends. Although shut out of power by Metcalfe, the Reformers tightened their party organization and triumphed in the election of 1847.

The La Fontaine–Baldwin government has been called the first true party government to exercise power in the Canadas. It was the first in a long line of bifurcated ministries representing the reality of linguistic duality at the highest political level. Given the Canadas' turbulent and violent political past, the transfer of power from the governor to the party in the assembly controlling the executive council was suitably symbolized by the passage of the Rebellion Losses Bill in 1849, which promised to compensate French Canadians and even some rebels who had suffered property damage in the rebellion. Coming on the heels of

TORONTO, CANADA WEST.

'Toronto, Canada West. From the top of the Jail'. This was one in a series of panoramic views of Canadian cities widely reproduced around the middle of the nineteenth century. Edwin Whitefield. AO 2420.

Britain's repeal of the Navigation Acts and its seeming abandonment of loyal colonists, the Bill aroused the fury of old Compact tories and anglophone merchants in Montreal. Some advocated annexation to the US. When Lord Elgin, the governor general, signed the legislation over Tory cries, Samuel P. Jarvis, an elder Toronto Tory, prayed 'they would . . . string him up as a caution to other traitor governors.' Others did more than pray. They burned the Parliament Buildings in Montreal, pelted Elgin with ripe tomatoes and rotten eggs, and attacked the homes of Reformers like Hincks. Larratt Smith, an up-and-coming Toronto lawyer, recorded the following in his diary in March 1849:

William Lyon Mackenzie is back in town [the state had issued a pardon to all rebels] . . . This evening his effigy, with those of Robert Baldwin and William Hume Blake, was burnt by a Tory mob. . . . The howling mob, which included two city aldermen, smashed in the house of Mackenzie's friend Mackintosh and attacked and stoned the residence of George Brown, editor of the Globe newspaper; then, worn out by its exertions, the rabble sullenly withdrew.[20]

Even Tory vigilantism could not turn back the clock. By 1850, the seeds of Canada's modern political system had been sown.

Not that Baldwin and La Fontaine reaped

the rewards. Their efforts to resolve cultural and political issues were only partly successful. Like the Rebellion Losses Bill, religious and educational matters sparked strong opposition. Of particular concern to Protestants in the 1840s was the rise of Ultramontanism, a movement within the Roman Catholic Church marked by intense devotion to the Pope and aggressive assertion of the church's primacy over the state. When La Fontaine gave in to Catholic demands for control in areas such as education, many Upper Canadians looked askance—ignoring the fact that Lower Canadian Reformers established Protestant institutions as well.

In Lower Canada, elementary schools financed by the state and run by the church increased dramatically in number, as did the religious communities that were the main source of teachers. In an attempt to head off anger and anxiety in Protestant Upper Canada, Baldwin and La Fontaine passed a secular public schools act and secularized the Anglican King's College, creating the University of Toronto. Nevertheless, Protestant fear of Catholic hegemony continued to grow, fanned by the influx of Irish Catholics occasioned by the potato famines, and the principle of 'voluntarism'—that all religions should be supported by the voluntary contributions of their members, rather than the state—grew increasingly influential.

That principle found an effective and outspoken advocate in George Brown, a successful businessman who was editor of the Toronto *Globe* and soon to become the voice of Reform in Upper Canada. When the census of 1851 revealed that Upper Canadians outnumbered Lower Canadians, Brown joined forces with the 'Clear Grits'—Reformers who opposed any religious teaching in schools and wanted to eliminate all official privileges for the French language—to push for representation by population instead of equal representation for each section. Pointing out that legislation regarding schools was often passed on the strength of Lower Canadian votes, over the objections of Upper Canadian representatives, they argued that the imposition of Lower Canadian cultural institutions on the upper province vitiated the compromise at the heart of the Union—a compromise that recognized the distinctiveness of each section and in effect demanded quasi-federal political arrangements to facilitate separate social and cultural development in the two sections. Framing the issue in sectional terms garnered Brown and his followers significant electoral support in Upper Canada; however, arguing in terms of a Protestant crusade against 'papal aggression' made compromise ever more difficult to achieve. By the early 1860s, the schools question would be the single most divisive issue in Canadian politics and a major cause of the political stalemate that characterized the last years of the Union period.

Economic issues were another source of division for the Baldwin–La Fontaine administration. During the 1840s and early 1850s, most political leaders in both Upper and Lower Canada agreed that the state should actively promote improvements in transportation—first canals and then railways—in the St Lawrence corridor to encourage settlement and growth. New loans from Britain in the 1840s facilitated the completion of an impressive canal system by the end of the decade. Initially Baldwin and La Fontaine supported

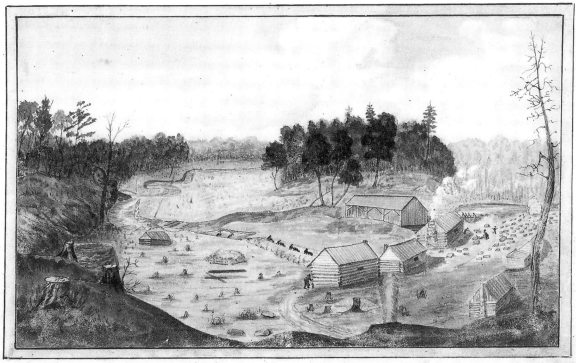

Brewer's Lower Mill;— view down the Cataraqui Creek & Clearing made for the Canal. Sketch taken in 1829.— Excavation for the Lock just commenced.

Thomas Burrowes, 'Brewer's Lower Mill; view down the Cataraqui Creek & Clearing made for the Canal. Sketch taken in 1829. Excavation for the Lock just commenced.' In 1827, the first estimate for building the Rideau Canal was £169,000; the final cost was £822,804. Between 1826 and 1832, some 9,000 men laboured on the Welland and Rideau canals each year. Human costs were high: of the 1,316 men who worked on a small section of the Rideau between Kingston and Newboro in 1830, some 500 died from disease and work-related accidents. The pay was poor, and those who survived the notoriously dangerous working conditions were cast aside as soon as the project was completed. AO C1-0-0-0-67.

the Guarantee Act of 1849, which provided state backing for British loans to select colonial railways, but in time both men became increasingly wary of promoting unrestrained economic growth. By contrast, Hincks and other economically aggressive politicians were pushing for further legislation that would increase the legal rights of chartered companies and extend government guarantees to

other railways. As a result, they began to part company with Baldwin and La Fontaine.

In 1851 Baldwin and La Fontaine retired, leaving their party in the hands of Hincks and Augustin-Norbert Morin, a lawyer-politician from Canada East. Economically, the new government was determined to take a back seat to no North American jurisdiction. In 1847, three years after the telegraph had become

The first locomotive built in Upper Canada. Called the *Toronto,* it was built at James Good's Locomotive Works in Toronto in May 1853. The photograph dates from the mid-1870s. Photograph courtesy of the Canada Science and Technology Museum, Ottawa. CN16257.

commercially feasible, most of the major centres in Upper Canada were linked by it. Railway growth was equally swift off the mark. In addition to passing financial legislation (especially the Mainline Railway Act of 1851) to facilitate borrowing abroad, the government guaranteed the loans of the St Lawrence and Atlantic Railway east of Montreal, the Great Western Railway through the Upper Canadian peninsula, and the Ontario, Simcoe and Lake Huron Railway (later the Northern Railway) north of Toronto. By 1852, municipal governments as well as railroad corporations were allowed to borrow with the backing of the provincial government. Thanks in part to this enabling legislation, British capitalists invested some $70 million in Upper Canadian railways, and more than 2000 kilometres of track were laid in the 1850s, of which more than half belonged to the Great Western and the Grand Trunk—railroads designed, in part, to serve as links between the eastern seaboard of the US and the states of the midwest.

Railways created demand for manufactured items—from rails and spikes to engines—and facilitated the expansion of local markets. In fact, the railways became effective industrial producers themselves: in 1861 the

View of the accident on the G.W. Railway near Dundas, on the morning of the 19th March 1859.
From a sketch taken on the spot.

Great Western Railway accident near Dundas, March 1859. In large black headlines, newspapers routinely reported on 'Frightful' or 'Fearful' railroad collisions. Between September 1853 and October 1854, 79 people were killed and 70 injured in 17 accidents on the Great Western line. A commission of inquiry cited locomotive engineers who ran over cattle for sport, gravel trains that ran on main passenger lines in disregard of published timetables, and a 'system of management unusual on the continent and ill-adapted to the circumstances and magnitude of this enterprise.' It concluded that managerial practices were haphazard and inconsistent.
MTRL JRR T16587.

Great Western employed over 2,000 people and the Grand Trunk over 3,100, and in 1870 two of the three largest industrial companies in the new province of Ontario were railways.[21] Nevertheless, from a political perspective railways, like religion and culture, did little to bind the two sections of the Union. The Grand Trunk, headquartered in Montreal, was originally chartered to provide the central link between the eastern and western roads, creating the backbone of a provincial system. But

its managers had larger ambitions: they wanted to consolidate ownership and control of the entire system in their own hands. Quickly absorbing the St Lawrence and Atlantic lines, they began merger talks with the Great Western. When those talks failed, the Grand Trunk sought help from its political friends, and in 1854 the provincial legislature altered the company's charter to allow for the construction of a line west from Toronto to Sarnia. With this extension running parallel to the Great Western line, the Grand Trunk no longer complemented the latter: now it would openly compete, in a market barely able to sustain a single line.

The Grand Trunk's ambition to redirect the commerce of Canada West through the St Lawrence corridor was naturally popular in Canada East, but it also attracted support in the Kingston area, which depended economically on the St Lawrence. Political leaders elsewhere, particularly in the southwest, regarded the Grand Trunk as a corrupt extravagance that threatened their own railway, the Great Western. George Brown, a staunch friend of the latter, became an increasingly shrill critic of the Grand Trunk in general and in particular of its political friends: John A. Macdonald of Kingston and George-Etienne Cartier of Montreal.

The mid-1800s marked a significant stage in the development of state and business enterprise. The push for development capital emerged from within the colony and paralleled similar initiatives from nearby American states. Local political and merchant promoters set the financial rules—and profited personally—to a surprising extent. Among them was Sir Allan Napier MacNab, the Hamilton businessman who, as premier of the Canadas in the mid-1850s, boasted that 'All my politics are railroads.' MacNab pocketed at least $400,000 (in modern dollars) from shady railway deals, while Hincks and Macdonald were only two of many who benefited from inside information and their political positions. Such activities did not escape the notice of Brown and the Grits. When Hincks became involved in a series of financial scandals, Reformer William McDougall suggested that the government was

on the verge of being abandoned to 'Railway speculators, hungry lawyers and stock jobbers'.[22] As social and political discontent rose, George Brown stood ready to capitalize on it.

From the outset, the provincial government had agreed to guarantee the debts incurred by railways and municipalities. By 1859, acting under the Municipal Loan Fund Act, business leaders in 20 Upper Canadian centres had borrowed $7.3 million, of which $1.2 million was overdue. By the early 1860s, both Toronto and Hamilton had amassed debts of $3 million for purposes not covered by government guarantees. In all cases, the provincial government had to take steps to prevent bankruptcy. In the wake of this borrowing, municipalities curtailed spending on clean water, sanitation, social assistance, and fire protection, reducing the quality of life for the urban poor in particular. When a 'soup kitchen' opened in London, Upper Canada, in 1859, it fed 70 poor families.[23]

In the late 1850s the state and private business alike confronted dramatic structural change. In that decade roughly half of all businesses in Hamilton and Brantford failed: bankrupts often pulled up stakes and moved to evade their debtors and try their fortunes elsewhere. Only two of the 15 banks chartered in Upper Canada before 1867 continued operations into the 1870s. Just before Christmas 1863, the Bank of Upper Canada dismissed 30 of its oldest officers, and three years later, the colony's oldest chartered bank closed its doors for good. 'I dont apprehend any immediate disasterous [sic] result from the Event,' a prominent colonial politician confided, 'beyond loss to the shareholders. . . .' Still, that loss exceeded $3 million and dramatically

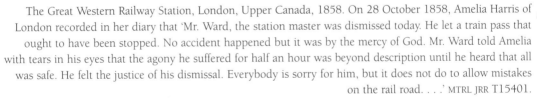

The Great Western Railway Station, London, Upper Canada, 1858. On 28 October 1858, Amelia Harris of London recorded in her diary that 'Mr. Ward, the station master was dismissed today. He let a train pass that ought to have been stopped. No accident happened but it was by the mercy of God. Mr. Ward told Amelia with tears in his eyes that the agony he suffered for half an hour was beyond description until he heard that all was safe. He felt the justice of his dismissal. Everybody is sorry for him, but it does not do to allow mistakes on the rail road. . . .' MTRL JRR T15401.

affected the lives of shareholders like Lydia Payne, a widow living in England who owned 215 BUC shares and 'depended on [her] stock . . . for support in [her] old Age.'[24] Railway companies defaulted on government-backed loans. By the end of the 1850s, the colony's three largest railroads were petitioning the government for relief and half of the government's revenues went to pay interest on debt, largely connected with railways. By that time, government and private finances were virtually indistinguishable.[25]

Workers and their families were far from passive in the midst of such change. At least 15 strikes occurred on the Welland Canal between 1843 and 1849, and at least nine on the Great Western Railroad between 1851 and 1856. In a phrase that captures the transitional nature of the era, one Great Western Railroad engineer recalled that railroad strikes were as common as the 'croaking of the frogs'. In 1853–4 alone, Upper Canada saw 40 strikes led by skilled workers protesting the introduction of machinery and demanding higher wages. As moulders, tailors, joiners, machine workers, printers, and firemen formed unions, a new set of class distinctions, between labourers and owners/employers, began to emerge. Similar experiences—in the workplace, in living conditions, in the family—helped to create a sense of working-class consciousness. In Toronto, even skilled workers found it increasingly difficult to own a home. Different economic groups began to concentrate in specific districts of the city. As on the farm, where larger families meant greater productivity, urban families at the lower end of the economic scale tended to have more children than those at higher levels. Increasingly, though, the labour necessary to maintain the family was done outside the home, under the supervision of strangers. By 1871, women represented more than one-quarter of the employees in Toronto's five largest industrial groups, and children accounted for another ten per cent. Women and children made up just under half of Ontario's tobacco workers, and in industry generally, women and children—some under ten years of age—often worked 60 hours a week for meagre wages.

Meanwhile, the state-sponsored educational system proved less effective at controlling unruly adolescents than its promoters had hoped. Local school boards were slow to adopt the state's slate of texts. In rural areas especially, it was often the religious and ethnic background of the teachers that determined whether a family would send its children to school at all. Moreover, rising educational

costs were making it increasingly difficult for children from lower-income families to attend school past the primary grades.

More privileged members of society also worried about their offspring. Amelia Harris, the matriarch of Eldon House in London, Upper Canada, kept a diary that members of the household were expected to read. In it she advised that 'No child can ever secure their own happiness by going in opposition to a mother, even if that mother is wrong.' A firm advocate of the separate spheres doctrine, she professed that she had 'never in [her] life left home even for a few hours without reluctance'. Much of her diary is taken up with worrying over her children's welfare and devising ways to set their lives on 'proper' courses. Such concern was widely shared.

In 1851, almost 45 per cent of the colony's population was under the age of 16. As in the 1830s, when the influx of young women and men from settled rural areas into urban centres had contributed to the rise of the institutional state, increasing efforts were made to control unruly elements. In the 1840s, municipalities had begun to pass bylaws designed to enforce new social norms. Now temperance movements flourished, police became more efficient, and 'vagrants and vagabonds' were summarily dealt with (in Hamilton the latter made up half of all those jailed between 1843 and 1851). Yet by the close of the 1850s, despite both the proliferation of asylums, poor houses, penitentiaries, and schools, and the professionalization of urban police forces and court systems, 'vagrants', criminals, the insane, and the poor seemed impossible to contain.

Church membership expanded greatly in this era. In 1842 more than one in six Upper

John Howard, Toronto Bay from Taylor's Wharf, 1835. No female skaters are visible in this scene. By the 1860s, however, 'lady skaters [were] springing up in all parts of Canada'—a development that may have reflected the proliferation of skating rinks. 'Many a match has resulted from attentions first received there,' observed Forbes Geddes of Hamilton in October 1862. In the same diary entry Geddes noted that the city was soon to have at least one new rink: 'This will be the Aristocratic Resort. Another one for the "unwashed" is talked of to be constructed at the East end.' Colborne Lodge, Toronto.

Canadians had no church affiliation; by 1872 that figure would fall to only one in every hundred. Before 1840, John Strachan had forcefully proclaimed the importance of the role to be played by the church in aid of the state, but in 1856, he sharply demarcated the two: the 'church and the world [are] two societies as distinct from each other as if each of the par-ties comparing them were of different natures.' The Gothic revival in church architecture symbolized this otherworldly message. For many, it seems, the social and economic dislocations that accompanied the advance of industrial capitalism brought a profound sense of unease. To temper the excesses of this secular life, otherworldly assistance was required.[26]

In part because of the general social and economic turbulence, fissures widened within the Reform alliance. As Brown took over Reform leadership in Upper Canada, moderate Reformers from Lower Canada, led by Morin and Cartier (a former *patriote* who had become a lawyer for the Grand Trunk railway), broke away and joined forces with a group of Upper Canadians made up of some old Tories like MacNab and, more important, some younger moderate conservatives like the lawyer and businessman John A. Macdonald. Representing the triumph of common economic goals over religious and ethnic differences, this new alliance of moderate conservatives from one side and moderate Reformers from the other won the election of 1854 and established a pattern that would remain the norm in Central Canadian politics for the next four decades.

Even as new political coalitions emerged, railways and the state alike slowly began to professionalize and systematize their operations. British investors sent skilled British managers to upgrade the railways' managerial control and operating systems, and the Canadian state passed legislation aimed at encouraging stricter, more centralized control of labour and general operations. At the same time the state reorganized its internal operations to better meet the demands of the emerging industrial sphere and an increasingly complex international financial world. In addition to setting up an internal audit system, it signalled the beginnings of an independent commercial policy by adopting a tariff structure that did not simply favour British imports. A more modern bourgeois state was emerging, one that a decade later would provide the context for Confederation.

For the moment, however, the political structure of the 'united' province was in serious danger of collapse. Although the new bourgeois party had won the election, the majority of Upper Canadians were not prepared to respect French Canadians' cultural differences, and they rejected a party that gave priority to business over the preservation of Protestant 'rights'. Now they rallied around the incendiary leadership of George Brown, who with the Clear Grits hoped to relegate Catholics and francophones to the sidelines. 'We are,' Brown wrote, 'obliged to hold them [French Canadians] accountable for many of the anomalies and much of the wrong which now disgrace the system. They have evinced no forbearance, no generosity, no justice. . . .' The election of 1858 ended in deadlock when Brown's Reformers carried a large majority in Canada West and Cartier's Bleus carried an equally large majority in Canada East. The uneasy Reform/Rouge alliance could now command roughly the same support as the Bleu/Conservative alliance. The Cartier-Macdonald government fell and a new administration was hastily cobbled together under Brown and Rouge leader Antoine-Aimé Dorion. Yet within hours of forming the government, Brown and Dorion were defeated on a confidence motion. Brown and his Upper Canadian colleagues retreated into resentment and bitterness as Macdonald and Cartier reconstructed their Conservative administration.

The most important new player proved to be Finance Minister Alexander T. Galt. Although he had been a liberal, Galt had close connections with the predominantly Bleu business community of Montreal, and as an early promoter of the St Lawrence and Atlantic

HANDKERCHIEF

1. Laying it on Right Check ....
2. Laying it on Left Check ....
3. Drawing it out of Pocket ....
4. Putting it over Right Shoulder ....
5. Putting it over Left Shoulder ......
6. Waving it with Right Hand ......
7. Waving it with Left Hand ....
8. Covering your Face ....
9. Holding it at your Right Side .....
10. Holding it at your Left Side ......
11. Placing it around your Neck ......
12. Crumpled up in the Right Hand ..
13. Crumpled up in the Left Hand ....
14. Dropping it ....
15. Folding it once ....
16. Kissing it ....
17. Tieing it in a Knot ....
18. Holding it open in front of you ....
19. Throwing it up ....
20. Putting it in pocket ....

FLIRTATION.

1. I love you.
2. I hate you.
3. Do you love me?
4. Follow me.
5. Not just now.
6. Will you go out to-night?
7. I'll call for you.
8. I don't want your company.
9. Do you want an Introduction?
10. Never mind an Introduction.
11. May I see you Home?
12. Yes.
13. No.
14. Come now or never.
15. Call me by my right name.
16. The same to you.
17. Remember you are engaged.
18. If you speak I will.
19. Will you see me Home.
20. Good-by.

Courtship practices in nineteenth-century Ontario were more liberal than is often assumed. Many diarists, male and female, recorded late-night parties, and some courting couples spent quite a lot of unchaperoned time alone together. After staying out 'past dusk' with her male friend, one woman remarked that they were 'raising quite a commotion in this illustrious village'. Handkerchief flirtation was one way of circumventing the gossips. MTRL Broadside Coll. 1873.

Railway he held (with Luther Holton and Casimir Gzowski) the construction contracts for the Grand Trunk line west of Toronto. But he was even more interested in western expansion—a subject near to the heart of his new political opponent, George Brown. Galt's immediate economic concerns won out over his reformist orientation, and in 1858 he joined the Conservative government with a distinct agenda of his own: expansion of the colonial union to include the Prairie West. His first priority, however, was to contain the financial crisis signalled by the near bankruptcy of the Union's three major railways.

At a time when 80 to 85 per cent of all the government's revenue came from customs duties, tariffs on US goods were a crucial concern. Since 1855, the Reciprocity Treaty had allowed free trade in natural products but not manufactured goods. Now, in order to increase revenue, foster some local industrialization, and protect the commerce of the St Lawrence, Galt proposed to change the way tariffs were assessed, replacing specific duties with a comprehensive system of *ad valorem* rates. In late 1858 he canvassed all boards of trade in the union for their comments on his plan. Most Lower Canadian boards supported the plan, thinking that it would increase commerce over the St Lawrence River. For that very reason the Toronto board objected and defended the older system of specific duties on the grounds that it was more helpful to 'the commercial body of Western Canada who desire to have the option of two markets'.[27]

That reference to 'two markets' provides an oblique comment on the commitment to reciprocity among Upper Canada's business class. In the past, businessmen had generally assumed that they needed access not only to the US itself but also to Europe by way of both the St Lawrence and the Erie Canal system in the US. When the Reciprocity Treaty took effect in 1855, exports of goods covered by it had doubled (from $8.5 million to $16.5 million) and imports of goods covered by it had quadrupled (to $7.7 million). The beneficiaries of these increases were concentrated in Upper Canada, especially in the southwest. After the depression of 1857, Montreal merchants began to protest that the treaty was diverting trade away from the St Lawrence; in effect, as E.J. Charleton put it, Lower Canada

was being 'sacrificed . . . to Upper Canada Agricultural interests'. Thus Charleton, for one, enthusiastically supported Galt's plan as a 'national policy for the national advantage'.[28] Thus too, like so many policies before it, Galt's commercial policy further intensified sectional conflict.

By 1859 the intensity of that conflict was threatening to split the Reform party. Whereas the more militant Reformers, mainly from the southwest, demanded simple dissolution of the Union, their counterparts east of Toronto—more directly affected by commercial activity along the St Lawrence—wanted to resolve the sectional division. Matters came to a head in 1859, at a Reform party convention. Whatever his personal antipathy for separate schools, the Grand Trunk, or Galt's new tariff, Brown insisted on the economic unity of the St Lawrence–Great Lakes system, and continued to advocate representation by population as the solution to sectional conflicts. Taking the lead, Brown steered the convention towards a new proposal for a federal union. Debate focused on one key resolution:

> That . . . the best practicable remedy for the evils now encountered in the government of Canada is to be found in the formation of two or more local governments to which shall be committed the control of all matters of a local or sectional character and a general government charged with such matters as are necessarily common to both sections of the Province.[29]

To appease the advocates of sectional autonomy, the term 'general government' was replaced with 'some joint authority'. Even though the Colonial Office had rebuffed Galt's demand for a broader union, the confederation option was now clearly on the table. Still, nothing substantive could be achieved without a majority from both sections, and for the moment the sectional rivalries remained too intense.

What broke the logjam was the American Civil War. After an initial economic dislocation, wartime demand in the US led to an economic boom in Canada. But the war brought political risks as well as economic opportunity. Although many Canadians, particularly Reformers like Brown, supported the abolition of slavery, most followed Britain's lead in favouring the South. Relations with the US deteriorated as a result of incidents like the St Alban's raid, in which Confederate agents operating out of Canada East attacked St Albans, Vermont. With the 10-year term of the Reciprocity Treaty due to expire on 31 December 1863, the American Congress began to consider the question of renewal. The danger that non-renewal would pose to Canada West's economy was foremost in George Brown's mind in early 1864, when C.J. Brydges, general manager of the Grand Trunk, approached him to discuss political prospects.

Brydges had been acting as Macdonald's political go-between with Maritime politicians regarding a proposed Intercolonial railway, a project dear to the Grand Trunk. Now, in talks with Brown, Brydges tried to link his own interest in the Intercolonial with Brown's interest in western expansion. He offered Brown the chair of the Canada Board of the Hudson's Bay Company and—as he later reported to Macdonald—did his best to convince the Reform leader that 'nothing could be done

about the Northwest without the Intercolonial'. Assuring Brydges that he was less opposed to the Intercolonial than others imagined, Brown also commented that 'the action of the Yankees on reciprocity . . . put an entirely new face on the question, and that it ought to be taken seriously into consideration.'[30] The key to Confederation had been found. Within four months, Brown, Macdonald, Cartier, and Galt had formed a new coalition government committed to a broader union of the British North American colonies.

Politics aside, the coalition of 1864 brought together two hitherto separate groups of the Anglo-Canadian business elite. On the one hand Galt and Thomas D'Arcy McGee represented that sector associated with the Grand Trunk and Montreal, while John A. Macdonald and his law partner in Kingston, Alexander Campbell, were closely involved with many of the Upper Canadian financial institutions active in railroad financing, and Macdonald was fast friends with C.J. Brydges of the Grand Trunk. This group, centred on the Grand Trunk, favoured eastward expansion via the Intercolonial. At the same time, however, the Grand Trunk was open to westward expansion; indeed, its president, Edward Watkin, had been actively working with the colonial secretary in an effort to arrange the purchase, from the Hudson's Bay Company, of a right-of-way to the Pacific coast.

George Brown, on the other hand, represented the industrial and financial interests of Montreal's rival, Toronto, and the more prosperous interests in rural Upper Canada who, as good land became increasingly scarce, were pressing for expansion to the uncharted prairies. Although Brown, through the *Globe*,

Eliza Harris, 'Go it Chaps', *c.* 1846. One wonders what Eliza's mother, Amelia Harris (see p. 112), thought of young ladies who indulged in such hoydenish behaviour. J.J. Talman Regional Collection, D.B. Weldon Library, University of Western Ontario, Eldon House Diaries I1056.C45, no.15, 1994.

frequently criticized the Grand Trunk for sloppy construction and financial mismanagement, he was far from averse to all railroads, and publicly supported the Grand Trunk's main rival, the Great Western (which rewarded Brown by building a station on land he owned in Lambton County).

Complementary and at times overlapping business interests formed one thread that helped to bind the coalition together. A second thread was shared attitudes towards democ-

racy. Both Macdonald and Brown were elitists, opposed to the notion of political equality, without faith in the ability of the masses, and in favour of privilege for the propertied. This elitism was reflected in Macdonald's insistence on a strong central government. As he told one of the conferences leading to Confederation, local or provincial governments must be kept weak in order to secure 'a strong and lasting government under which we can work out constitutional liberty as opposed to democracy'.

For many of the Fathers of Confederation, the rights of one minority in particular took precedence over majority rule. Which minority should be protected? Certainly not the Native people. Macdonald was quite clear on that point when he wrote to the electoral returning officer of the district of Algoma in Ontario in October 1867: 'I drew the clauses relating to Algoma in the Union Act, but I really forgot all about the Indians. Had they occurred to my mind I should certainly have excluded them.' Accordingly, the returning officer refused to accept any Native votes in the subsequent election. Having made his view of democracy clear during the Confederation debates ('Classes and property should be represented as well as numbers'), Macdonald specified his preferred minority in connection with the establishment of the appointed Upper House or Senate (the North American version of the British House of Lords): 'the rights of the minority ought to be protected and the rich are always fewer in number than the poor.'

George Brown was equally opposed to democracy. In the US, Brown pointed out, 'the balance of power is held by the unreasoning ignorant mass, to swing them is the grand aim of the contest and as truth, character, statesmanship, honest policy and fair argument would be thrown away upon them, both parties by consent—nay of necessity—resort to other expedients.' Not surprisingly, this successful businessman and large landowner numbered among his political supporters some of the richest and most powerful of Toronto's business and social elites. The pro-Confederation forces in the Canadas were united by geography (centred on the St Lawrence–Lake Ontario transportation corridor); by business, commercial, and social interests; and by common economic and political problems. Those elites, linked as they were to powerful financial interests in England, became the moving force behind Confederation.[31]

The coalition, formed in June 1864, acted with dispatch: in September of that year they arrived—uninvited—at Charlottetown, where they took over a conference that had been organized to discuss Maritime Union. Here they presented their broader vision: a federation of British North America. In a letter to his wife, the exuberant Brown described his arrival at Charlottetown in almost imperialistic terms:

> About noon . . . we came suddenly on the Capital City of the Island. Our steamer dropped anchor magnificently in the stream and its man-of-war cut evidently inspired the natives with huge respect for their big brothers from Canada. I flatter myself we did that well. . . . Having dressed ourselves in the correct style, our two boats were lowered man-of-war fashion—and being each duly manned with four oarsmen and a boatswain, dressed in blue uniform, hats, belts, etc., in regular style, we pulled away for shore and landed like Mr. Christopher Columbus who had the precedence of us in taking possession of portions of the American continent.[32]

The broad picture that the Canadians sketched—a strong central government, weak local governments, an appointed Upper House, a debt equalization scheme, and a subsidy program—was accepted at least in principle by a majority of those present at Charlottetown. The details would be hammered out at Quebec.

St James Church, York, 1816. The artist George William Allan described York's first Anglican church as 'a miserable scratch of a thing'. MTRL T30854.

An opponent of the Confederation scheme described what happened there:

They went [to Quebec] taking with them several ladies who they knew are always in favor of union. They had nice times going up and nicer after they got there; all they did was in secret, confidential. . . . They had a fat time, dinners balls champagne suppers and when surrounded with such influences did they form a new Empire. After sitting 16 days the wonderful creature [Confederation] made its appearance.[33]

The Canadians' control of the conference was virtually complete. They prepared the draft res-

olutions for each day's agenda; the secretary was Macdonald's brother-in-law; the chairman was Etienne Taché, from Lower Canada; and Canadians made all the major introductory speeches. The Canadians were reluctant to compromise on any of their proposals. Should peripheral areas such as Prince Edward Island and Newfoundland fail to agree, so be it; they could be brought in later. The 72 resolutions produced at Quebec became the backbone of the constitution that, after minor modification at Westminster in 1866–7, would be enacted into law by the Imperial parliament as the British North America (BNA) Act on 1 July 1867.

On one issue, however, the Canadians did

have to bow to their counterparts from the east: New Brunswick's Samuel Tilley and Nova Scotia's Charles Tupper. As Tilley put it, 'We won't have the Union unless you give us the Railway.' In addition to a promise that the new government would complete the Intercolonial, Tilley secured the right both to increase the colony's debt before Confederation and to borrow money at a reduced rate of interest, pending the new government's assumption of debts. Since Canada's debt far overshadowed that of the Maritimes, even George Brown could hardly object. These concessions allowed Tilley and Tupper to raise money immediately for local railroad construction and thus to go some way towards pacifying the anti-Confederates.

Nevertheless, the Canadians left little room for doubt as to the roles they expected the various partners to play in the new nation: the Maritimes would supply minerals, coal, fish, and an opening to the sea; the west would (eventually) supply wheat; and the Canadas would supply manufactured goods. Or, as George Brown put it, 'our farmers and manufacturers and mechanics shall carry their wares unquestioned into every village of the Maritime Provinces and they shall with equal freedom bring their fish and their coal and their West India produce to our 3 millions of inhabitants.' Economic affairs, including banking, currency, bankruptcy, shipping, railways, trade and commerce, and immigration policy, would be concentrated in the hands of the central government, while jurisdiction over social and cultural matters would remain local.

Brown had staked his reputation on 'rep by pop', and acceptance of this principle was the *sine qua non* of his participation in a coalition government. Yet the virulence of his anti-

St James Cathedral, York, in the early 1850s. By 1880, Gothic-style churches loomed over Ontario's secular cities, towns, and villages, where, as *The Canada Farmer* noted in 1865, 'straightforward square houses' predominated. AO 3963 C11-49-0-5 (750)1.

Catholic, anti-French attacks on separate schools made it impossible for the francophone delegates to agree to it: no French Canadian could advocate placing his culture in the hands of an unchecked anglophone majority from Canada West that would only be reinforced by the English-speaking majorities of the Atlantic provinces. The solution to the impasse was a strong provincial government with jurisdiction over 'our language, our laws, and our religion'. During the Union, a quasi-federal system had grown and had solidified within a legislative union. Confederation would now create two new governments to give expression to this basic political reality. The de facto pursuit of separate cultural and social agendas in Canada West and Canada East became the de jure constitutional reality in Ontario and Quebec.

Both sections, however, contained minorities: English-Protestant in Canada East and Catholic—both English and French—in Canada West. In the latter especially, the sometimes vitriolic rhetoric surrounding separate schools posed serious concerns. Recognizing that provincial autonomy for francophones inside Quebec would severely weaken the position of their religious and linguistic confrères outside the province, Cartier insisted on a federal guarantee of minority rights. Brown and other Reform leaders, despite their long-standing opposition to separate schools, agreed, but insisted that such rights be specific, not general. Accordingly, the 'Fathers of Confederation' provided protection for the linguistic rights of French- and English-speakers at the federal level and in Quebec (eventually Section 133 of the British North America Act); the rights of the Protestant minority to their own schools in Quebec; and the rights of Catholics to their own schools in Ontario. Where appropriate, the same rights would be extended to the minorities in the Maritimes, particularly New Brunswick.

These compromises eased the widespread fear that Confederation would weaken minority rights. Yet, as with much else in the British North America Act, other interpretations were possible. George Brown, for one, was jubilant at the conclusion of the Quebec Conference: 'All right!!!' he wrote to his wife, 'constitution adopted—a most creditable document—a complete reform of all the abuses and injustice we have complained of!! Is it not wonderful? French Canadianism entirely extinguished!'[34]

One other general question that prompted much debate at Quebec and thereafter was the appropriate balance of power between the federal and provincial governments. John A. Macdonald pointed to the US Civil War to underline the dangers of a decentralized federalism based on 'states rights'. Although Macdonald understood that a highly centralized union was out of the question, he worked assiduously at the Quebec and London conferences to expand the powers of the central government to their maximum limits. In the end, he believed he had obtained all he could have desired, and said as much in December 1864:

> I am satisfied we have hit upon the only practicable plan—I do not mean to say the best plan . . . . we have avoided exciting local interests, and, at the same time, have raised a strong Central Government . . . . If the Confederation goes on you . . . will see both the Local Parliaments and Governments absorbed in the General Power, This is as plain to me as if I saw it accomplished now [—] of course it does not do to adopt that point of view in discussing the subject in Lower Canada.[35]

Although Macdonald accepted a federal compromise—'not,' as he said, 'the best plan'—he believed he had achieved what he wanted: a strong central government and weak provincial governments. This conclusion turned on four key issues: whereas in the US all residual powers belonged to the states, in Canada they were assigned to the central government; the lieutenant-governors of the provinces were to be federal appointees; and the federal government had the power both to disallow provincial legislation and to pass remedial legislation. On each of these points Macdonald found a reliable ally in George Brown. The post-Confederation debate would turn on whether, as Macdonald believed, (a) these were general powers, available under all circumstances, and (b) the lieutenant-governors were agents of the federal government, as opposed to the Crown.

If so, the federal government had enormous clout. If not—as Cartier and many Reform leaders insisted—the provinces would be fully autonomous within their jurisdictions.

For the moment it was enough to agree on the basic economic and political agenda, and work towards acceptance of Confederation in the Maritimes. Yet the relative balance of power between the central and provincial governments remained ambiguous. It would be only a matter of time before a centralizing prime minister in Ottawa would have to confront a powerful Ontario jealously guarding its autonomy.

CHAPTER SEVEN

Ontario in the New Dominion: 1867–1905

$\mathcal{F}$rom the start, Ontario was the strongest province in the new nation. Almost half of all Canadians lived there. With 82 of 181 seats in the federal legislature, its debt burdens eased, its economic interests mollified, westward expansion imminent, and the French problem muted, the province seemed to have little to gain from tampering with the Confederation agreement. But politics dictated otherwise. The coalition government that had carried Confederation could not last. Conservatives outnumbered Reformers nine to three in the cabinet, and John A. Macdonald passed out jobs and favours lavishly to Conservatives. Reformers soon became restive: in December 1865, George Brown left the coalition (although he continued to support Confederation), and he and the Ontario Reformers gradually edged back towards their old sectional policies. Blithely ignoring Brown's resignation, Macdonald continued to emphasize the image of the government as a coalition.

For the new Dominion government—in essence just an expanded version of the Union government of the two Canadas—it was business as usual. Ottawa remained the capital, and the same public employees managed the new civil service from their existing offices. Not so in Ontario. In the new provincial capital, Toronto, the government had to start from scratch with new offices and a new staff. Many pre-Confederation laws would have to be re-passed as provincial statutes. But none of this could be accomplished until after Ontario had elected its first government. And here, like Sydenham during the Union's first general election, John A. Macdonald left little to chance.

Claiming that a non-partisan coalition was far superior to self-interested parties, Macdonald shrewdly recruited John Sandfield Macdonald to head the Ontario Conservative party. A Scottish Catholic with reform roots and Conservative friends, Sandfield had never supported Confederation, but he accepted it as a *fait accompli*. In an era when federal and provincial elections were held within the same period (though not on the same day), the two Macdonalds made a formidable team. John A. managed the raising and distribution of election funds, timed the votes for individual constituencies to create a bandwagon effect in

John A. Macdonald and John Sandfield Macdonald. George Brown's newspaper, the Toronto *Globe,* reflected a common perception of Native people when it compared the two Macdonalds to 'Indians on the war-path. . . . Their movements are secret, they come apon their prey unawares, and they try to dispatch him in a hurry' (quoted in Noel, *Patrons,* 216). NAC C134560 / NAC C406.

favour of the Conservatives, situated polling stations far from Reform strongholds, and appointed partisan returning officers. Intimidation and bribery were widespread, and George Brown declared the process 'absurd and undignified'. But it was effective. The Conservatives carried Ontario by a wide federal margin and won a strong provincial majority.

Close ties existed between the two governments. Five members of the Ontario cabinet also sat in the federal assembly. Both Sandfield and John A. Macdonald desired 'harmony' between the two governments. And both were determined to keep Brown and the Reformers—now beginning to call themselves Liberals—from gaining power at either level. Sandfield Macdonald's government passed some noteworthy measures, including a Free Grant and Homestead Act, designed to attract Americans to Ontario's newly opening north; an election act that broadened voting rights and restricted voting to one day; and an education act that made primary and secondary schooling free and, up to the age of 16, compulsory. But the Liberals, now the province's official opposition, characterized Sandfield Macdonald as little more than a federal puppet. They called for an end to dual seats and argued that 'subordinate' federalism must be replaced by a more equal relationship. 'No outside control by the Lower Canadian French,' the rallying cry of the Upper Canadian Reformers, now became, 'No domination by the federal government.'

When, in 1869, the federal government granted a discontented Nova Scotia 'better terms', Ontario's Liberal leader, Edward Blake, leapt into action: Ontario's taxpayers would bear the cost of any change in constitutional arrangements, yet they had not been consulted; it was because Upper Canada lacked control over its destiny that the Union had failed, and Confederation had been intended to remedy that situation. Now, however, 'The former evils so far from being removed by Confederation will be intensified, the just expectations of the people will be disappointed, sectional strife will be aroused, the federal principle will be violated and the Constitution will be shaken to its base.' All provinces must consent to any changes in the Confederation agreement, Blake concluded.[1] Ontario's Liberals had found their platform.

The last straw for the Liberals came in 1870, after the Red River Métis under Louis Riel resisted Canada's efforts to annex their territory. In response, Macdonald's federal government passed the Manitoba Act, creating a new bilingual and bicultural province that resembled Quebec far more than it did Ontario. Once again the French seemed to be dominating—now in a part of the country that many Ontarians considered their special preserve. Western settlement had been a primary goal of Confederation, and Ontarians saw the prairie region as a natural extension of their own

province. 'We hope to see a new Upper Canada in the North-West Territory,' Brown's *Globe* proclaimed in 1869, 'a new Upper Canada in its well regulated society and government—in its education, morality and religion.' The intellectuals of the Ontario-based Canada First movement carried this credo to extreme lengths with their vision of a 'super race' reigning supreme in the continent's north.[2]

The Liberals were impatient for the next election. When, in 1871, it finally came, they campaigned as if their opponents were John A. Macdonald's federal Conservatives. Sandfield Macdonald's close links to the latter were no advantage in Ontario and his plans for opening up the province's north seemed woefully insufficient. The election results were close, too close. Blake moved a want of confidence motion that passed by a single vote, making him premier and initiating a period of unbroken Liberal dominance that would endure for more than three decades. With his sights on a political career in Ottawa, Blake remained in office only long enough to persuade Oliver Mowat to succeed him as leader, in 1872. Mowat was always intensely partisan in his approach to politics, and he believed the secret to governing Ontario lay in careful 'management' of the business of government. Like John A. Macdonald, he was a product of the Union period. Both men believed in a strong executive role and the need for close control of patronage; both preferred the political centre and favoured moderate compromise over confrontation. But neither would back away from a clash of wills. On one issue—the constitutional distribution of power—Macdonald and Mowat alike were single-mindedly committed to their respective positions.

The boundary between the pre-Confederation Province of Canada and Rupert's Land, the Hudson's Bay Company land bought by the federal government in 1869–70, had long been a source of dispute. If the northwest was not to be part of Ontario, precisely where was the boundary to be drawn? Even the two arbitrators charged with settling the dispute could not agree and in 1872 submitted separate reports. A year later the federal Conservatives fell from power. The provincial Liberals and the federal Liberals under Alexander Mackenzie formed a new three-man arbitration board that reported in 1878, supporting all of Ontario's demands. All that remained was for the two governments to ratify the agreement in their respective legislatures. Ontario stood to gain some 285,000 square kilometres of new land, and as far as Mowat was concerned, the matter 'was settled'. But before Mackenzie could ratify the agreement, the Conservatives under the redoubtable John A. triumphed in the 1878 federal election. Not only did Macdonald refuse to implement the arbitration award, he extended the Manitoba boundary east to cover the disputed territory.

So intense was the dispute in the Lake of the Woods–Rainy River area that the federal and provincial governments each sent their own law agents, who ended up arresting each other! The region was mainly boreal forest with, everyone believed, enormous timber, mineral, and even agricultural potential. Under the BNA Act, Crown lands and natural resources fell to the provinces, and timber licences and royalties on mineral exploitation were major sources of provincial income. But the Manitoba Act reserved Crown lands and natural resources to the federal government in

Oliver Mowat. Although trained in John A. Macdonald's law office, Mowat did not share Macdonald's political views, and the two once came close to blows during a debate in the Legislative Assembly. Mowat had entered the coalition cabinet in 1864 as postmaster general, but after the Quebec Conference Macdonald offered him a judicial position—effectively depriving the Reform party of a very able politician. But Mowat did not stay out of politics for long. In 1872 he accepted an offer from the departing Blake of the leadership of Ontario's Liberal party; he would serve as the province's premier for the next 24 years. NAC PA28631.

both Manitoba and the Northwest Territories. Whoever controlled the disputed territory would control economic development and benefit from a substantial increase in revenue. The winner would also gain control of numer-

Mending a birchbark canoe, Northwest Angle, Ontario, 1872, albumin print. Most early photographers of Aboriginal people were looking for 'exotic' subject matter. Thus pictures of more quotidian activities, such as farming, are rare. NAC PA74670.

ous opportunities for political patronage—in the establishment of municipal government, the granting of liquor licences, the appointment of judicial and other officials—that could be used for partisan purposes. The importance of the latter became clear in the provincial election of 1883. While the Ontario Liberals charged that the federal Conservatives were flooding the province with patronage appointments in an attempt to unseat Mowat, Ontario Conservative leader William Meredith argued for increased municipal autonomy—a move

that would threaten patronage positions under Mowat's control. New sources of patronage in the north could give the premier a way of increasing power without antagonizing already entrenched municipal interests. In the end Mowat did hang on to power, but his majority suffered a significant cut.[3]

Small wonder that Mowat chose to personally argue the boundary case in the courts. He prepared well: his legal department amassed five volumes of documents and maps relating to the disputed area, whereas the federal government's file consisted of only one committee report. Mowat himself set the questions that the final court of appeal, the Judicial Committee of the Privy Council in England, would consider—questions that privileged the 1878 arbitration findings in Ontario's favour. In July 1884, the Privy Council backed the province almost without qualification. Some 100,000 people cheered Premier Mowat on his return to Toronto.

Macdonald had been bested; but he fought on. 'Even if all the territory Mr. Mowat asks for were awarded to Ontario,' he warned before the court made its decision, 'there is not one stick of timber, one acre of land, or one lump of lead, iron or gold that does not belong to the Dominion.' When the federal government signed Treaty Three with the Ojibwa in 1873, Macdonald asserted, the state had acquired the rights to all the natural resources in the treaty area. In so doing he effectively acknowledged that First Nations peoples had indeed owned the land and resources before the treaty. In fact, the Royal Proclamation of 1763 had said as much; but until now no colonial or Canadian court had ever supported that position. 'We say,' Mowat replied, 'that there is no Indian title at law or equity. The claim of the Indians is simply moral and no more.' Mowat argued that the Proclamation was 'provisional' and had been repealed by the Quebec Act of 1774.

The result was a legal battle called the St Catharines Milling case. The federal government had granted the St Catharines Milling and Lumber Company the right to cut timber in the disputed area. Arguing that control of that resource belonged to the province, not the federal government, Mowat sued the company.

The case ended up in the Privy Council and again Mowat won. The powers of the federal government were further weakened. In 1889, Macdonald ratified the court's decision and Ontario assumed untrammelled rights to the land and resources of the vast new territory. A further agreement between the two governments in 1912 extended the boundary to its current position. Had the federal government been able to convince the courts that the First Nations did own the land before entering into Treaty Three, Macdonald would have prevailed. But the federal lawyers called no representative of the Ojibwa to testify. Nor did they ever use available historical material effectively to refute Ontario's claims concerning the 1763 Proclamation—even though its provisions had been validated by many Upper Canadian leaders (including Governor Simcoe) in the treaty process of the 1790s and later. Had they been called, the Ojibwa would have made strong witnesses. During the Treaty Three negotiations, Ma-we-do-pe-nais, an Ojibwa chief, had said:

> All this is our property where you have come . . . This is what we think, that the Great Spirit has planted us on this ground where we are, as you were where you came from. We think where we are is our property. The sound of the rustling of the gold is under my feet where I stand; we have a rich country; it is the Great Spirit who gave us this; where we stand upon is the Indian's property and belongs to them.

In July 1888 the Privy Council did acknowledge that, before the treaty, the First Nations had a right of occupancy, 'a personal foundational case in many decisions regarding Native title. Nevertheless, the decision that First Nations' right to land was only 'usufructuary'—restricted to occupancy—meant that Native people were treated as second-class in relation to white Europeans, who could claim ownership. As Victor Savino, an Indian land-claims lawyer, noted a century later, in the St Catharine's case 'Indians were used and fructed.'[4]

The Ontario boundary dispute helped to rally support behind those who, like Mowat, believed that Confederation had created a largely decentralized federation. As a member of the pre-Confederation cabinet, a delegate to the Quebec Conference, and an active participant in the debates over the relative powers of the central and provincial governments, Mowat had been as much a 'Father of Confederation' as Macdonald. Now, as premier of Canada's largest province, he took the lead in the evolving process of constitutional interpretation. In addition to the boundary dispute, Mowat personally argued Ontario's case in a number of other precedent-setting appeals before the Privy Council; he won all of those cases and in the process defined the constitutional limit on the federal power to disallow provincial legislation. Together these cases confirmed the older Reform view, first articulated in the Reform Convention of 1859, of a decentralized federalism in which each province remained sovereign within its constitutional jurisdiction. Ontario's overwhelming victories dealt a severe blow to Macdonald's goal of a politically centralized Canada. The disputes were far from over, but now that its territorial ambitions had been satisfied, Ontario no longer had any serious quarrel with the federal system. Ever since the days

Lucius Richard O'Brien, 'Lords of the Forest', 1874, watercolour on paper. Just as a magnificent tree reaches the end of its life cycle and falls, so must the noble savage—or so this painting suggests. Such rationalizations of the impact of the European invasion on the New World were popular in the late nineteenth century and beyond. Art Gallery of Ontario Acc.72/19.

and usufructuary right, dependant upon the good will of the Sovereign', but still it granted all rights of ownership to Ontario. In the twentieth century St Catharines Milling became a of the Loyalists, when Britain had granted them land at the expense of the Native people, Upper Canadians had seen themselves as occupying a position of special favour. In championing territorial expansion, Mowat and the Liberals laid claim to the Loyalist mantle. From now on, Ontarians would tend 'to identify the national interest as their own'.[5]

Even as Mowat chopped away at federal power, he moved to centralize political power inside Ontario. In exchange for forgiving or paying down municipal debts, he assumed many hitherto local functions and the appointment-making power that accompanied them, then instituted a centralized appointment process that rewarded deserving local party activists and helped to link the centre to the peripheries. The efficient, smoothly running, patronage-based political machine he created was one the provincial Conservatives could only dream of emulating.

Nevertheless, by the 1880s longstanding conflicts over religion and language were about to resurface. Education was a particularly sensitive area in this regard. While the BNA Act had given Ontario and Quebec jurisdiction over their own school systems, it also guaranteed educational rights that 'existed in law and in practice' at the time of Confederation. In other words, Ontario's separate school system, while it need not be expanded, could not be restricted or abolished. In the aftermath of the uprising of 1870, many Ontarians mistakenly interpreted the French-speaking, Catholic Métis people's resistance to arbitrary annexation of their territory as a conflict over issues of religion, language, and schools.

In 1870 the provisional Red River government headed by Louis Riel had executed Thomas Scott, an Orangeman from Ontario. To many Ontarians, Riel became a murderer as well as a rebel. When Premier Blake issued a warrant for his arrest, Riel left the country. In 1885, however, the controversy resurfaced when Riel returned to lead an abortive Aboriginal–Métis rebellion in Saskatchewan. This time he would be tried and hanged for treason.

In Quebec Riel was a hero; the Québécois cheered Wilfrid Laurier, the future Canadian prime minister, when he proclaimed, 'Had I been born on the banks of the Saskatchewan I would myself have shouldered a musket.'[6] In the heat of the Riel affair, Quebec's premier, Honoré Mercier, offered the Jesuits in his province compensation for land the British had seized from them following the Conquest of 1760. He then invited the Pope to arbitrate the settlement.

Protestant extremists loudly condemned this papal intrusion into Canada's domestic politics, and several Conservative MPs from Ontario requested that the federal government disallow the Québec legislation, known as the Jesuit Estates Act. When the request was refused, an organization calling itself the Equal Rights Association attracted widespread support from Ontario Protestants. By 1891 anti-Catholic feeling had escalated to the point that a more militant group, the Protestant Protective Association, established itself in Ontario. The PPA membership pledge required followers to 'denounce Roman Catholicism' and oppose the participation of Catholics in public life.

The extremism of the PPA may in part have reflected the new visibility of Ontario's urban

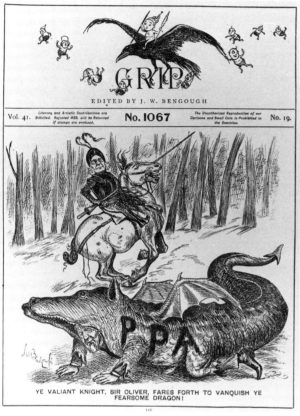

J.W. Bengough, 'Ye Valiant Knight, Sir Oliver, Fares Forth to Vanquish Ye Fearsome Dragon!', *Grip*, 12 May 1894. In the elections of 1894, Conservative leader Meredith (depicted here under the skin of the PPA dragon) tried to use anti-Catholic rhetoric to defeat Mowat's Liberals; but the premier never wavered from his moderate principles of compromise and tolerance. Mowat insisted that Ontario would respect minority rights as guaranteed by the Confederation agreement. He won the 1894 election, albeit with a reduced majority. William Ready Division of Archives and Research Collections, McMaster University.

Irish Catholics. By the late nineteenth century they were more likely than any other religious group except Presbyterians and Methodists to own houses and land. Moreover, Ontario's Catholic leaders understood that their flock

had arrived—'made it'—in the urban milieu. They began to adopt a more open and accommodating attitude to the wider community within which they lived. While still protective of separate schools, they preached denominational peace and the cultivation of positive links between Catholics and Protestants. Three weeks after he had been stoned by members of the Orange Order in Toronto in 1889, Catholic Archbishop John Walsh promised to 'inculcate in our boys the best sentiments of patriotism and love of country, *for this is their country*, . . . despite the injustice preached against us at the present time—an injustice which will not, which cannot prevail in a free country.'[7] Throughout, the moderate Mowat had stood by the commitments he and his Reform colleagues had made to the separate schools at the time of Confederation. But Ontario's Conservative party had flirted with the PPA. When Meredith resigned after losing his third election, his successor, George F. Marter, touched off an internal power struggle by announcing that he favoured the abolition of all separate schools. In 1896, James P. Whitney, the new rising star of Ontario conservatism, defeated Marter and committed his party to improving relations with the province's Catholic minority. Under Whitney, the separate-school issue for a time ceased to occupy centre stage in Ontario's partisan contests.

Nevertheless, other issues continued to pit Liberal Ontario against Conservative Ottawa. The provincial rights movement promoted the notion that Ontario's economic interests were not being adequately served by federal policies. A case in point was the rail industry. In fact, Ontario's northern railways and associ-

Guelph horseshoeing forge, *c.* 1860. In 1861 sawmilling and blacksmithing were Ontario's two largest employment sectors. Even so, individual sawmills or blacksmith shops rarely employed more than five workers.
Guelph Public Library.

ated manufacturing companies, especially in
southern Ontario, were richly subsidized by
the federal government. Yet bias was suspected
when in 1881 a Montreal-based company won
a decade-long fight over control of the
Canadian Pacific Railway. Similarly, Ontario
industries dependent on imported raw materials (such as coal) complained that the 1879
National Policy of high protective tariffs
favoured the coal-producing Maritimes and
promoted an east-west flow of trade that benefited Montreal over Hamilton and Toronto,
which had no direct link to the continental
railway. In time, those industries would

become vociferous defenders of the National
Policy's tariff structures, but rural Ontarians
remained adamantly opposed.

It is true that in the 1870s a depression
throughout the Atlantic economies had initiated a general decline in commodity prices.[8]
Dependent on exports of agricultural and lumber products, Ontario's economy, like
Canada's, was tested by fundamental changes
in market conditions. But the price decline
was not evenly distributed; prices for wheat
and barley and some vegetable and animal
products fell unevenly. Furthermore, Canada's
terms of trade improved in this period as the

W. Cruikshank, 'Provincial Ploughing Match, Hamilton, 1876', *Canadian Illustrated News*, 9 Dec. 1876. The era of the hand-held plow was passing; to succeed commercially, farmers had to adopt more advanced technology. NAC C64727.

wholesale prices of imports fell and overall export prices held relatively steady.[9] Declining prices for wheat and barley reinforced a trend towards mixed farming that had already become apparent in the 1850s. 'As far as Ontario is concerned,' the Toronto *Globe* predicted in 1878, 'the end of exporting wheat is not far off.' In fact, wheat continued to generate more profits than dairy products, but milk and butter also became major cash products for farmers. Expanding export markets were a

catalyst for the development of a cheese industry shipping to both the United States and Great Britain, and by the late 1860s, as one observer noted, farmers had 'cheese-on-the-brain'. Even when butter exports began to decline in the 1880s—in part because of poor quality, some thought—domestic consumption continued to grow.[10]

Oliver Mowat carefully cultivated rural Ontario constituencies where the Liberals had traditionally enjoyed strong support. Rural voters rewarded him with majorities in every election he fought. The Department of Agriculture, one of the largest provincial ministries, spent thousands annually researching the newest developments in agricultural technology and encouraging farmers to keep pace with the latest innovations. Agricultural Societies—funded in part by provincial grants—dotted the province, and a new Agricultural College opened at Guelph in 1874. Generally, then, the agricultural sector prospered during the late nineteenth century. But it could not provide sufficient employment for Ontario's growing population. Mechanization required capital investments beyond the reach of many marginal farmers, particularly those working the less productive land in eastern Ontario; farmers who could afford new equipment often became cash poor and unable to purchase land for their children. Increasing numbers of rural people moved to the cities to seek work in new manufacturing industries. The largest centres grew the most rapidly, and by 1911 the majority of Ontario's population lived in cities. In the face of rural depopulation, farm organizations lobbied to protect the quality of social as well as economic life in the countryside.

By 1871 Ontario was responsible for more than half of Canada's industrial production. Most of its manufacturing industries were still in primary production, characterized by widely dispersed small shops situated close to their raw materials. But already, Toronto and Hamilton dominated industrial production. Manufacturing was concentrated in a belt that ran from Oshawa west along the north shore of Lake Ontario. The recession of the 1870s led to many business failures and a consolidation

of industrial capital that foreshadowed the dramatic mergers of the late nineteenth and early twentieth centuries. A classic example was the agricultural implements industry. At Confederation, such implements were produced in small 'factories' scattered throughout the province, many of them little more than upscale blacksmithing shops producing and repairing a wide assortment of goods. By 1881 Ontario had 144 such small, independent, family operations owned by men like Hart Massey and Alanson Harris.

Massey built his business through aggressive marketing; he even exported to Britain. Harris, on the other hand, was an innovator whose company created such state-of-the art equipment as the open-ended binder. In 1890, the two firms merged and moved to a new, larger factory in Toronto. The merger gave Massey-Harris an overwhelming competitive advantage in the Ontario market. Over the next two decades, the company absorbed many smaller producers (including some American firms), expanded its line of products, and became Canada's largest producer—and exporter—of agricultural implements. Its only real competition was the American International Harvester (itself the product of a similar merger), which had jumped the tariff wall and opened a branch plant in Hamilton.

Manufacturing reshaped itself during this period. Diversification and mechanization led to rapid increases in the value of production. Yet because of increased labour productivity, continued immigration, and rural depopulation, even this growth could not create enough jobs. In each year following 1873, more job-seekers left Ontario than entered it. Although the closing decades of the nineteenth century

SS *Cumberland* at Northern Railway Wharf, Collingwood Harbour, 1876–7. Between 1870 and 1909, the federal government spent over $25 million on grants to northern Ontario railways, but much of the money went to southern Ontario manufacturers of rails and rolling stock. CSTM/CN X39357.

had brought significant economic growth, many Canadians had expected more. Emigration had slowed population growth. And while farmers had adjusted to economic realities, depopulation had frayed the fabric of rural Ontario. Nevertheless, by century's end, Ontario possessed an advanced industrial economy poised for spectacular expansion when economic conditions in the Atlantic economy improved.

One of Mowat's main challenges was how best to use the great economic potential of Ontario's new northern territory, which included the districts of Muskoka, Parry Sound, Nipissing, and all points north. Ontarians were far from knowledgeable about their north's economic assets. In 1882, the *Globe* optimistically asserted that the disputed boundary territory alone contained no less than '60,000,000 acres of fertile land'—a preposterous estimate (by 1891 less than 142,000 acres would have been developed for agricultural purposes and over three-quarters of that total was unimproved pasture or woodlots).[11]

Roast yards at Copper Cliff, near Sudbury, 1890. 'The ore is run through crushers . . . and taken over an elevated track to the roasting yard,' reported the Royal Commission on the Mineral Resources of Ontario in 1890. 'The fire is set to kindling material in the draught openings, and as it spreads and the heat increases the sulphur of the ore adds to the fuel, sending up a heavy, yellowish cloud of acrid smoke. The heap burns from thirty days to seven weeks.' Not until the late twentieth century would environmental concerns begin to restrain southern Ontario's enthusiasm for northern resource development. NAC PA200965.

Under Mowat's leadership, systematic northern development began. The government surveyed 107 townships, settled 25,000 people on some 3,000,000 acres (1,200,000 hectares) of land, and spent $2.75 million on building and servicing 7350 kilometres of colonization roads. The aim was not simply to facilitate farming. Despite many attempts to promote agricultural colonization, the worth of northern Ontario, as Mowat realized, lay

elsewhere. Politicians pandered to people, and in 1871 only one per cent of Ontario's population lived in the north. Exploitation of the north enabled Mowat to finance southern Ontario's dramatic economic development without resorting to 'the bugbear of direct taxation', and helped to ensure his political longevity.[12] In much of the United States, resource rights went to the purchaser of the land, but in Ontario and Canada, these rights

Workers at Silver Islet mine, *c.* 1880s. Silver Islet, on Lake Superior near Thunder Bay, was the north's most successful silver mine in the nineteenth century. Between 1870 and 1884, one 24- by 20-metre outcropping located a kilometre and a half off the shore yielded 3 million ounces of fine silver worth some $3.5 million. AO F1132-2-1-2 ST1237.

remained in the state's possession. Entrepreneurs had to pay the state for the right to cut timber and mine minerals. For example, the commissioner of Crown Lands would auction off the rights to a section of timber lands for a set time period, and the successful bidder would also pay ground rent and stumpage dues on the timber cut. To maximize returns, Mowat timed these auctions to correspond with favourable economic conditions in the industry. Between 1867 and 1899, payments from mines and forests represented close to a

third of provincial revenues, and most of that income came from northern development.[13]

Clearly Mowat spent money in the north in order to make money; between 1872 and 1896, the Mowat government realized, after all expenses, some $17,000,000![14] This profit, made in the north and spent in the south, made possible healthy surpluses throughout Mowat's premiership at a time when most other provincial governments struggled with deficits. It also allowed Mowat to indulge an agricultural population extremely averse to direct taxation. Although some northerners complained about the unequal flow of capital, their small numbers made them easy to ignore. The decision to invest northern capital in the south skewed the trajectory of northern development. During the Mowat era, the north experienced extensive growth but little diversification. Mowat's policy also ushered in a long period of only loosely supervised resource exploitation. Most northern lumberers were financially vulnerable and not even remotely interested in implementing the conservation measures that some of their more wealthy southern counterparts in the Ottawa Valley were promoting. A bureau of Forestry was not created until 1898, after Mowat had left the provincial government. Up to that time a clerk of Forestry, initially resident in the department of Agriculture and then in the department of Crown Lands, handled forests as if they were a cash crop, properly 'part and parcel of farm management'. The clerk focused most of his energy on the impact of deforestation on southern Ontario's farm economy, encouraging Arbor Days, when communities would plant trees along roadways. Even as tourists travelled north to enjoy pristine forests, Mowat's economic policies were making short work of them.[15]

New technologies and the rapid expansion of the industrial factory system altered the very nature of work and with it the social conditions of those who laboured for wages. Deskilling of labour was a feature of mines in the north no less than of factories and farms in the south. At Silver Islet, technological advances allowed mine managers to lessen their reliance on skilled Norwegian and Cornish miners, men who, in management's eyes, tended to be too independent. The company recruited cheaper, relatively unskilled workers from mining camps in Nova Scotia and Illinois. 'If miners are plentiful,' William Frue, the mine's general manager, advised, 'make up the number from mixed nationalities.' Such policies made it difficult for labour to form a unified front against management. Management exercised strict control over the labour force: the Islet had its own five-cell jail and jailer; alcohol use was carefully monitored (three drinks per day); camp watchmen were ever present; clergymen were provided; and, of course, the company store and bunkhouses ate up roughly half of the miners' monthly pay. At Copper Cliff's nickel-copper mines, managers employed mass-mining techniques, 'so the work of "mining" consisted mainly of drifting and quarrying with Ingersoll air drills.'[16] Miners lost status; only surface labourers at the mines received lower pay. In order to control the men, Copper Cliff's management separated them from the wider community. The Company profited from housing and land leases: in 1889, the manager noted a return of 20 per cent on the rental of small houses. The workforce was ethnically diverse: non-Anglo-Saxons lived in ramshackle ghettos at the town's edge; management enjoyed separate and more substantial quarters.[17]

Technological change also had an impact on farm work. As farms mechanized, women's work in particular became deskilled and devalued. Before the late nineteenth century, many women earned money milking cows, tending livestock, and manufacturing cheese and butter; Lydia Chase Ranney, a craftswoman who, with her husband, manufactured cheese on their Oxford County farm, oversaw up to 14 apprentice dairymaids in any one season. Even in the twentieth century, cheesemakers would wield great power in rural areas; as Bertha Pope, Ontario's only solo female cheesemaker for much of that century, noted in 1967, she had the power to accept or reject the milk products supplied to her factory by the region's farmers. But she was the exception: after about 1870, when cheese production shifted to factories (farm production was halved in that decade), men generally replaced women as manufacturers, and women merely toiled as labourers within the factories.[18]

As historian Margaret Derry has explained in wonderful detail, the process of change in butter manufacture was more prolonged. In the 1870s and 1880s, farmers and exporters attributed a decline in export demand for butter to poor quality, which they blamed on the central role played by women in the manufacturing process. Yet the domestic market for butter was buoyant. The low export demand may simply have reflected differences in taste: the British did not like salty butter and Canadians apparently did. For a while milking continued to be seen as a nurturing, female task—women's work. After 1890, however,

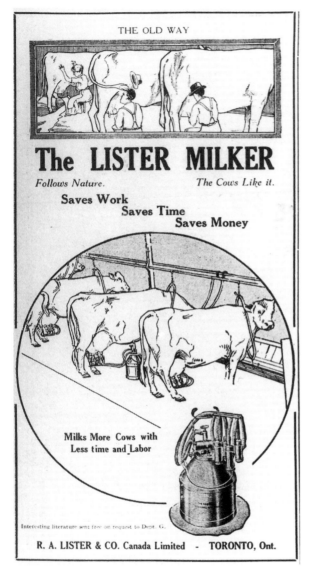

THE OLD WAY

The LISTER MILKER

Follows Nature.   *The Cows Like it.*

Saves Work
    Saves Time
        Saves Money

Milks More Cows with
Less time and Labor

Interesting literature sent free on request to Dept. G.

R. A. LISTER & CO. Canada Limited - TORONTO, Ont.

The Lister milker, *Farmer's Advocate,* 19 June 1919. 'If you want to know how to treat a cow you must first study how to treat a woman,' one agriculturist advised in 1891. 'First study the human mother, and when you have got the laws that govern her in the exercise of her maternity you have arrived at the laws that govern the bovine mother' (cited in Derry, p. 36). By the 1890s, however, the emphasis was shifting from maternity to machinery. According to this advertisement, 'The Old Way' meant discontented cows and spilt milk. Special Collections, Univ. of Guelph Library.

men began to supplant women as milkers, and women were increasingly relegated to cleaning the milk pails; after all, as one writer in the *Farmer's Advocate* put it in 1885, 'for washing and keeping things clean, [men] were not equal to women.'

With the advent of the milking machine, the dairy cow came to be seen as 'not only an animal, but . . . a machine'. In 1895, a writer in the *Canadian Livestock Journal* went even further: 'The modern dairy cow in her best form is a highly artificial animal. The more artificial she is the better. The dairy cow has been trained and made over by the hand and brain of *man* for a perfectly natural purpose, for giving milk, yielding butter, and making money.' It was only a small step to conceiving of the farm as a factory.[19]

Skilled artisans working in the small manufacturing shops that dotted southern Ontario traditionally exerted considerable control over their work. But specialization in manufacturing output eroded this shop-floor control. As machinists came to specialize in either brass or iron, stoves or agricultural machinery, skill sets narrowed and employee interaction became increasingly limited. Whereas before, the craftsperson had been responsible for a wide range of tasks related to the production of an item, increasingly those tasks were compartmentalized. Less-skilled labourers did work that craftsworkers had done in the past. And such labour was abundant. The great numbers forced into the cities by rural depopulation were only too willing to take on such jobs, often in the face of resistance by the craftsworkers. A disgruntled Toronto tailor did not mince words: 'Between science and progress the working classes are ground as

The Toronto House of Industry, 1890. Institutions like this offered unemployed men rudimentary lodging in return for work such as street cleaning. Increasingly, workers were losing control over their livelihoods. In March 1889, the Toronto *World* reported that, at the local House of Industry, unskilled labourers rubbed elbows with an engineer, a stone mason, a clerk, a fuller, and a baker, among others. AO C336 #1597 5346.

between millstones.' 'The over-production of machinery,' Joseph Dickson, a carriage maker in Chatham, believed, 'has caused a great many men to be thrown out of work. I know they have one machine in the waggon shop here that takes the place of about twenty men.' Furthermore, the long, hard Canadian winter insured that many jobs were seasonal. 'In the trades,' the federal government's *Labour Gazette* correspondent noted in the autumn of 1901, 'many are just now "between seasons" and are a little slack. . . . This by many of the men is looked forward to as an annual rest.' Much of the construction industry, which employed about a quarter of the urban workforce, shut down during the winter months. Employment in transportation picked up significantly during the late fall but declined precipitously during the long winter. Work in food canning was concentrated into a three-month period at the end of the growing season. Even in industries such as agricultural implements, production slowed during the late summer, fall, and early winter.

Seasonality masked a more insidious trend. Only about a third of the urban unemployed lost jobs due to seasonal conditions. The remaining two-thirds were out of work because of factors more closely associated with the evolving industrial economy. In 1901, one in seven of Hamilton's wage workers worked less than nine months of the year.[20] The Canadian labour market was becoming increasingly insecure. Families were vital lines of defence against the impersonal workings of the labour market. In his walk through a Toronto working class area in 1894, a *Globe* reporter came upon

> *a very neat house [in which] a carpenter was found, a big, strong man eager to work, who had done nothing for months. The signs of poverty were only too apparent, and on being questioned, he admitted that his family were in want. His wife, by going out to work, earned enough to provide food, but not enough to buy fuel or pay rent. A neighbour gave him some shutters to mend, the first work he had had for sometime.[21]*

When asked where his wife was, Mr Gloynes, an unemployed Toronto labourer, provided a similar answer: 'She is out working. She makes eight or ten dollars a month scrubbing and doing chores.' The vast majority of working-class wives did not work for wages, however. A man was expected to make a 'living wage', an income sufficient to maintain his family free from poverty. A proper woman, according to the cult of domesticity, was expected to run the house and raise the family. Because of these social dicta, wives (and their husbands) may have been reluctant to admit to census takers that they earned wages. Working-class wives raised children, tended chickens and pigs, tilled gardens, and, given adequate space, took in boarders. The younger children helped. Such non-waged contributions were often crucial to urban working-class family survival. Children also contributed financially.

When a family had children 14 and older in the house, then, on average, those sons and daughters contributed an impressive 40 per cent of the family's income. But even with such support, many families teetered on the brink. In 1901, almost 20 per cent of Hamilton's working-class families had income close to or below the poverty line. General labourers were at the highest risk of poverty. Nearly two-thirds of labourers' families without children over the age of 14 lived below the poverty line.[22] In the early stages of the family life cycle, most of these families coped financially. When children arrived, so, too, did poverty. Some families made ends meet by sharing the rent for a house with another family.

Skilled workers reacted to the deterioration in labour conditions by organizing trade unions to pressure employers and labour councils to lobby government. The unions of the 1860s and early 1870s were often locals of either British- or American-based international unions, organizations that viewed the unskilled as potential competitors rather than collaborators. Workers pressed for a nine-hour day. In 1872 the Typographers struck in support of their demands. George Brown, erstwhile Liberal leader and publisher of the *Globe,* the most important Liberal paper in the province, organized the Master Printers Association in an attempt to break the

Collecting coal by the railway tracks, Toronto, *c.* 1900. Despite efforts to regulate child labour, children from poor families were often working for wages before they reached the age of 14. Many others helped in the house, hawked newspapers on the street, or, like the very young girls shown here, scrounged for coal or scrap metal. John Kelso photo. NAC PA181961 Acc. 1975.069.

Typographers union. One dissenting Conservative paper, the *Leader,* granted the union's demand and continued to publish throughout the strike. As the tension and rhetoric escalated, Brown and his Master Printers Association went to the courts, and 12 strike leaders were charged with conspiracy in restraint of trade, a common law offence. John A. Macdonald immediately moved to score political points against an old rival by passing the Trades Union Act of 1872. Modelled on British legislation, the Act exempted collective bargaining from restraint of trade provisions of the common law. The strike leaders in Toronto were freed. With this boost to its morale, the union won the strike and established a nine-hour day in the printing industry.

The Trades Union Act is frequently cited as labour's Magna Carta, but its significance proved far more symbolic than real. Although it enshrined collective bargaining, the Act assumed that most unions would incorporate under the civil law. Incorporation, however, made unions vulnerable to civil suits for damages; courts could rule that business losses as a result of strikes were recoverable through civil action. Since the system of collective bargaining relied on economic sanctions—either the strike or lockout—the threat of such rulings jeopardized the system. As a result, unions refused to incorporate, and many employers in turn refused to negotiate labour 'contracts', which could not be enforced in the civil courts. The Trades Union Act not only failed to address the basic issue of civil liability, it also defined as criminal offences a number of standard union practices, including picketing during a strike. Although these criminal provisions were only occasionally enforced, the Act nonetheless limited the effectiveness of labour's only economic weapon, the strike, and it did little to improve the province's deteriorating industrial relations.

Recession led to a contraction of the labour market in 1873. Union membership declined and municipal labour councils collapsed under the pressure of unemployment. Not until the end of the decade, when the economy showed some signs of real growth, did the trade union movement begin to recover. Heeding the call of the Toronto Trades and Labour Council, various municipal labour councils organized a special convention in 1883 to discuss the need for a new national federation of labour. In 1886, a second convention placed the Trades and Labour Congress (TLC) of Canada on a permanent footing. Limited initially to Ontario unions, the TLC soon included most labour organizations across Canada. In 1886, a second labour organization, the Knights of Labor, burst upon the scene. While other unions played on

the pride and 'respectability' of craft, often arguing that skills represented 'property' and thus, in a property-based economy, gave the workers who possessed them the same rights as capitalists to participate in the decision-making process, the Knights questioned the capitalist system itself. Often their critique mixed romantic notions of a pre-capitalist world of independent commodity producers with more modern ideas anticipating both the co-operative and socialist movements of the twentieth century. The Knights' rhetoric promised far more than the organization could deliver. It called for the inclusion of women and unskilled labourers and condemned strike action, but most Knights' locals included only skilled male workers, and many locals were involved in work stoppages. These strikes produced few concrete results and led to disillusionment among members. Renewed economic recession in 1887 dealt the *coup de grâce*.

The Knights disappeared almost as suddenly as they had appeared, but they had shaken middle-class Ontario. Newspaper editorials worried about the 'class question' and the meaning of the new labour militancy. John A. Macdonald also took notice. Labour organizations had complained for years about the deteriorating social conditions that had accompanied industrialization. The federal Royal Commission on Relations of Labour and Capital was created to investigate the social problems of the emerging industrial order.

The Royal Commission attempted to put a gloss on working-class life, noting some improvement on nearly every issue. Yet hours remained long, factories were still unsafe and unsanitary, and women and children not only continued to be employed in large numbers but were often physically abused while on the job. By the time the Commission delivered its final report to the federal government in 1889, there was no longer much debate about the seriousness of the social consequences of industrialization. But labour conditions fell within the provincial jurisdiction. It remained for Mowat to act.

The Employers' Liability Act of 1886 regularized the system by which injured workers could recover compensation from employers. It consolidated, but did not alter, existing practice. Injured workers still faced the daunting and difficult task of proving that their injuries resulted from employer negligence. The civil law principles of assumption of risk and contributory negligence favoured employers in the civil courts. Nor did the 1886 Ontario Factories Act do much to improve conditions on the factory floor. The Royal Commission had expressed concern about the moral vulnerability of young women and children working with men. The Factories Act restricted the employment of children, limited the hours of labour for both women and children, and made a number of pronouncements designed to improve working conditions in factories and shops. The province even appointed a female factory inspector. Yet those industries—such as food canning—that did employ large numbers of children under 14 received seasonal and other exemptions. Similarly, women and children under 18 could not be required to work longer than 10 hours per day or 60 hours per week—but these were already the standards in most industries, and in any event, employers could request partial exemptions here as well.

Toronto's leading employer at this time was the apparel industry. Three in four gar-

Nine-Hour March, Hamilton, 15 May 1872. Labour organizations throughout the province threw their support behind the Typographers in their strike for a nine-hour workday. NAC NL22324.

ment workers were women, and as in other industries, they received about half the wages of men, even though they were doing comparable work. 'I don't treat the men bad,' one clothing manufacturer in Toronto admitted in 1897, 'but I even up by taking advantage of the women.' The industry operated via outwork. Independent contractors bid for the right to 'manufacture' clothes. Bidding was cutthroat, and the women and girls in whose 'low, damp basement[s]' and attics the cutting and sewing were done received minimal pay on the basis of piecework. Girls and women who worked in clothing factories rarely had the opportunity to become skilled at their trade. One employer commented, 'I have twenty or twenty-five girls working for me and not one of them could make a coat right through.'

Numerous investigations into this system were conducted. Typically, investigators concluded 'the contracting system tends inevitably to the lowering of wages and degrading the conditions of labour.' In this context, the insufficiency of the Factories Act was apparent. 'Women and children work many more hours daily than would be permitted in shops and factories under the regulation of the [Provincial] Acts.' Well into the twentieth century, it remained common to see 'large numbers of women and children winding their way up and down Bay street [Toronto], carrying bundles in their arms or on perambulators.' 'Some of the poor creatures,' another observer affirmed, were 'hardly able to walk.' Those areas where women dominated as wage earners tended to be those most resistant to government supervision, however nominal.[23]

More generally, the enforcement of regulations governing working conditions presented great difficulties. The Act required employers to keep factories clean, ventilate workrooms, provide sanitary facilities, and install safety guards on all dangerous machinery. However, it failed to provide a standard against which conditions could be measured. 'Sanitary facilities' could mean a single outdoor privy to serve several hundred employees. No one had authority under the Act to determine which

machines were dangerous, what safety devices needed to be installed, the amount of space required per worker in workrooms, or the amount of air circulation. With depressing regularity, factory inspectors investigated and reported on inadequate conditions, but in the end the Act proved unenforceable.

Nor is it clear that the province ever intended to enforce rigorously its new Factories Act. The government initially appointed only three inspectors for the whole province. By the first decade of the twentieth century, there were ten, yet the Factories Inspection Branch remained understaffed and underfunded. Inspectors, meanwhile, believed that more could be gained through 'education' and public reporting than through prosecutions. Despite the ever-increasing volume of their reports, inspectors prosecuted few. When inspectors found underage children, they charged the parents, not the employers. With the Factories Act, the government established its right to regulate the conditions of labour, but failed to effectively exercise that right.

Other social problems outside the workplace received little attention from Mowat. Liberal ideology was laissez-faire. Poor relief, for example, had traditionally been a local responsibility, yet the new municipal laws enacted following Confederation made such programs optional. No Ontario municipality taxed itself to support public relief programs. A majority of citizens insisted that the problems of poverty should be addressed through private rather than public initiatives.

Private initiatives were invariably controlled by boards made up of religious activists. Minorities such as the Catholic and Jewish communities established direct control over their own social service networks for their co-religionists. Among Protestants, internal denominational divisions required shared control. Ministers, wardens, deacons, and others from several denominations served together on boards of directors of a wide variety of charitable organizations. Local churches often had 'poor funds', but the amounts were small and disbursements irregular: in 1893, for example, the Baptist Church in the small town of Thorold took money from the poor fund for general expenses. Religious notions often impeded the evolution of a public social welfare system.[24] Protestants commonly believed that poverty was a punishment for sin. Social Darwinists insisted that hierarchical social structures and economic inequality were part of the natural order. Thomas Conant, a well-known Ontario author, asked in 1898, 'Is it wise to foster the growth of a class of persons whose filth and foul disease are the result of laziness and their own vice?'[25] Yet Christians also fervently believed that charity was their duty.

The key was to distinguish between the 'deserving' and 'undeserving' poor. Many citizens believed that religious leaders were best suited to make this distinction, and they opposed public aid. Most private programs concentrated their efforts on the needs of children and women, who could more easily be identified as victims and therefore deserving. Such beliefs were rooted in discriminatory social notions about women's and men's roles and helped perpetuate gender inequality in other aspects of social life.

The plight of the dependent elderly suggests how difficult it was to distinguish the deserving from the undeserving. Until the Mowat era, community groups such as the

Woman selling pencils, Toronto, 1918. Elderly people without children to assist them were particularly vulnerable to poverty. COTA SC244, Item 676.

Ladies Aid Society had provided essential help to impoverished senior citizens in the form of 'outdoor relief'—donations of food, fuel, and clothing. As the middle-class turned against poor-relief measures in general, the government decided that the most efficient solution was to provide institutions where cheap care, and, for some, rehabilitation, could be offered. Mowat's Charities Aid Act of 1874 channelled money away from outdoor relief and towards private charities that supported institutional relief. Publicly assisted charity institutions increased from four in 1866 to nearly a hundred in 1900. Almost none specialized in care of the aged, but many soon complained of being deluged by 'the decaying and decrepit'. In fact, Ontario's institutions housed a paltry 4 per cent of the province's senior citizens. The government knew this, but in the declining economy of the 1890s it, like other North American jurisdictions, claimed that charity for the aged faced a financial crisis. The solution was to deny institutional care to all senior citizens with living relatives. This policy, the government argued, would not only save money but reinforce traditional family values. It was a con's game. The government was not close to a state of financial crisis. Most senior citizens were able to look after themselves, and families, far from abandoning their elders, were extremely active in caring for them. The tragedy of Mowat's penurious policy was that the truly poor elderly usually had families equally poor.[26]

Poverty was often equated with sloth, vice, and laziness, and for the working-class poor, it could be a short step from being denied state succour to incarceration in a state penal institution. Mowat's answer to the perceived problem of what the Toronto *Globe* termed 'a criminal class' was the establishment in 1874 of the Central Prison, designed to punish those sentenced to less than two years and thus not admissible to the federal penitentiary at Kingston. The Central Prison aspired to be 'a terror to evil-doers'. Working-class men, especially the unskilled, dominated the prison's population. Whenever possible, convicts were expected to work and pay for their upkeep.

Whippings, frugal diets of bread and water, and extended periods of isolation typified the custodial regimen. This grim approach was a legacy of the dissatisfaction felt by mid-century Upper Canadians for costly institutions that seemed unable to effect rehabilitation and social reform. Other jurisdictions in North America and Great Britain had much more ameliorative penal systems in the late nineteenth century than did Ontario.[27]

In 1880, the Mowat government established a second 'special' reformatory designed to put to hard labour another recalcitrant portion of the population. The Mercer Reformatory for Women was not simply designed for female inmates: it was also run by women. Its inmates were overwhelmingly of an unskilled working-class background, often servants. Most were sentenced on moral charges, not, as in the case of the Central inmates, on property charges. In striking contrast with Central, punishments were few and rarely severe. 'Our aim has been to govern with kindness,' Mary Jane O'Reilly, Mercer's superintendent, affirmed, 'and we have found this the most effectual way of influencing them, treating them as human beings who have a claim upon our charity as well as our justice.' One of O'Reilly's staff noted that their intent was 'to bring the girls up as if they were at home. . . . I never lock up my rooms. The front door is always open and Mrs O'Reilly's quarters are the same.'[28]

Prisons were also seen by some as fitting institutions for the socialization of Native people. In 1873 in Brantford, the home of the Six Nations, the proportion of Native people in the local jail matched the proportion in the population as a whole; by 1901 the proportion

The Andrew Mercer Ontario Reformatory for Females, 1903. Administrators at the Mercer emphasized reform
rather than punishment. Their maternal-feminist approach reflected the patriarchal attitudes of the time, but at
least they treated their charges with humane consideration. AO Govt. Doc PS (29th Annual Report of the
Inspector of Prisons and Public Charities, Ontario Sessional papers, 35 [1903], 87).

of Native people in jail was more than twice their proportion of the total population. Native people considered incarceration cruel and unusual punishment. Most were arrested on charges of drunkenness and jailed because they could not—or would not—pay a fine. In many localities, Native people in general were considered to constitute a 'criminal class'.[29]

The state also looked to education to cultivate appropriate citizens. Just as Native children were sent to special residential schools, in many communities Black children were relegated, despite their parents' protests, to segregated schools. Schooling taught that poverty

was self-inflicted; individuals were the architects of their own misfortunes. The uneducated became increasingly defined as socially unacceptable and suspect.

John Sandfield Macdonald had passed legislation that made school attendance compulsory up to the age of 16. Mowat provided uniform textbooks so the government could oversee their 'fitness'. He also introduced the kindergarten, a 'garden of children' where moral values could be cultivated from the earliest age. The children of working-class parents remained somewhat less likely to attend schools than their middle-class counterparts, in part because

Amherstburg parade, 1 August 1894. The anniversary of Emancipation Day, 1 August 1834, when Britain abolished slavery throughout its empire, was often an occasion for Ontario's Black communities to assess social progress. In 1899, Reverend A.W. Hackley of Chatham asked, 'What has the negro of Kent County done that he is unable to go into the ice cream parlour? What has he done that he should be so ostracized from restaurants?' (in Colin McFarquhar, 'A Difference of Perspective: Blacks, Whites and Emancipation Day Celebrations in Ontario, 1865–1919', *Ontario History* XCII [2000], 151). AO ACC2537 S 12008.

some school boards exacted a fee of 10 to 12 cents a month per child. While this charge could be waived for the poor, 'that,' Hamilton's trades council noted, 'looked too much like beggary and the other children in the schools would soon know of it and point their fingers at the poor ones.' Texts were expensive and kindergartens were very slow to take hold outside Toronto. Daily attendance continued to be lower in rural than in urban centres.[30]

School attendance was more seasonal in rural than in urban areas, although literacy levels were similar. As good rural land became harder to find in Ontario, parents limited their families' size and young adults delayed marriage. As early as 1850, young people began extending the time they spent in their parents' home. For middle-class parents, rural and urban alike, the home was a place for nurturing and inculcating respect and respectability.

School playground, *c.* 1900. In 1876 John George Hodgins published a manual on school architecture in which he maintained that no schoolhouse intended for girls should be more than two storeys high. 'What is the testimony of the oldest and most thoughtful teachers of our State in regard to the influence of excessive stair climbing? That it is evil, and only evil, and that continually.' 'Stair climbing very frequently gives rise to female complaints [and] is very injurious to many girls especially as the period of puberty approaches. . . .' If a school had to have more than one storey, Hodgins concluded, 'the ground floor should *invariably* be reserved for the girls.' John Kelso photo. NAC 181923.

Parents thought schools should perform the same function. A concern for their children's material future also underlay the importance placed on education by both rural and urban families. Parents increasingly provided in their wills 'cash and an education' for certain of their children—daughters as much as sons.[31]

Given later marriages, many parents realized that their daughters might need to work for a considerable time. The teaching profession offered non-factory employment for those daughters. Female teachers received less in wages, so school districts were keen to hire them. Schools sought single, not married, women. Women were thought to be more natural nurturers than men, who were seen to be more aggressive and sexually passionate. The most nurturing teachers, then, would be unmarried women who were not distracted by raising children of their own and who, having presumably not known sexual passion, could be trusted to offer students physical nurturing—touching, hugging, and so on—in a way that men could not. In this way social constructions of gender difference determined participation in the work of schooling just as in the work of farming, in some cases facilitating and in others limiting the possibilities for women and men alike.[32]

Work was the crucible within which men proved their worth: 'it is in the hurry, the bustle, the turmoil of a busy active existence,' John Scrimger, a Galt liveryman, told members of the local Mechanics' Institute, 'that we see the man. Then we can discern whether he is an upright, virtuous, and noble character that may command our admiration and respect, or whether his be a nature that repels us, and fills us with contempt and aversion.' By contrast, women were expected to exercise their finest qualities—beauty, sincerity, warmth, purity, domesticity—in the cultivation of the home, the 'little heaven on earth'. The only acceptable public activity for married women was charitable work with churches or benevolent societies. Like housework, this was a selfless labour of love; monetary recompense could only sully such work.[33] But times were changing, however slowly. In the late nineteenth century, the Married Women's Property Laws gave wives the right to own and manage property and conduct business free from their husbands' interference. At the time, few women owned property and conservative judges often refused to grant married women the potential agency inherent in the Property Laws. But soon more women began to write wills, and

fathers began writing wills that put daughters on a more level footing with sons. The Property Laws created confidence that property ceded to daughters would now remain in their hands after marriage. A significant increase in landed property ownership by women—married, single, and widowed—followed the passage of those laws.

Many women began to run their own businesses. By the turn of the century, urban women in the workforce were as likely to be self-employed or employers as were urban men. Some of these women may have been simply fronts for husbands who transferred their property to protect it from confiscation by creditors. Yet courts were increasingly strict about such activity. Such attempts to defraud actually provided some married women with an opportunity to take control of their lives. In 1904, when a Mr Cammell of Hamilton sued his wife for recovery of property, she testified that he had deeded a hotel to her in order to avoid paying creditors. She ignored him, paid the debts, upgraded the property, and made the business a success. The court ruled in her favour. Granted, such women were a minority. It is true, too, that women who were self-employed or employers earned far less than their male counterparts (though more than female employees) and often were self-employed simply because wage work was not available to them. Nevertheless, the Property Acts were the most important legislation affecting women's rights passed in Ontario in the late nineteenth century.[34]

Church and benevolent work provided an opportunity for women to work together in larger, more overtly political arenas. Temperance reform engaged the energies of many. Middle-class women dominated the Women's Christian Temperance Union. The WCTU looked to education and legislation to reform drinkers. When, in 1884, single and widowed women with property received the right to vote in municipal elections, members of the WCTU urged them to vote for local prohibition, a right ceded to municipalities by provincial legislation. The WCTU was the first organization to lobby for women's suffrage at the provincial and federal levels, arguing that women's special nurturing qualities could help reform society as a whole. In this period, few women argued that they had an inherent right to vote; rather, voting was seen as a means to realize specific reform agendas. Yet, for many WCTU members, even this maternal feminist approach to reform was much too 'radical'. 'I am more than sorry,' the WCTU 's superintendent of franchise work lamented, 'that all our women are not in hearty sympathy with this department of our work.'[35]

Labour leaders argued that a 'love of liquor' was not what drew working men to taverns. Rather, they explained to a Royal Commission on the Liquor Traffic in the early 1890s, 'the love of sociable society; and the comfort that is found in the places where the sale takes place . . . often . . . not to be met with in their own homes' was the principal attraction. 'Discomfort, badly cooked food and ill-ventilated dwellings have much to answer for in connection with intemperance. Attention to these matters, *and more especially* to the training of the female portion of the population in a knowledge of domestic economy and household duties, the undersigned are satisfied would have an elevating and most beneficial effect.'[36] In the hierarchy of the fam-

SWINE.

WHEREAS great inconvenience or damage is experienced by the Public from Swine running at large within the limits of the Town of Niagara, Be it therefore, and it is hereby enacted by the President and Board of Police thereof, that all Pigs found running at large within the limits aforesaid, shall be liable to be impounded under the following

REGULATIONS.

1. That it shall be the duty of all Bailiffs and constables, and all other persons are hereby empowered, to drive to the Pound all Pigs found so running at large, and it shall be the duty of the Pound Keeper to receive and detain the same, and if not claimed at or before the expiration of 24 hours from the time of impounding, then it shall be the duty of the Pound-keeper to advertise the same for Sale, such Sale to take place 48 hours after such advertisement shall have been posted on the market, and in three other conspicuous places in the Town, and if the proceeds of such Sale shall exceed the charges then the overplus shall be paid to the owner of the animals sold, if claimed within one month, and if not so claimed, to be applied to the public uses of the Town.

2. And be it further enacted, That any owner of a Pig or Pigs shall be liable to a Fine of not less than 2s. 6d. nor more than 5s. with costs, for each Hog or Pig, every time it is suffered to run at large, within the precincts of the said Town, and that the oath of one credible witness will be sufficient for a conviction before any Member of the Board.

3. And be it further enacted, That the follow- ing shall be the Fees for all services performed under this Act :—

For driving to the Pound each Pig,		1s. 3d.
" Receiving each Pig.		0 7½
" Keeping and feeding each Pig for each 24 hours impounded,		0 7½
" Advertising each Pig.		1 3
" Selling each Pig.		1 3

4. And be it further enacted, That any Fin and Costs which may arise from an infringement of this Act, shall, if not paid, be levied in the usual way, by to of the Goods and Chattels of the offender ; and, in default of any Goods and Chattels, every such offender shall b liable to be imprisoned in the Jail of the District for a period not exceeding eight days.

5. And be it further enacted, That all By-Laws repugnant to this Act shall be repealed.

ALEX. DAVIDSON, President.

Police Office, Niagara, 6th June, 1849.

Proclamation versus pigs, Niagara, 1849. Well into the twentieth century, many working-class urban families kept livestock to help make ends meet, and even well-off city dwellers maintained large kitchen gardens. Municipal regulations were largely ignored. Mackenzie-Lindsey Poster Collection, AO 5289 C233-1-1-2080.

ily, men enjoyed far greater rights and exercised far greater power than women or children. While many families worked together to survive, and both middle- and working-class families did protect and nurture children, there was also much abuse, exploitation, and inequality within families. Ontario court records document a persistent pattern of wife beating, or as the *Ottawa Citizen* reported on one case, 'reconstructing' a wife 'with a hard wood log'.

A basic assumption in common law was that 'wives did not require the explicit protection of the law because they were under the guardianship of their husbands.' That assumption applied to children as well. Neighbours often aided wives who were being beaten by their husbands outside the home, and they would testify to hearing the sounds of beatings within a home, but they rarely intervened in what they—and the law—saw as private patriarchal space. Courts believed that 'moderate correction of his wife [and children] for . . . misbehaviour' was allowable. 'Proper castigation,' one judge affirmed, is normal. Besides, 'it is not for magistrates or courts,' he concluded, 'to step in and interfere with the rights of a husband in ruling his own household.' Wives, especially working-class wives, had little recourse before the law. Some courts did fine and jail abusive and deserting husbands, but that was of little help to impoverished women and their children. Some husbands simply refused to pay fines or post sureties as security for good behaviour, choosing jail instead. 'Why,' a prison inspector lamented in 1877, 'a ruffian who is constantly beating his wife should not be *sentenced* to jail for a certain period with hard labour, instead of his electing to be *detained* there in utter idleness . . . is beyond my comprehension.' Most often, criminal courts merely gave suspended sentences and counselled mediation. Deserting husbands were rarely required to continue support payments; this changed with the passage of the Deserted Wives' Maintenance Act

of 1888, but enforcement was very spotty. Divorce was almost impossible for poor women, as it required an act of the federal parliament to effect and the grounds for such an application were extremely limited. Violence was one ground, but as a judge pronounced in 1873, 'the law . . . lays upon the wife the necessity of bearing some indignities, and even some personal violence, before it will sanction her leaving her husband's roof.' [37]

The poor were disadvantaged at almost every turn. Public health reformers had long campaigned to restrict the keeping of domestic animals in urban areas. The first to be banned were pigs (the mainstay of working-class families), long before cows (the choice of the middle class). For example, like many wealthy families, the Harrises of London's elite kept both pigs and cows and cultivated a large garden on their spacious urban estate, and not until 1937 did London prohibit the raising of cows within city limits. Banning domestic animals represented a serious economic loss for many poor families. Such reforms insured better public health standards, but at the cost of eliminating a key non-wage option for supplementing meagre industrial wages. [38]

Many environmental problems beset urban Ontario in the late nineteenth century. In 1878, a Select Committee of the Provincial Assembly reported that the water supplies of three-quarters of 80 responding municipalities were contaminated by human waste from privies, disease was widespread, and little or nothing was being done about it. Existing provincial legislation allowed for the collection of information and inspection but provided little in the way of enforcement. Municipalities were reluctant to assume costly responsibili-

J. Winterborn, 'Roxburgh Place, Residence of A. Marshall, Esq.', watercolour, 1868. This orderly farmstead was located in Oxford County, in southwestern Ontario. The artist was apparently a schoolteacher in Blenheim Township. Courtesy Michael S. Bird.

Morningstar Mill, St Catharines. Photo Peter Fowler.

Tom Thomson, 'Autumn Foliage', oil on wood, 1916. NGC. Purchased 1918.

Mennonites on their way to church, Waterloo County. Photo John de Visser.

Carl Schaeffer, 'Summer Evening in Town, Hanover', watercolour on paper, 1942. In the shadow of the city's major industry, families tend vegetable gardens, cattle, and chickens. The Edmonton Art Gallery Collection, purchased with funds provided by the Winspear Foundation.

The Horseshoe Falls, from the Skylon Tower, Niagara Falls. Photo Andrew Leyerle.

ties: dead animals in the street did not require a garbage collector; rather, Kingston's local paper advised unhappy ratepayers to await the arrival of 'a few carrion consuming crows'.

In 1882, the Toronto *Globe* lamented that the city's water system provided at best 'drinkable sewage'. In the 1890s, Sudbury's sewage was dumped raw into two creeks that ran through the centre of town. A report prepared for the town of Belleville in 1878 described the sewage system as 'overcharged cesspools, neglected privies, and filth laden sewers'; wells and springs were drying up because of 'the indiscriminate destruction of trees that formerly covered the ground' and 'the general adoption and extension of land-drainage'; and the nearby River Moira 'was completely unfit for domestic use owing to the peat colour of the water'. Lake Ontario's Bay of Quinte also fell short: in the warm months 'large tracts of its surface resemble[d] a lawn rather than a lake.'[39] Mowat's government tightened its supervision by establishing a Provincial Board of Health. But the board often found itself powerless in the face of local municipal councils that refused to raise local rates to establish adequate sewage systems and water supplies. In 1884, Toronto granted only $500 to its local health board to oversee sanitary conditions for the city's nearly 100,000 people. In the absence of effective provincial enforcement, private concerns took some municipalities to court. In 1893 the Town of Walkerville, in the words of a Grand Jury, 'wilfully and injuriously did construct, make, build and maintain certain sewers and drains' that conveyed waste to the Detroit River, which became 'greatly filled, impregnated, polluted and fouled with the said refuse matters and substances'; the waters

were 'corrupted, fouled, offensive and unhealthy to the great damage and common nuisance' of users and residents. Walkerville and Windsor paid to clean up the mess and revamp their local sewage systems.[40]

A movement to reform city government gathered force. Historians have debated the motives that lay behind the actions and rhetoric of city reformers. Did they have the interests of the community as a whole at heart, or did they represent the needs of a more narrowly focused elite? In the case of municipal water issues, it seems clear that changes occurred only after one or two unwelcome events transpired. Following a big fire, municipal councils were quick to upgrade water transmission facilities; after an epidemic, sewage systems and water quality would be upgraded. In both cases, the first step was often the purchase, from private interests, of local water systems. The money for such initiatives usually came from increased municipal property taxes. But not all ratepayers benefited equally. Water mains and pipes reached industries and wealthy residents first and the poor much later. Moreover, even as fire insurance companies pressured local councils to reform water transmission services, they routinely increased costs to residents who lived in areas with substandard systems. Thus, in many municipalities, industrialists and well-off residents also benefited from lower fire insurance rates, while those least well off, not connected to the new system, suffered from higher premiums. The benefits of municipal reform eventually trickled down, but it was a slow process and many died waiting.[41]

Nor did death by infectious diseases such as tuberculosis and scarlet fever strike the rich and poor equally. In Hamilton, the lowest mortality rates 'were found among that segment of the population least exposed to overcrowding and environmental blight and living in the areas with the highest per capita property values.' In the 1870s, life expectancy for Belleville's lower-class residents (most of whom were Catholic) was about 37—some 10 years less than for the better-off Protestants. Catholic infants actually had a lower death rate than Protestant infants, because Catholic mothers protected their babies from poor water by breast-feeding for a longer time. But this cultural difference could do nothing to protect against overcrowding, poor nutrition, and unsafe sewage facilities.[42]

The new century would bring even more fundamental change as economic growth dramatically quickened the pace of industrialization and urbanization. At the turn of the century, cities grew at an ever-accelerating rate, placing even greater strains on housing stock, water and sewage systems, and other urban services. As social conditions further deteriorated, old notions of laissez-faire could not contain demands for reform. The social consequences of industrialization demanded a more sustained and systematic reform response.

CHAPTER EIGHT

The Making of Industrial Ontario: 1905–1923

'A new order of things [has] come,' wrote William Meredith, the retired leader of Ontario's Conservative party, to the newly victorious Conservative premier, James Whitney, in 1905. For the first time since 1872, a Conservative government led Canada's most powerful province. Rural Ontario had been the Liberals' stronghold, but the urban population had skyrocketed even as rural population growth slowed. By 1911 a majority of Ontarians would live in cities and work in manufacturing rather than farming and primary industries. While these trends began in the late nineteenth century, their trajectories soared in the first decade of the new century. Manufacturing output in Ontario's major cities almost doubled—the greatest increase of any time before the Second World War.[1]

The era of the talented generalist gradually gave way to that of the trained specialist. Technology and efficiency became the watchwords of success and progress. The State became more interventionist, albeit reluctantly and unevenly, and increasingly relied on specialized, scientific advice. Reformers, while still strongly religious in orientation, allied with the scientific and medical communities in their efforts to preserve and cultivate an appropriately productive and moral citizenry.

Amidst this fast-paced change, however, continuities were evident. Four out of every five Ontarians had been born in Canada, and most, including Whitney himself, had grown up in small-town or rural Ontario. Some of the province's largest industries—agricultural implements, cheese and butter, tanning—were rural-based. As the rural population ebbed, support for traditional rural ways swelled. 'It is from our ranks,' one rural activist maintained, 'that the effulgence of freedom has ever sprung.'[2] As late as 1921, two-fifths of Ontarians still lived in the countryside, and many who lived in cities had moved there from rural areas. Politicians ignored rural voters and values at their peril. Meredith continued as premier until his death in 1914. His Conservative successor, William Hearst, lasted five years before being overturned by the United Farmers of Ontario, the last Ontario government elected specifically to uphold the verities of rural life.

Although the last decades of the nineteenth century provided a strong base on

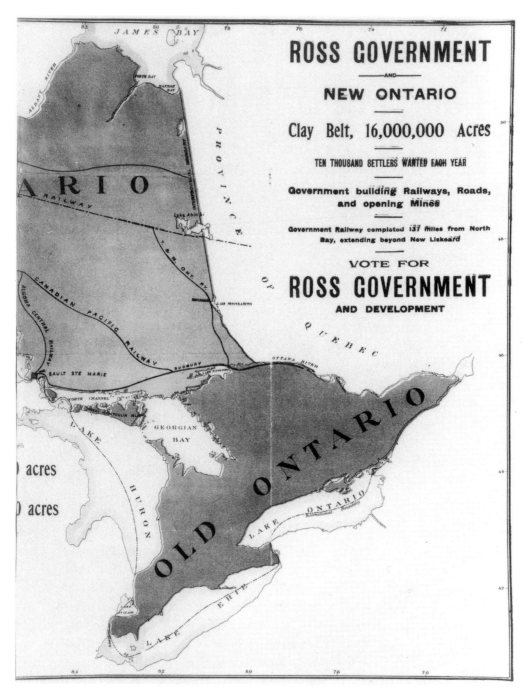

Map of Ontario, 1904. At the turn of the century, the rural life continued to be seen as a panacea for the problems of an urbanizing, industrializing society. Governments hoped that the recently surveyed (1900) clay belts of the 'New Ontario' would attract many agriculturists, immigrants and Ontario-born. AO C233-1-1-2230, 5296.

which to build, accelerated growth in Ontario depended on favourable changes in the Atlantic economy. The new century brought an end to economic stagnation and ushered in a period of rapid capital accumulation. Technological changes provided incentives for the investment of that capital in Canada. As the traditional agricultural, forestry, and primary manufacturing sectors expanded, new industries, particularly in mining and secondary manufacturing, emerged. The provincial economy became not just bigger, but significantly more diverse.

In 1902, the Grand Trunk Railway began building through northern Ontario en route to the west coast, and the Liberal government commenced work on a north-south line, the Timiskaming and Northern Ontario Railway. Exports boomed, primary manufacturing of non-ferrous metals grew, and the development of the sulphite process in paper-making breathed new life into Ontario's forest industries—the Abitibi Pulp and Paper Company's plant at Iroquois Falls would soon be one of the world's largest.

Ports through which a railway passed, such as the Lakehead, served as gatekeepers between the west and the east, much as the Algonkians had for the Huron and more northern peoples in the period before European settlement. The cleaning, sorting, and transhipment of wheat became an economic mainstay of the Lakehead region. By the end of the 1920s, the Lakehead had become the world's largest grain port.[3]

Neither mining nor paper-making, however, proved as significant as the development of the hydroelectric industry. Ontario depended on costly imported coal from the

Gold miners, South Porcupine region, *c.* 1910. Railway construction led to the discovery of rich silver reserves at Cobalt; large gold deposits discovered at Porcupine and Kirkland Lake soon put Ontario ahead of the Yukon as Canada's foremost gold-producing region. Mining was dirty, dangerous work, and many gold miners contracted an incurable disease known as silicosis, caused by prolonged exposure to silica dust particles. AO ACC9160 S13751.

United States. If Ontario was to emerge as a major manufacturing centre, a cheap source of domestic energy would have to be found. The development of the hydraulic turbine, the dynamo, the alternator, and high tension wires, which allowed hydroelectricity to be produced and transported cheaply and efficiently from generating stations to industrial cities, provided that energy. Increasingly, manufacturers harnessed hydro's power.

This widespread growth attracted people as well as capital. Between 1896 and 1914, immigration increased sharply to both Ontario

Waiting for dinner at the cook's shanty in a logging camp in the Ottawa Valley, *c.* 1905. At the turn of the century, provincial revenues from timber exceeded government income from any other source. NAC PA106194.

and the Prairie provinces. As settlement advanced in Manitoba, Saskatchewan, and Alberta, Ontario's manufacturing companies responded to enlarged markets for capital and consumer goods. Although the hitherto dominant clothing industry grew, it lost ground to secondary iron and steel industries, which by 1911 employed more workers than any other sector in Ontario cities. Increased mechanization and the adoption of labour-saving machinery, meanwhile, led to a stabilization of the workforce despite continued growth in the volume and value of production. A major depression in 1913 briefly interrupted the extraordinary pace of economic growth, but war in Europe quickly ended the slump. Between 1916 and 1918, the Imperial Munitions Board awarded Canada over $1 billion in contracts for war matériel, 60 per cent of which went to Ontario. Such extensive investments even revitalized the industrial base in many small Ontario towns that had been economically dormant at the turn of the century.

Industrial production continued to be concentrated primarily in Toronto and the surrounding region—the 'Golden Horseshoe', as Ontarians came to call the arc of territory extending from Hamilton to the west and Oshawa to the east. Industrial jobs in turn drew migrants both from abroad and from the surrounding countryside into the largest cities. South-central Ontario became Canada's single largest consumer market, a magnet for yet more investment. As finance and trade grew ever more sophisticated, more lawyers, middle managers, and clerks were needed. Large retail department stores appeared.[4]

Government bureaucracies also began to expand in this period, and with the harnessing of hydroelectricity, the state gradually assumed a more interventionist stance. While formerly, simple statutes and court cases had been sufficient to resolve most issues to do with the use of water, by the 1920s, regulatory and administrative agencies were in place. The experts who staffed them attempted, often in direct response to pressure groups—the strongest of which were lumber and hydro companies—to sort out competing use rights to water. Citizens with environmental concerns only slowly coalesced into effective lobby groups.

Aboriginal people were accorded few if any rights in this area. Treaty Nine, signed in 1905 and 1906 between Native people in the 'new' north and the Ontario and federal governments, was even less generous than Treaty Three, negotiated in the 1870s. On the Mattagami and Abitibi rivers, Native rights to rivers were removed in favour of private corporate hydroelectric development. Much of the Mattagami band's traditional hunting area, burial grounds, and village were flooded; the only compensation for the loss of traditional lands was 25 cents an acre. Subsistence-based hunting rights meant little in the future envisioned by miners, foresters, and hydroelectric engineers. The province, through the Hydro Electric Power Commission, would not take over such development until 1933.[5]

In the eyes of federal authorities, for Native people to make independent economic decisions was tantamount to Native self-determination—an unthinkable notion. Forests were often cut without the sanction of the bands that had been granted the land as reserves. The Garden River band at the Sault was even denied the right to cut timber on its own reserve, because the federal Indian agent felt that the only proper economic activity for his charges was farming.

Native people resisted such provincial interference into their sovereign affairs, with occasional success. The Garden River band had a rocky bluff known as 'wild man's stone' which it worked with local entrepreneurs, who provided band members with jobs as well as money for the rock and gravel resource—a rare opportunity for the band to move out of farming. The Garden River people's success in protecting the bluff from government appropriation set a precedent for future diversification and became a story retold throughout the twentieth century. The Dokis, a small band on the French River, managed to resist government pressure and keep control of an extremely valuable timber reserve for which, in 1883, they had been offered a meagre $4

Ojibwa women stretching a tanned skin, Long Lake, 1916. Many young Native men were away at war in this period. In Ontario, as in other parts of Canada, Native people enlisted in the armed services at a rate at least equal to that of the general population, even though they were not citizens. The Six Nations people at Brantford, however, refused to fight unless they were requested to do so by the Crown; throughout the war, they ignored all requests to enlist from officials at the provincial and federal levels. CMC 36690.

per person per year. When in 1906, after the death of a longstanding chief, band members finally agreed to sell, they netted $1.1 million—$600 per person per year—and 'became per capita the richest Indians in Canada'.[6]

Ontario's First Nations were becoming increasingly assertive in the protection of their rights. They especially resented residential schooling. From the 1870s the federal government had been taking Native children from their families and placing them in the 'care of strangers' in the hope of 'civilizing and assimilating them into white society'. Anglican, Catholic, Methodist, and other religious bodies eagerly administered the state-funded pro-

gram. In 1913, two Mohawk parents complained about whipping, hair shearing, poor food, and inadequate visitation rights at a local residential school. When the government ignored the complaint, one father, supported by the Six Nations council, took the school's principal to court. The jury awarded the father $100 ($5,000 had been asked for) in compensation for his daughter's having been kept on a water diet for three days and $300 for a whipping administered to her 'on bare back with raw hide'. The principal was replaced and punishments made less severe—one government official felt the children were being 'disciplined to death'. It was only a partial victory, but not one that the government wished to see repeated; Ottawa refused to release funds to the Six Nations council for the payment of court costs.[7]

Assertive action by the Mohawk nation was far from unusual. In 1919, Lieutenant F.O. Loft, a Mohawk leader, had convened the first congress of the League of Indians at Sault Ste Marie, calling for 'absolute control in retaining possession or disposition of our lands'. Fittingly, given the prominence of women in Iroquoian society, it was a Mohawk woman who, in 1921, directly confronted the Ontario government on the central principal at issue: Native sovereignty. Eliza Sero, a 52-year-old Mohawk widow who had lost a son in the First World War, took a provincial fishery inspector to court for confiscating her seine fishing gear and prohibiting her from fishing in the Bay of Quinte without a licence. Fishing in the Great Lakes was big business in Ontario, which formed the northern shore of all but one of the five Great Lakes. The number of fishers had increased from 2,000 in 1879 to over 3,200 in 1920, and improved fishing technology meant larger catches. Since competition for fish in the Quinte area was intense, the local white community could only have been pleased with the inspector's actions.

Seine nets were less damaging to fish stocks than gill nets, and the licensing system had been instituted in the late nineteenth century partly as a conservation measure. But Sero's position, argued in court by white lawyers, was simply that she was a member of a sovereign nation and not subject to the laws of the whites. The presiding judge at the Supreme Court of Ontario, William Renwick Riddell, was on record as opposing the very concept of treaties as the product of negotiation with sovereign First Nations. 'In Ontario,' he wrote several years later, 'there never has been any doubt that all the land, Indian and otherwise, is the king's, and that Indians are subjects in the same way as others. There are no troublesome subtleties in Canadian law.' In pronouncing in favour of the province, he asserted that seine fishing was not, in any case, a traditional Indian practice—conveniently overlooking the fact that Ontario's First Peoples had been using seine nets for at least five hundred years. Eliza Sero died in 1937 at the age of 68. We do not know if she continued to fish. We do know that the Mohawk people continued to fight for the acknowledgement of their sovereignty.[8]

Women were leaders on other fronts. Young farm women led the great exodus from rural Ontario to the cities between 1890 and 1910. 'I've talked wid dozens of girls and I'll put ye woise,' Mrs Murphy explained to Mrs Thompson in the *Farmer's Advocate* in 1918:

'Take it from me if ye want girls on the farm ye must be afther makin' the farm more attractive nor it is now. Wan thing is the lack of conveniences. The danged men have everything they want . . . and the women is still carryin water and churnin and washin jist like the women as come over on the Mayflower. Thin, again, the girl wants some company. On most farms her only chance is to flirt wid the hired man. . . . And there is wan more thing and that's the biggest trouble of all.'
'And what's that' says some wan.
'The long hours' says Kathlane.[9]

The exodus of young women to cities caused consternation not only to those who saw rural life as Ontario's backbone but to a

Women workers, International Malleable Iron Company, Guelph, *c.* 1920. By the 1920s, wages had improved and the workweek was shorter than it had been in 1900, but women were still paid much less than men. Guelph Public Library Archives.

group of Protestant social activists—medical doctors, charity workers, and church ministers—committed to raising the moral tone of Canadian society. Members of the so-called purity movement, part of a larger, loose-knit reform group known as the Social Gospellers, looked askance at single women working, living, and moving around big cities like Toronto without suitable chaperones. Young, single working women, often exploited in the workplace, became figures of suspicion outside it,

and as the numbers of nickelodeons, vaudeville theatres, saloons, and dance halls in Toronto increased—from 5 in 1900 to 112 in 1915—policewomen were hired to keep an eye on them.[10] From this perspective, the proper employment for working girls was home service.

For some single women, this dreary prospect was the only one available. In order to enter the country, single Finnish women had to agree to work as domestics. Black women too

Modifying a percussion fuse, Russell Motor Car Co., Toronto, *c.* 1917. The First World War had a major impact on women's work. At first women's war effort was restricted to fund-raising and prodding reluctant men to enlist, but in late 1915 and early 1916, when enlistment drives intensified, many women began to take men's jobs, in factories and even banks. However, most stayed in industrial work only until the men returned from the war. NAC PA24640.

were segregated in the domestic sector. As Caribbean-born Violet Blackman recalled of Toronto in 1920, 'You couldn't get any position regardless who you were and how educated you were, other than housework because even if the employer would employ you, those you had to work with would not work with you.' 'Really and truly,' Marjorie Lewsey recalled, '[Black women] weren't allowed to go into factory work until Hitler started the war.'[11]

Most working women were single, and it was often assumed that all they required was pin money. Ghettoized in low-wage, low-status occupations, frequently the last hired and first fired, women were paid much less than their male co-workers, even in sectors where they did the same jobs. Hitherto a rarity, by 1921 female typists and stenographers accounted for nearly half of Canada's clerical workforce, but they earned just over half the salary of male clerks; even by 1971, the wage gap would narrow only slightly.[12]

In 1907, 400 primarily single women between the ages of 17 and 24 walked off their jobs at the Toronto offices of the Bell Telephone Company in protest against low wages, harsh working conditions, and long hours. Moral purity advocates chastized Bell for endangering the future of the 'race'. A better system was needed, one Methodist minister preached, one that would not 'strain women beyond their capacity and impair the interests of the unborn'. Twenty-six doctors testified to the dangers faced by the young women in Bell's employ, and a report of a Royal Commission on the strike warned that 'the breaking point of the operator's health is not far from the breaking point of efficient work.' While they did not win any of their major demands, the strikers did force Bell to rethink its often oppressive managerial practices, introduce cafeterias, and undertake consultation with the workforce.[13]

In 1913, two thousand Hamilton garment workers, many of them women, struck at the city's four largest clothing factories and, after two weeks, won a victory. A strike in 1912 against Timothy Eaton and Company fared less well. 'Those [involved] are almost entirely Jewish,' *The Ladies' Garment Worker* noted, 'and the chief slogan by which it was hoped to cut off public sympathy was the report . . . that this is "only a strike of Jews."' The 'slogan' worked. The future of the wrong race was at issue, and moral purity advocates stayed away. Timothy Eaton arrogantly proclaimed that the action was 'nothing but a hold up game' and that the strikers could forget about their jobs—jobs already being done by Yorkshire-bred strikebreakers, both male and female.[14]

Rising labour militancy and the rapid growth of trade unions in the 1890s led to the creation of both provincial and federal Departments of Labour, which attempted to set a minimum budget necessary to maintain 'health and decency' for a family of five. Yet by the end of the Great War only skilled railway workers—locomotive engineers, conductors, firemen, and brakemen—earned more than the government's estimated minimum. Average wages for adult male wage earners represented less than 75 per cent of what was required.

Still, there were some improvements in the standard of living for Ontarians during these years. Changes in the structure of the labour force shifted many from lower-paying to higher-paying jobs. And slowly, the hours of labour began to decline, from ten hours per day, six days per week, to nine hours per day with a 'half-holiday' on Saturday. During the war, the trend towards shorter hours accelerated dramatically. Employers, pushed by government studies, factory inspectors, and trade unionists, gradually recognized that industrial fatigue seriously impaired morale and thus productivity. Between 1917 and 1919, Massey-Harris reduced the workweek in its Toronto factory from 60 to 48 hours without any decline in production. It was a classic example of 'welfare capitalism'; reform, employers discovered, was profitable. By 1920, the standard workweek in virtually all industries had been reduced to 48 hours; in some it stood at 44. Real wages may not have improved, but workers spent far less time in the factory to earn those wages—and a little overtime at time-and-a-half increased incomes for many workers.

The wretched working conditions existing

Employee picnic, Gilson Manufacturing Co., Waterloo Park, 1922. To ease employee dissatisfaction—and combat union organizing efforts—without raising wages, many companies began to offer recreational activities such as singing clubs and annual picnics. Guelph Library Archives, Industrial Souvenir Web site.

at the turn of the century began to be corrected. Factory inspectors had argued for years that better safety measures, improved ventilation, and less-crowded workrooms would pay dividends in the form of higher efficiency and productivity. The war brought new reform voices, including the Canadian Manufacturers Association, and major employers led the way in workplace innovations such as lunchrooms, midday meals at cost, and pension plans

designed to tie workers to their jobs and thus reduce the cost of labour turnover.

In addition, many companies sponsored sports teams, capitalizing on a vibrant tradition of community- and provincial-level competition in games such as baseball (the most popular), hockey, tennis, and lacrosse. In each case, companies' efforts were supported by provincial associations, which used the opportunity to establish rules and award prizes to regulate behaviour and foster allegiance to community and state. Company teams allowed business to keep an eye on their workers even during their increased leisure hours.

Initiatives of this kind multiplied at the height of labour unrest, between 1918 and 1920; in many cases, they were designed specifically to blunt the bite of organized labour. Industrial Councils, on which management and worker representatives sat, were meant to substitute for unions. While not all workers supported such measures, many did, rendering united worker action of other sorts more difficult. As the 1920s progressed, Ontario's industrial workers increasingly saw welfare capitalism as the most feasible among a limited set of options.[15]

In public health, little had changed since the last quarter of the nineteenth century. Cities had grown far more rapidly than housing stock or basic urban services. Slums expanded at an alarming rate. In 1909, the infant mortality rate—the single most sensitive measure of general health standards—rose in Toronto to an appalling 180 per 1,000 live births—twice the level for Rochester, New York, a city of comparable size and economic structure on the other side of Lake Ontario. Toronto was dumping untreated sewage into the harbour and pumping untreated water back into the city's water system. Reform demands finally produced results. The city moved its water intake; began to filter and then chlorinate water; situated its sewage outfall six kilometres from the main harbour; and built sedimentation tanks to provide primary treatment. By 1910, Toronto's sewage outflow was no longer poisoning the drinking water.

For public health, it was a time of activist

state intervention informed by scientific specialists. Medical practitioners began to campaign for new programs based on principles of preventative medicine. Reformers insisted that boards of health must intervene to prevent the outbreak of disease, not merely respond to crises. John W.S. McCullough, a prominent reform advocate who became the chief medical health officer of the Provincial Board of Health in 1910, and Charles J. Hastings, who became Toronto's medical health officer in 1911, lobbied successfully for increased health budgets at both provincial and local levels.

A particular concern for Toronto's Board of Health was the relation between sanitation, milk, and infant mortality. In May 1912, Hastings ordered inspectors to test milk and dump 'into the sewer all milk which is obviously dirty'. They dumped 900 gallons in that month alone.[16] In 1913, Toronto required that all milk sold must be pasteurized, and over the next five years, the infant mortality rate fell dramatically. Yet it was not until the late 1930s that provincial legislation required that *all* milk produced in the province be pasteurized.

An aggressive campaign to upgrade Toronto's housing stock also began in 1912. The local board condemned many slum houses as 'unfit for habitation' and attempted to eliminate outdoor privies. Unfortunately, indoor plumbing was as costly as a small self-built house (see p. 180)—beyond the reach of many working-class people. By 1920, after an extensive public works program, sewage and water facilities reached every house in Toronto, and by 1941, 90 per cent of urban households had indoor toilets—though almost 90 per cent of Ontario farms still used outdoor privies.[17]

In other areas of social policy, the provin-

Pollution, Toronto harbour, *c.* 1912. In 1912 the Ontario Board of Health was empowered to require that municipal governments erect sewage treatment plants and enforce water purification measures. With chlorination the incidence of typhoid dropped dramatically, but untreated waste from Toronto—and virtually every other municipality on the Great Lakes, in the US as well as Canada—continued to pollute the region's water systems. CoTA SC244, Item 1122A.

cial government remained laissez-faire. But new religious reformers, rejecting the nineteenth-century notion that poverty was the 'wages of sin', argued that low wages, unemployment, overcrowded housing conditions, poor public health, and other deteriorating social conditions in Ontario's burgeoning industrial cities bred immorality as surely as they bred disease. The Social Gospel movement's 'missions' began to offer the services

that would in time form the basis of Ontario's social welfare system.

Houses of Industry already provided some 'indoor' as well as 'outdoor' relief to destitute individuals and families. Social Gospel volunteers expanded this limited poor-relief system by creating new institutions such as the Young Men's and Young Women's Christian Associations, and University Settlement houses provided community recreation for children,

LET TORONTO FIRST DO ITS DUTY

Jack Canuck, 'Let Toronto First Do Its Duty', 3 August 1912. A new breed of religious reformers argued that the solutions to poverty and immorality lay in improving conditions by, for example, eliminating slums. CoTA Fonds 251.

cheap meals for the poor, and a wide variety of programs and classes to help the poor do more with less. Volunteers also helped men, women, and children acquire new skills that might translate into better jobs, and their efforts touched thousands of lives.

Prohibition appealed to the basic ideology of Social Gospellers as few issues could; it promised to eliminate public drunkenness, reduce crime, and improve social conditions for the poor. Social Gospellers quickly became the backbone of the movement. Initially, temperance advocates had demanded moderation, if not voluntary abstinence. But soon zealots demanded government intervention to prohibit the manufacture, sale, and consumption of alcohol. The Canada Temperance Act (1878) had allowed a 'local option', whereby a municipality could ban the sale of alcohol within its boundaries. Some municipalities did so, but this option satisfied few. Prohibition activists stepped up their campaigns, and in 1894 the province held a plebiscite asking, 'Are you in favour of the immediate prohibition by law of the importation, manufacture and sale of intoxicating liquors as a beverage?' Over half of all eligible voters cast a ballot, and the majority were in favour (65 per cent in rural areas and 58 per cent in urban areas), but the government refused to be bound by the results.[18] Nevertheless, by the time of the Great War prohibition dominated the reform agenda and was a central issue in provincial elections.

The feminist movement too gained strength before the war, partly as a result of the growing temperance movement. A paternalist society, Ontario at the turn of the century still recognized few civil rights for women, and most had little choice but to acquiesce to discriminatory legislation. Some progress was made, particularly in medicine, towards improving women's access to higher education and professional training and opportunities to practise their professions. But little could be expected so long as women were denied the basic democratic right to express their political voice. Suffragists had been working to gain the vote since the 1870s, but it was not until temperance advocates, notably the WCTU, became active in the suffrage cause in the 1890s that the movement gained the weight it needed to begin making significant progress. The organizational overlap of suffrage, prohibitionist, and Social Gospel groups provided both institutional strength and ideological cross-fertilization.

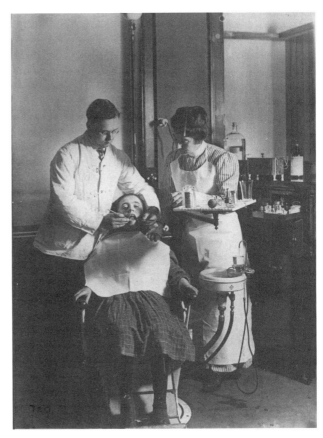

A dental inspection, *c.* 1905. An activist state informed by scientific specialists led to intensive reform efforts in the area of public health. This photo, by the Ministry of Health, was meant to encourage regular check-ups.
AO.RG10-30-2,3.02.3

'Maternal feminists' suggested that granting women the right to vote would transform the political landscape by injecting a more caring, maternal influence into the decision-making process. As Nellie McClung, a leading Canadian suffragist, put it, 'When women ask to vote, it is in the hope that they may be able with their ballots to protect the weak and innocent.'[19] The Social Gospel, prohibition, and suffrage movements, working together, achieved their greatest influence and success during and immediately following the Great War, and women exercised their right to vote in Ontario's affairs for the first time in October 1919. But the political culture of the province in the early decades of the new century would, for a time, cushion the impact of that precedent-setting political moment.

In Ontario, as in other provinces, sitting governments have rarely been unseated, and by 1905, the Liberals had enjoyed 33 uninterrupted years in power. What, then, can account for the triumph of James Pliny Whitney and his Conservative party? No doubt one important factor was Oliver Mowat's resignation in 1896 to join the new Liberal cabinet in Ottawa under Prime Minister Wilfrid Laurier. Not only did Mowat's successors lack his political touch, but increasing industrialization and urbanization favoured the Conservatives, who had traditionally enjoyed the support of urban voters, particularly those of the middle class. When, despite these disadvantages, the Liberals survived a very close election in 1902, Whitney worked hard to strengthen his party's provincial organization. He dismounted from 'the Protestant horse', moderating his views on Catholic and French-language schooling, and—having lost an election early in his political career as a result of corruption within his own party—he became an advocate for electoral reform and a moral watchdog on Liberal electioneering practices.

Whitney's numerous charges of Liberal corruption led to a series of election investigations in 1904, one of which revealed that the election of a Liberal in Sault Ste Marie had been effected by dint of bribes (money and whiskey), 'bogus bibles' (used to swear in voters), and coercion (by a local railway company, of its employees). Perhaps the last straw was the discovery that 20 Americans had been brought over from Michigan by steamboat and persuaded with liquor and money to vote for the Liberals. Editors of small-town liberal newspapers looked askance. The 1905 provincial election turned on charges of government corruption, with Whitney asserting that he was 'honest enough to be bold!' He won an overwhelming victory, and the once-powerful provincial Liberals were reduced to little more than a corporal's guard in the legislature. Whitney was to win three more elections before his death in 1914.

Like Mowat, Whitney ran his own show. 'The Members of the Legislature must not imagine that their duty is simply that of delegates to repeat what they hear in their own localities and nothing more,' Whitney believed. 'The duty of the Legislature is to help to show the people what it is right to do in the interests of the people themselves.' Whitney meant what he said. As many disgruntled backbenchers found to their chagrin, he was there to lead, not be led.[20]

Openly pro-business and pro-development, Whitney's government proved highly innovative and at times progressive. The creation of Ontario Hydro is a revealing example of Whitney at work. Ontarians heralded hydroelectricity as the 'white coal' that promised, in the words of the Hamilton *Spectator,* 'A Smokeless City in a Coalless Province.' Hydro, proclaimed the Toronto *Globe*, represented 'the subjugation and enjoyment of nature'— Niagara Falls. No one opposed hydro development, but debate emerged over who was to

Disinfecting railway cars to prevent the spread of foot-and-mouth disease, 1906. The campaign for cleanliness and good health extended to rural areas and their products. Growing knowledge of the causes of disease led to a new emphasis on prevention. Foot-and-mouth disease is still a serious threat to livestock. John Boyd photo. AO C7-3.

control the means of production: government or private companies? And, if government, municipal or provincial?[21]

By 1903, 126 Ontario municipalities owned gas, water, and electric-light facilities. Municipal control of these facilities was also common in the United States. Yet in 1906, the Whitney government chose a revolutionary option: provincial control. Whitney's biographer, Charles Humphries, argues that this action exemplifies the emergence of a 'progressive' conservative political party in Ontario. In

contrast to his Liberal opponents, who favoured a monopoly in the interests of capitalists, Whitney pushed for a monopoly in the interests of consumers—among whom, of course, would be capitalists using provincially controlled hydro production to operate their enterprises.

Whitney had co-opted the left. As historian Viv Nelles has pointed out, 'from the outset the crusade for public power was a businessman's movement. They initiated it, formed its devoted hard core membership and . . . provided it with brilliant leadership.' In the

United States, the left was strong, and business feared socialism; in Ontario, the left was relatively weak and gave middle-class business interests no reason to fear state ownership.

With cheap, state-controlled power, Ontario's petite bourgeoisie could better their collective position in society; and the state could become a major player on the North American manufacturing stage. Behind the scenes, Whitney worked hard to bring the financial and business elite, who advocated private monopoly, to the bargaining table with representatives of the business middle-class. Only when reconciliation seemed impossible did Whitney take the final step. Aided by the energetic leadership of Adam Beck—past mayor of London, cigar-box manufacturer, and a member of Whitney's cabinet—Whitney in 1908 created Ontario Hydro, under Beck's control, to generate and distribute electricity throughout the province.[22]

The move solidified Whitney's progressive reputation, but two other measures were, in their own ways, equally innovative. Under recent Liberal administrations, the premier had virtually managed the University of Toronto. Whitney stabilized funding and created a structure that fostered independence from direct government control. Nor did he ignore the working class. Responding to intense pressure from trade unions for protection in the face of numerous industrial accidents, Whitney enacted a new Workmen's Compensation Act in 1914. Unlike Mowat's 1886 legislation, the Act went far beyond employer's liability and provided automatic compensation to injured workers through a government fund administered by a public board. Ontario's workers saw this as a major

triumph. For Whitney, it was a way of consolidating the urban vote, of maintaining and strengthening the coalition of interests from which he drew his support.[23]

When it came to issues of religion and language in Ontario's school system, however, Whitney stumbled. Although he had tried to improve relations with the Catholic community, he was 'typically Ontarian in his outlook and sensitivities'; as a young politician he had been an unabashed supporter of Meredith's anti-Catholic, anti-French electioneering tactics, and in 1890 he had proclaimed Ontario to be 'an English province . . . in every respect.'[24] Whitney's deep-seated bias was revealed after the provincial Ministry of Education in 1912 found a number of bilingual separate schools in the Ottawa Valley and northeastern Ontario to be substandard, particularly in teacher training and English-language instruction. The government might have responded by working with the Franco-Ontarian community to address these problems, but it did not. Instead it introduced Regulation 17, limiting the use of French in Ontario's schools. The result was a marked deterioration in French–English relations.

Whitney's overwhelming electoral victories no doubt reflected his identification with programs that promoted economic growth, but the disarray of the provincial Liberals—unable to find either a viable leader or a viable issue—also contributed. Between 1905 and 1914, internal party squabbling twice led to the resignation of the Liberal leader in the middle of a provincial election. In the 1914 election, the Liberals campaigned for prohibition as if it were the only issue. The demise of the once-powerful Liberal machine came in 1917 when N.W. Rowell, the provincial leader,

'Aliens' under armed guard sawing wood at Camp Petawawa, *c.* 1916. During the First World War many Canadians of German and Ukrainian descent were treated as 'hostiles' and shipped to remote internment camps. Most German-Ontarians lived in and around the town of Berlin, which in 1916 changed its name to Kitchener. Similarly, Toronto renamed streets such as Bismarck Avenue, which became Asquith. A.A. Chesterfield Collection, Album #2, Queens University Archives.

resigned in order to join the 'coalition' Union government in Ottawa headed by Conservative Prime Minister Robert Borden.

Following Whitney's death in 1914, the premiership fell to William Hearst, northern Ontario's most prominent cabinet minister. Hearst lacked his predecessor's talent for dealing with interest groups. Rowell's policies as Liberal leader had driven virtually all the so-called liquor interests into the Conservative camp, but Hearst was a devout Methodist who sympathized with the prohibitionists. In 1916 his government passed the Temperance Act—alcohol could be purchased only by the bottle and on a doctor's prescription—and delayed a referendum on the issue until war's end. When the Conservatives 'abolished the bar . . . they completely destroyed their organization in the city,' one contemporary observed. 'The barroom has been the back-bone of the Conservative organization for many years.'[25] Nor could Hearst satisfy the mammoth egos of important party members such as Adam Beck.

An ardent imperialist who strongly identified with British political and cultural ideals, Hearst wholeheartedly supported the war effort and deferred to Ottawa's leadership in that area. Although there were pockets of Italians and other non-British immigrants in Toronto, Germans around Berlin, and French and Scandinavians in the North, fully 75 per cent of Ontario's population claimed to be of 'British' origin, and Hearst could count on general backing for his stance. Nevertheless, 76 per cent of Ontarians were native-born, and they were quick to object when federal policies seemed to threaten the province's interests. At a time when political leaders like Mowat, Whitney, and Hearst were moving to centralize power and establish a strong bureaucracy staffed by experts, recruitment for war service was decentralized, largely dependent on local volunteers, and recruiting propaganda stressed community as much as national pride.[26]

With the armistice, however, support for the war effort no longer masked opposition to other federal policies, and this opposition rebounded on the provincial Conservatives. In October 1919, the Hearst government fell to an unlikely combination of agrarian progressives and urban labour. The *Globe* believed it had witnessed a 'political revolution' on the part of voters.

Agrarian discontent was hardly surprising. Farmers had long faced economic difficulties as production costs rose far faster than income, and their problems intensified under the inflationary and other pressures of the war economy. Indeed, many rural men had refused to enlist; as the reeve of Huron County saw it, the government wanted to take 'our farm hands who make money for the country' while letting 'shiftless young men continue to hang around towns and cities'.[27] Poor farmers, with 10 acres or less, protested with their feet, while those in the middle class stayed put and commenced political action. Farm leaders opposed protective tariffs that kept costs high and farm incomes low. In 1914 E.C. Drury, a university-educated farm organizer, and J.J. Morrison, a capable, hard-nosed agrarian advocate, helped found the United Farmers Organization (UFO). Maintaining that rural depopulation had led to decreased political influence, decreased land values, and higher mortgages, they argued for the expansion of co-operatives, a progressive income tax, and the nationalization of banking to improve the collective lot of struggling farm families. By 1918, with a membership of 25,000, the UFO moved into politics.

Farm women too were attempting to better their position. Mechanization had not lessened their work; if weaving, spinning, and cheese making were increasingly done outside the farm household, poultry raising, vegetable growing, dairying, and canning more than filled the potential void. While their urban counterparts used their husbands' money to run their homes, farm women earned their own money. 'Men like to pet their wives and make children of them,' one wrote in 1908. 'They seem to inherit the patriarchal air . . . We love to be petted but we want to be treated as an equal in the partnership of life.'[28]

Rural women began to organize to deal with economic and social change. Most of the province's teachers were women, two-thirds of whom were employed by rural or small-town boards. In 1918, the Federation of Women's Teachers' Associations of Ontario formed to push for equal pay for equal work. A scant year later, the association represented one-third of the province's women teachers.

An older women's organization, the Women's Institute (WI) had been founded in 1897, and by 1919 it was one of the largest in Ontario, boasting 900 branches and 30,000 members. The WI provided rural women with

Students at a school for the blind knit socks for soldiers in the trenches, *c.* 1916. Everyone was expected to contribute to the war effort. A.A. Chesterfield Collection, Album #2, Queen's University Archives.

an opportunity to develop leadership skills and a heightened sense of common problems. Its leaders were largely conservative, small-town, middle-class women who believed that the answer to rural decline lay in pursuit of the domestic ideal: farm women needed to stop working for money and concentrate on home management. It seems, however, that WI leaders did not have absolute control over members. The leadership counselled against push-

ing for women's suffrage, but many branches went their own way: 'We have got the suffrage microbe,' a member from Massey, Ontario, declared. 'Headquarters may give all the orders they like . . . [but] our Institute . . . has been the best medium we have had to spread the suffrage doctrine.'[29]

A more radical group, the United Farm Women of Ontario (UFWO), was founded in 1918, and—without support from the UFO—

To everyone's surprise, the United Farmers Organization swept the 1919 provincial elections; this celebratory placard was placed on the legislature's doors the day after the vote. But the coalition government that the UFO formed with the Independent Labour Party would not last long. AO ACC 13079 S17192.

by 1921 reached a peak of 6,000 members. The UFWO assumed as its main task the education of rural women for political action. In rural newspapers and at rural meetings, members stressed the necessity of class consciousness as a precursor to political action. The UFWO put the primary blame for the harsh conditions of rural life on men—'with all the political power in their hands [they] have made a terrible muddle of affairs'—but they also criticized women's passivity.

Male rural leaders tended to stress other problems. Both traditional political parties, farmer leaders argued, represented the interests of urban business. According to the UFO's Morrison, parties abetted 'the power of the vested interests that are destroying [what] . . . our pioneer fathers wrested from the wilderness.' In 1919, with a membership of 48,000, the UFO nominated its own candidates and, with only 22 per cent of the popular vote (less than either the Liberals or Conservatives), won 45 seats in the provincial legislature. Much to the surprise of Drury and Morrison, neither of whom had run in the election, the UFO had suddenly become Ontario's largest party.[30]

Farmers were not the only discontented newcomers to the provincial legislature. The province's industrial workers saw their standard of living deteriorate during the war as costs increased far more rapidly than wages. Rents escalated. Craftsworkers lost ground as deskilling accelerated. Ontario saw more strikes between 1916 and 1919 than in the previous 15 years. Within established unions, membership numbers grew, and many new unions were formed. Women workers continued active: in one case, a strike in the metal industries included women. Nor was all this activity restricted to the industrial heartland of southern Ontario. In the north, forestry and mine workers organized and struck; gold miners in South Porcupine held out for seven months in 1912–13 against strikebreakers, detectives, and state pressure; and a street-railway strike in Port Arthur in 1913 led to bloodshed between police and strikers.

Whereas the United States and Great Britain included labour leaders in their wartime planning, Canada did not; perhaps this was one reason why the state's repressive instincts had unusually free rein. The federal government's War Measures Act denied the right of collective public protest, and police raids were carried out in some Ontario communities. Nevertheless, when labour leaders mounted a General Strike in Toronto, in 1919, many workers did not participate.

Compared to their counterparts in western Canada, Ontario workers had been treated relatively well, especially under the Whitney government. From their point of view, any problems had less to do with the political and economic system itself than with the people who currently managed it. This perspective has been called labourism, a set of beliefs anchored by the conviction that change for the

better was possible within the capitalist system. Now a new political movement reflecting this vision began to take shape among Ontario's non-unionized workers. Arguing that both traditional parties represented the interests of urban businessmen, the leaders of this movement called for a new party that could represent all people—not just the collective interests of organized labour—and be the harbinger of a new democracy. In response to their call, the Independent Labor Party (ILP) was founded in July 1919.

The ILP courted the female electorate. In Hamilton, women formed a separate Hamilton Women's ILP. In labour papers, working-class women attacked the notion of separate spheres and the image of the 'sentimental and false ideal of womanhood'. Yet labouring men continued to refer to these women's groups as 'auxiliaries', and women continued to knit socks for returning veterans and bake cakes for commemorative events. For women, the social, economic, and political space created by worker protest was not unbounded.[31]

Although the ILP ran far fewer candidates than its farmer counterparts, it did elect eleven members (defeating Adam Beck in London) and garner substantial votes in most cities except Toronto, where factional squabbling divided the labour vote. For some, political success in 1919 made strikes and militant unionism less necessary. While strike activity continued in Ontario in 1920, it seemed less spirited, less radical, more muted. In the face of renewed employer intransigence, it was certainly less successful. And, as quickly became evident, labour's political basket was not designed to hold all of labour's eggs.

With 55 seats between them, the UFO and

Coxwell Avenue, Toronto, 1912. Small houses like these were often self-built. 'My brother, dad and I built my house, then we built my brother's house,' Fred Purser, a factory worker in Hamilton in the 1920s, recalled. 'And when I die I've asked them to bury me there. Because for one little while that was my part of the world. I owned something, you know, that was me' (quoted on Web site 'Made in Hamilton, 20th Century Industrial Trail', site 19). CoTA, Arthur Goss, architect, RG8-18-5.

the ILP formed a 'Progressive' coalition government under E.C. Drury. Farmers supported Drury's rural credit plans, which included the establishment of the Provincial Savings Bank. Strong support also existed for the creation of the Ontario Athletic Commission in 1920—to regulate boxing and the "aggressive masculinity" it symbolized and to provide worthwhile alternatives to moving pictures and other popular entertainments of 'dubious' moral value.[32] But the Drury government never coalesced into an effective administration, nor did the

Progressives ever articulate a clear vision. Indeed, the UFO's Morrison denied that the movement was ever a political party: 'you cannot broaden out the political association [of farmers] because there is none.'[33]

Conflicts within the UFO and ILP were matched by difficulties between them. After electing so many of its members to the legislature, the UFO immediately questioned the wisdom of a coalition with labour. Both the UFO and the trade unions condemned Drury's plans to merge the two parliamentary caucuses into

Prohibitionists at work at Elk Lake. A note at the bottom of the photo reads: 'Blind pigs raided 160 kegs destroyed.' Such action was unusual; the law was largely ignored. AO F1194 S15000, 3001.

a single Progressive party. ILP members in industrial centres vigorously opposed the farmer-dominated coalition's anti-tariff stance. Labour became even more disillusioned when Drury refused to concede the eight-hour day to striking workers at Ontario Hydro. Farm and labour leaders grew increasingly critical of the new government.

They were not alone. The right to vote had been granted to women in 1917 by Hearst and his Conservative administration. In 1919, rural women took immediate advantage of their new power by turning out in large numbers—in part because Hearst had scheduled the long-awaited referendum on prohibition for the same day as the provincial election—

and voting against his government. 'This election was the first time that the franchise was granted to women and I knew,' one UFO leader later recollected, 'that the farm women were strongly for temperance and would certainly go to the polls to vote for the Temperance Cause and when there would mark their ballot for the farmer candidate.'[34] The prohibition side won, but those who had pinned their hopes for broad social reform on prohibition were to be sorely disappointed. Many Ontarians simply defied the new law. Enforcement was spasmodic, doctors' prescriptions were easily obtained, and pharmacies ready to fill those prescriptions proliferated. Lured by the prospect of increased tax

A model kitchen, 1916. A provincial housing committee set up guidelines for the placement of rooms and appliances in working-class homes, believing that 'the workman's wife, with a family of small children, will appreciate the savings in steps which such an arrangement will assure.' COTA SC 18-10.

revenue, by the end of the 1920s the province would repeal prohibition and take control of alcohol sales itself.

In the 1920s more women than ever before were participating in organized sports—especially tennis and golf—and notions of female frailty were beginning to be dispelled. Yet most hopes for improvements in general social and economic conditions for women were disappointed. Although Drury enacted a minimum-

wage law for women in the workforce, no such protection was provided for men, and some observers have suggested that this move may have contributed to the institutionalization of gender discrimination in pay. While the presence of single working women in cities had been accepted by the late 1920s, concern now focused on married women. The passage of an act that provided an allowance for widows with *more* than one child proved to be a two-edged sword, since recipients were expected to stay home with their children and their behaviour was regularly monitored. As the government-published *Labour Gazette* explained, 'the allowance is considered a salary from the government to enable the mother to make good citizens of her children.'

Like industrial workers, mothers—'the workers in our greatest, most vital and most profoundly important productive industry'—attained value only through the products of their labour: their children. Mother's Allowances, Ontario's superintendent of Trades and Labour noted, were 'primarily in the interests of the child; the mother being only a secondary from the standpoint of the state.' Mothers became automata dedicated to the rearing of children (described as 'little machines' in government publications such as *The Baby*) who would grow up to be productive citizens and never represent any burden to the state. As the Act's first annual report noted, 'if she [the mother] does not measure up to the state's standards for such guardians [i.e. be efficient, thrifty, clean, industrious, non-complaining and, of course, loving], other arrangements must be sought in the best interests of the children.' Similar attitudes had underlain child care legislation, such as that concerning Children's Aid Societies, passed by Liberal and Conservative governments before the UFO.

In that it was more an entitlement than a charity, Mother's Allowance went beyond previous government welfare initiatives. Mothers had crucial roles to fill, and if they performed their tasks in the state-prescribed way they would be rewarded. But government allowances were never intended to provide enough to survive on: throughout the 1920s and especially during the Depression of the 1930s, widowed mothers were expected to find additional funds on their own, whether from employment or from family members. If the state were to provide sufficient money, politicians and bureaucrats believed, it would erode the 'incentive to effort' deemed so crucial by Ontario's laissez-faire governments. As one close student of this progam has concluded, 'By failing to come close to adequacy despite recognizing entitlement and need, mother's allowances thus became an ominous indicator of contradictions that would soon bedevil other welfare programs to emerge within Ontario.'[35]

So much for the hopes of the female labour activists who had dared to oppose the notion of separate spheres. Industry and science combined to reinforce and even increase gender specialization within Ontario's households. Ironically, it was not the ideals of the home that transformed the factory; instead, the ideals of the factory—such as the efficiency pursued through time-and-motion studies by the American engineer Frederick Winslow Taylor—invaded the home. Parental advice manuals provided rigid schedules for handling, feeding, playing, cleaning, sleeping, even crying! Nor did the introduction of new technologies speed up the housework. A new understanding of the role of bacteria in the generation of disease underpinned the emer-

Elsa Sillanpaa using a laundry wringer, Sault Ste Marie, 1927. Few families could afford the slick new machines coming on the market. AO F1405-15-105, MSR1097-11.

gence of a domestic science that promoted spotless homes. More, not less, work was needed to keep a home really clean.

The emergence of a medical science that advocated cleanliness coexisted well with a

State of the art: the Beatty washing machine, *c.* 1927. The Beatty Bros of Fergus, Ontario, were the first in North America to manufacture an agitator washing machine. The next year, Maytag brought its own model into production. Photograph courtesy of the Canada Science and Technology Museum, Ottawa.

religious reform movement that extolled moral purity. Homemakers were increasingly portrayed as fighting on the front line in the prevention of disease and fostering of virtue. By spending more time cleaning the home, cooking nutritious foods, doing laundry, and nursing and teaching children, homemakers could cultivate a physically and morally healthy family, and in the process put Ontario in the vanguard of an international movement against disease and moral lassitude. Ontarians wanted cleanliness and godliness!

Women, of course, did not always follow such proscriptions. While many families could not afford luxuries like a mechanical refrigera-

tor or vacuum cleaner, Joy Parr's study of consumption in post-war Canada suggests that women often privileged traditional homemaking devices over the 'new-fangled' items that producers wished to market. And many of Ontario's women resisted the 'mothering' call: family size, which had already declined dramatically in Ontario before 1890, declined by a further 36 per cent by 1930, a rate of decline which outpaced that of Canada as a whole. Still, the prevalence of such beliefs doubtless served to keep many married women in the home and delay, by many decades, their more widespread labour participation.[36]

And what of the ideals espoused so aggressively by the UFWO's leadership? During the 1920s, membership declined dramatically, with most women moving to the more conservatively led Women's Institute. Yet, in part because of this infusion of UFWO members, the WIs began to speak more forcefully on a range of issues. They demanded upgraded technology in the home and critiqued public health measures and educational systems—hardly what one might expect from contented, well-domesticated matrons. Such critiques were, nevertheless, bounded by their home focus. It would be close to a half a century before Ontario's rural women would again organize in an explicitly political manner.[37]

Although the social reform and feminist movements had lost much of their earlier vigour, neither entirely disappeared. Drury's coalition government suffered a different fate. Continued internal squabbling jeopardized any chance Drury might have had for re-election. It surprised no one when the Conservative Party under G. Howard Ferguson swept back into power in 1923 with more than half the popular vote.

CHAPTER NINE

Boom, Bust, and War: 1923–1943

$\mathcal{A}$ small-town Protestant imperialist from rural eastern Ontario, the new Conservative premier was a firm believer in 'economical' government with respect to both spending and legislation. G. Howard Ferguson supported essentially unfettered private enterprise (excepting Ontario Hydro, a 'special case') and restriction of public assistance to only the most needy. In 1927 he opposed Prime Minister Mackenzie King's plan for Old Age Pensions, delaying provincial implementation for as long as he could. When police magistrates urged him to implement a plan to relieve them of the 'depressing duty of committing friendless, penniless, offenceless and homeless old men to Gaol,' Ferguson replied that their families should look after them. This nineteenth-century mindset was increasingly out of touch with the dramatic economic and social changes sweeping Ontario.[1]

On linguistic issues Ferguson began with an equally old-fashioned allegiance to British traditions and institutions, 'one flag and one language'; when Ontario's francophone population rose sharply on the eve of the war, he described the increase as an 'invasion', a 'national outrage'. Yet by the late 1920s Ferguson had developed the political sense to moderate his views. In 1928 his government modified Regulation 17 to allow for French- as well as English-speaking school inspectors and adjustments to policy at the local level rather than across-the-board imposition of inflammatory measures. The resolution embodied a high degree of pragmatism. While Ferguson privately considered it simply a more effective approach to anglicization, he reaped political rewards for defusing a volatile political and cultural issue.[2]

A byword of Ferguson's administration was efficiency. Adopted from the corporate world, which saw Taylorism as a way to increase productivity while cutting costs, the idea of efficiency informed everything from conceptions of motherhood to ideas about conservation and park development. In the 1926 Ontario election, a central Conservative campaign booklet bore the title 'Business Methods in Public Administration', and administration by experts rather than legislation by elected politicians was Ferguson's preferred approach to governance. Efficiency became the answer to poverty and unemployment, with government welfare activities centralized in the Department of Public Welfare.

The premier, of course, presided over all. That was hardly new. With the exception of Drury, none of Ferguson's predecessors would have disagreed. This tendency to focus power in the office of the head of government had been a core component of Ontario's political culture ever since the lieutenant-governors of the pre-Confederation era. Ferguson advised his successor, George Henry, to provide 'distinctive courageous leadership, and dominate the Government and Party', and assured him that 'the average fellow likes to be dictated to and controlled.[3]

After unsuccessfully promoting the sale of a light beer known as 'Fergy's Foam', Ferguson ended the prohibition era by instituting government liquor stores, a move that did not please the die-hard drys, but at least held out the promise of government control and supervision. He gave relatively free rein to mining and forestry development, especially in northern Ontario, and little aid or encouragement to conservation of natural resources. Indeed, one of the province's major forestry enterprises, Abitibi Power and Paper Company, implemented a more farsighted northern forestry renewal program than any offered by the provincial government. The government distributed millions of tree seedlings in southern Ontario, but ignored the heavily logged back reaches of northern areas seen by few voters.[4] As in the Mowat era, the north existed to serve the south.

Although less dramatically than in the pre-1914 era, in the 1920s Ontario entered another period of sustained growth. Electrical

appliances and automobiles—classic examples of the 'consumer durable' industries located near south-central Ontario's primary markets—headed the list. The automobile industry dominated because of its extraordinary capacity to generate jobs, not only directly in the manufacture of vehicles but indirectly in primary steel production, parts production, and vehicle servicing. Automobile production added higher-than-average value to products, which in turn sustained relatively high wages. Yet unskilled labourers benefited most from the assembly-line production systems pioneered by Ford, which first set up in Ontario in 1904. The precursor to General Motors followed soon thereafter. By the end of the 1920s, automobile production had emerged as Ontario's single most important industry.

Ontarians took to cars like ducks to water. In the London region, well over half of summer traffic in 1914 was horse-drawn; by 1922, that had dropped to 3 percent. Farmers may have lagged behind urbanites in the purchase of household appliances, but they quickly outpaced them in the purchase of cars; by 1940, farm families were twice as likely as city dwellers to own a car. Decreasing prices in the 1920s—the Model T cost $650 in 1914 and $415 in 1926—made car ownership possible for many in the working class.

Increased auto use necessitated increased planning and regulation. Ontario established a Department of Public Highways in 1915, and road improvement and construction, financed in part by increased gasoline taxes, proceeded apace. As early as 1911, Hamilton employed plain-clothes police to apprehend speeders. Licensing of drivers commenced in 1927. Rural space became more accessible to urban

Sunnyside, Toronto, 1926. By the end of the 1920s, Ontario boasted the highest per capita car ownership in the world—next to the United States. NAC RD151.

dwellers, even as cities were forced to redesign interior roads and provide parking facilities. In 1926, Toronto's chief constable complained that the streets were 'just an open air garage'. Pedestrians and horses had to yield control of the streets to cars. Noxious exhaust fumes replaced blowing manure as a primary source of air pollution. 'Reckless walking' became punishable by fines. City playgrounds kept children off the streets where they used to play.

Car imagery became part of common rhetoric. Anyone wishing to make a case for the modernity and farsightedness of a particu-

lar policy or program did so by analogy to auto manufacture or operation. The car was the ultimate machine, against which all else was to be measured. The renowned physician Sir William Osler warned that the human body needed care; one should not 'neglect his machine, driving it too hard, stoking the engines too much'. The premier, however, stood apart from this enthusiasm. Ferguson never owned a car, and he sympathized with those rural dwellers who complained of the noise, dust, and intrusions of urban drivers in rural areas. At one rural church picnic, he

Fish merchant and children, Toronto, July 1929. Horse-drawn vehicles would continue to make home deliveries of milk, bread, and other staples for many years to come. M.O. Hammond photo. AO F1075.

asserted that the auto was a curse on human civilization. The next day, to his surprise, the Ford Motor Company threatened him with a lawsuit.[5]

Three decades of sustained economic growth ended abruptly in 1929. Between 1900 and 1929, the expansion of the consumer market had not kept pace with the even more pronounced expansion in the capacity to produce goods. Economic dislocations on both sides of the North Atlantic, meanwhile, led to a sharp

decline in the volume and value of Canada's exports. As exports collapsed, employment contracted, producing a further decline in consumer spending. And as consumer spending—already too limited to absorb increased production—declined, manufacturers faced growing inventories of unsold products. They in turn cut production and laid off workers. Layoffs brought further contractions in consumer spending, leading to more production cutbacks and, eventually, bankruptcies.

Ontario faced the Depression with the advantage of Canada's most diversified economy. Not all regions or workers suffered equally. For those who were able to keep their jobs through the Depression, falling prices—the cost of living declined by 20 per cent between 1930 and 1932—made a decent living possible. The risk of unemployment was lower in the service sector and greater in construction. It was also greater for younger workers, and older ones, and recent immigrants. Because women worked for lower wages than men, their risk of unemployment was lower as well. Unemployment was particularly high in northern resource industries: in the summer of 1931, two-thirds of Sudbury's men were jobless. The Depression devastated single-industry towns and cities such as Oshawa and Windsor, which depended on a declining automobile industry. Native men from the Six Nations reserve who had been working in Hamilton, Buffalo, and Detroit, often as high riggers, returned with their families to the reserve to live with relatives and grow their own food. Ontario's farms, spared the droughts that plagued the Prairies, had prospered in the 1920s, but declining prices in the 1930s rendered much farm work unprofitable:

Toronto Railway Company construction, King and Bay Streets, 1911. In 1929 *The Coupler,* a journal published by the Toronto Transit Commission, complained that a sharp rise in copper prices had inspired 'a very bold type of thief' to chip away the copper bonds from streetcar tracks. CoTA S8-6-26.

by the end of 1931, the government ceased foreclosing overdue farm mortgages because there was no one to buy the properties. Farm incomes declined by over 40 per cent in the four years following 1929.[6]

The Great Depression bottomed out in 1933. Estimates of unemployment during that winter ran at 20 per cent of Ontario's industrial workforce. Ethnic tensions in urban areas intensified. Jews represented some 45,000 of Toronto's half million residents and often lived in mixed ethnic neighbourhoods. In August 1933, following a baseball game between

Jewish and church teams—a common form of competitive recreation—in a west end park called Christie Pits, a group of local toughs known as the Pit Gang taunted Jews with 'Heil Hitler' chants and unfurled a huge swastika banner. A riot erupted that was quelled with difficulty by city police. Other ethnic minorities also became targets for racists and bigots.

By mid-decade, rates of business failure and personal bankruptcy began to slow as investment and employment gradually revived. As commodity prices stabilized and then increased marginally, corporate profits

Klansmen and burnt cross, Kingston, 13 July 1927. The American-based Ku Klux Klan gained little ground among Ontarians, who already had a well-entrenched (albeit more moderate) outlet for exclusionary views: the Orange Order. After hooded and cloaked Klan members attempted to separate 'a negro and his intended white bride' in Oakville in the late 1920s, the local paper applauded: 'it was really impressive how thoroughly and how systematically the Klan went about their task.' According to a Milton paper, 'if the Ku Klux Klan conducted all their assemblies in as orderly a manner as in Oakville . . . there would be no complaint.' The Toronto *Globe* and *Star* both praised the Klan's motives. In April 1930 Ontario's Court of Appeal sentenced one of the perpetrators to a three-month jail term for inciting a mob. The judgment did not mention the issue of race. NAC PA87848.

recovered. But wages did not. Despite measurable growth, the Depression had only eased, not ended. By 1939, the standard of living, measured in real wages, was only marginally better than it had been four decades earlier. Efficiency advocates found themselves without effective answers to the catastrophe of the Depression. Ferguson retired in 1930, leaving his successor, George Henry, to face unprecedented social and economic problems with little upon which to build.

Probably the most positive initiative to emerge during Henry's tenure as premier was one he had little to do with. With the construction of Highway 60 into Algonquin Park, several ecologically minded groups had

Native basket-sellers, Parry Sound, July 1931. Sales of Native crafts depended on tourism, which was hard hit by the Depression. M.O. Hammond photo. AO F1075 H2320.

formed to pressure the government for more enlightened park management. J.R. Dymond, a zoologist at the University of Toronto and co-founder, in 1931, of the Federation of Ontario Naturalists, argued that with proper supervision, environmental and utilitarian interests could both be served. The park's superintendent, Frank MacDougall, was open to a multi-use policy that would privilege conservation over timber and tourism. The scientist and government forester made a creative and formidable team. In the midst of the Depression, the foundations of Ontario's post–World War II parks policy were laid.[7]

On the pressing issue of relieving poverty, Henry remained bewildered. He rejected the idea of a provincial unemployment insurance program to assist urban workers on relief, instituting instead a program to encourage people to become farmers, generally in the north; it accomplished little. He attempted to bring 'efficiency' to the administration of ever-increasing relief expenditures, which in practice meant cutting payments. His answer to dissent and destitution was to invoke 'law and order'. Communists became the prime target. In close collaboration with R.B. Bennett's federal Conservatives, Henry and his attorney general engineered raids against Communist leaders in Toronto, deported alleged immigrant radicals, and ordered local militias to contain protests and put down strikers in several Ontario municipalities. In October 1933, police took brutal action to break up a demonstration in Port Arthur. Ivar Nordstram, one of the demonstrators, recalled the police

> *hitting people over their heads with fists and batons. The demonstrators dispersed in all directions. The police [on horseback] chased after them mercilessly. . . .While I was running I could see many men lying bleeding and unconscious. The Mounties seemed to be enjoying themselves riding after people. It was very unreal, like watching a British foxhunt, only here they were hunting people. Finally some cop noticed me and knocked me unconscious with a baton.[8]*

Responses such as these constituted overkill. Certainly the unemployed did protest and the Communists, through the Worker's Unity League, did agitate. But most such activity remained local and fragmented. In fact, as early as the mid-1920s organized labour seemed in retreat: membership had declined, most industrial unions had collapsed, and craft unions, desperately trying to defend the interests of a shrinking membership, had adopted a conservative stance. Hard times reinforced their conservatism. To resist wage cuts too vigorously was to run the risk of losing your job and earning no wage at all. 'What, strike in the 30s?!' exclaimed one Depression-era worker in the 1990s, 'You've got to be kidding!' 'We had it in mind,' another observed, 'that there were hundreds more out there looking for work.' 'They were all a bunch of scardy crows,' one female mill worker flatly concluded.[9]

Hard times reinforced the conservatism of the existing craft unions. Average strikes per year between 1930 and 1933 were less than half the yearly average for the century's first two decades. Although some collective violence did occur in the Depression's early years, it was the exception. More typical was the report of a police officer in Cochrane in 1931 to the effect that the local communist organization held its meetings in orderly fashion: 'The unemployed themselves have been very good during the past winter. . . . no disorder of any kind (as might be expected from men who are hungry). . . . The only useful thing we as Police Officers can do at the moment is to keep these unemployed moving.'[10] Portraying himself as a populist, the protector of the poor and dispossessed, Mitchell—'Just call me Mitch'—Hepburn led his Liberal party to a sweeping victory in 1934. In 1933, as opposition leader, Hepburn had roundly criticized Henry's decision to send troops to strike-torn Stratford:

> *The provincial government has seen fit to send artillery, machine guns and tanks to Stratford because the citizens are objecting to the treatment given them by wealthy manufacturers . . . They take all they can from the people and give as little as they can to the workers. My sympathy lies with those people who are victims of circumstances beyond their control and not with the manufacturers who are increasing prices and cutting wages at the same time.[11]*

During the 1934 provincial election, Hepburn claimed to 'swing well to the left, where some

Ontario Police Patrol officer, Toronto, *c.* 1925. During the Great Depression, 'Red Squads' intimidated and harassed suspected communists and provincial motorcyle police were used to repress dissent. A mass meeting in Toronto's High Park in August 1933 was contained by motorcycle police who encircled the crowd with their exhaust pipes pointed inward. Ministry of Education photo. AO RG 2-71 COT-156.

Grits do not tread', and as premier, he appointed a number of pro-union Liberals to his cabinet.[12]

By 1933, relief provision for the unemployed had drained federal, provincial, and municipal resources. The three levels of government blamed one another for inadequate relief funds. But they agreed on the necessity of rigorous evaluation of relief applicants. In 1932, a provincial inspector praised the attitude of East Windsor's relief administrators:

'These officers work on the theory that . . . most men squeal before they are actually hurt.' Municipalities where 33 to 45 per cent of the population was on relief—Windsor, Niagara Falls, Pembroke, and many Toronto suburbs, among others—often elected sympathetic councillors who, in attempting to provide adequate relief, pushed their municipalities into bankruptcy. The provincial government had no sympathy for what David Croll, the minister in charge of relief, called 'pampered, ineffi-

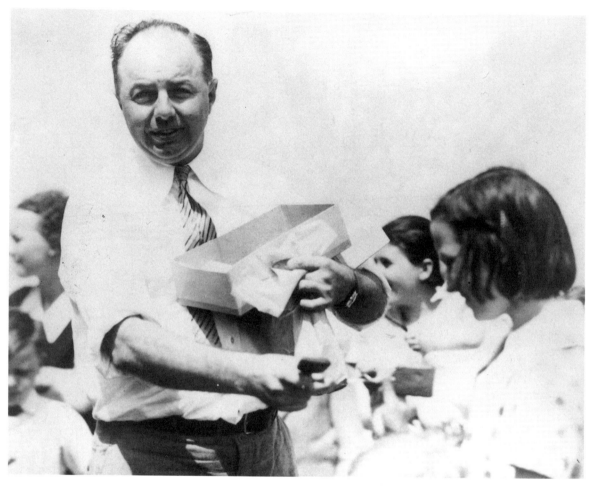

Premier Mitchell Hepburn and Hunger Marchers at Queen's Park, 1934. To receive public relief funds, one had to work, but the meagre assistance provided led to many strikes by relief workers. In August 1934, decrying the repressive tactics of his Conservative predecessors, the recently elected Hepburn promised protesters that they could meet in Toronto's public parks, then handed out a grand total of $90 in food vouchers and laid on free rides home in a convoy of trucks. NAC C19517.

cient and political cry-baby municipalities'. 'Relief for Workers, Nothing for Shirkers' became the motto of the welfare department.

Over the course of the Depression almost 200 relief strikes involving 24,000 workers occurred in the province. Protest focused on the uncharitable and demeaning treatment that relief applicants often received, especially in rural areas. Means, hygiene, and morality tests provoked rage and, on occasion, collective outcry. At times, workers of many kinds stood united against repressive authority, but class cohesion was much weaker in the larger centres, where ethnic, age, sex, and marital differences cut across class lines and under-mined efforts to develop a concerted worker response to Depression problems.

Like the Conservatives before them, Hep-burn's Liberals began to use state force to repress dissent. When in April 1935 relief recipients refused to work on public projects in Crowland Township, on the Niagara penin-sula, the mercurial Hepburn swung hard to the right, declaring a 'battle to the bitter end'. Falsely accusing the strikers of 'terrorization' and 'breaking heads and damaging property', he sent the provincial police to end the strike. He blamed 'professional agitators' who pressed 'for the day when Canada will be a communist state. . . . That day will never come,' he promised, 'in this or any other Anglo-Saxon country with the majority of people rural dwellers.'[13]

The relief strikers all lived in urban Crowland near a number of manufactories. But the local council was dominated by farm-ers who insisted that relief grants should be restricted to a non-subsistence level. Hepburn, who came from a leading farm family in south-western Ontario, could easily identify with the attitudes of Crowland's farmers, and perhaps he really did believe that the majority of Ontarians still lived in rural areas—though in fact by 1931, 61 per cent of Ontario's popula-tion was urban. On the other hand, in terms of influence Hepburn was quite correct: even though urban voters outnumbered them, the electoral system ensured that rural voters con-tinued to have a proportionately greater influ-ence in Ontario elections. Whatever else Hepburn was, he was an astute politician.[14] By 1937, the provincial government had broken the back of the relief movement.

Unemployed men, members of The Single Men's Association, parading to Bathurst United Church, Toronto, *c.* 1930. Ontario had experienced several economic depressions before the 1930s—in 1873, 1893, 1913, and 1921—but they paled in comparison to the Great Depression. In 1931, Ontario's unemployment rate reached 38 per cent, the highest in the country. Single men were the hardest hit. NAC C29397.

Unemployment was a family affair, and women and children often stood alongside the men on the picket lines. The ideal of a male breadwinner bringing home a family wage had always been difficult for working-class families to achieve, but many aspired to it. The Depression made that goal difficult to realize

Assembling a Mantle Modern radio, Westinghouse Electric plant, Hamilton, 1947. During the Depression, Anne Mackness, with a child of seven and an unemployed husband, wore gloves when she applied for an assembly job at White Radio in Hamilton, so that the interviewer 'wouldn't see my wedding ring'. She got the job. Married women who worked were often seen as taking jobs from men. NAC PA205829.

even for many middle-class families. As male employment dropped, female employment increased. In some cases unemployed men simply left town, too depressed and demoralized to cope. Often married women had to work to support their families, drawing critical commentary from government and even from associations representing professional women, such as the Canadian Federation of Business and Professional Women's Clubs and the National Council of Women in Canada. The Trades and Labour Congress urged all married women who could afford it to leave their jobs.

May Hoyle left Eaton's in 1938 after working there as a stenographer for eight years. 'I loved it. I really hated to leave work but in those days you just didn't work once you were married.' Some unions pressured management to fire married women, regardless of their seniority and skill, before men and single women. And many companies and municipalities, including London, Ontario, did so. When the Toronto Board of Education passed a 'marriage ban' for female teachers, most of the province's school boards followed suit. In the thirties, only 5 per cent of teachers were married women; in the same decade, the proportion of male teachers soared.

Skill sets, availability of work for men, and local cultures all affected employment patterns in this period. In 1936, at Penman's in Paris, Ontario, married women represented 40 per cent of the female work force; women possessed the skills the company needed, and the local community offered only marginal employment for men. Married women appear to have been able to find and keep jobs in the clothing industry more easily than in other industrial sectors. More commonly, however, as one journalist observed, 'Nowadays, any stick seems good enough to beat the business girl with.' While magazines in the 1920s advocated that single women should work prior to marriage, that changed in the Depression. 'When I went to get a job at 16,' Vida Richard recalled, 'I was told by some smart-aleck man, and not just one but many—why don't you get a man and get married?' Such attitudes rendered widows with children, who had to survive on a partial Mothers' Allowance, extremely vulnerable, yet they dared not publicly complain: local supervisors were quick to retaliate by decreasing or terminating their allowances.[15]

Only Prince Edward Island granted proportionately fewer Old Age Pensions than did Ontario in the 1930s. Moreover, those Ontarians who received such assistance rarely got the full $20 a month allowed by federal legislation. Local, especially rural, boards employed rigorous means tests. Appeal processes were not widely known, and when they were pursued, they often proved futile. In the interests of cost control, Ontario centralized pension payments in 1933 and instituted even more draconian means tests.[16]

The Depression years saw the growth of radical movements ranging from the moderate-socialist Co-operative Commonwealth Federation (CCF) to the agrarian-based New Canada Movement (NCM), a precursor of the more broadly based Canadian Youth Council, to more radical Communists. Art Haas, recalling his membership in the New Canada Movement, a primarily rural organization influenced by the Social Gospel, said: 'I know that in 1932 I had a great sense of the inequality of our system and that sense is with me 56 years later. I am sure that it was the motivation that kept me interested in improving the conditions of the underdog.' Ivar Nordstram recalled that 'in the study groups in the Scandinavian Hall [at Port Arthur] I learned to make sense of the world through a class analysis of society. . . . No, the '30s were not tragic years for those of us who became part of the Movement. They were only tragic for those that didn't.' 'The way the union talked,' Mary Fox, a Depression-era worker in Hamilton, remembered, 'I had such great belief in them. . . . I am sure unity brings strength. . . . We all thought that.'[17] Both CCFers and Communists looked to the trade unions as the primary organizations to defend industrial workers. Critical of the conservatism of existing craft unions, they joined forces with advocates of industrial unionism inside the labour movement to push for major changes in organized labour in North America.

Striking lumberworkers outside a Finnish Hall, Thunder Bay, *c.* 1933. The clenched fist symbolized solidarity and resolve. Everett photo. AO MHSO fonds, F1405-15-73 MSR7456.

In the United States, President Roosevelt's New Deal, which required all employers to bargain collectively with unions, provided a catalyst for the rebirth of the labour movement. In response to the rising tide of militancy among North America's industrial workers, the craft-dominated American Federation of Labor expelled its militant industrial unions, which in 1935 organized themselves into the Congress of Industrial Organizations. The new CIO launched major organization drives in the steel, automobile, rubber, and electric industries, and by 1937 had established itself as a major force in labour-management relations in the United States. Canadian unionists had strong attachments to international organizations—the majority of Ontario's unions were local branches of American-based AFL unions. The sudden success of the CIO in the United States inspired Canadian workers to organize their own CIO unions.

In 1935, Hepburn's government passed the Industrial Standards Act, which encouraged the institution of minimum wages and standard working conditions within various industrial sectors. The Act promised stability within industrial areas by preventing cutthroat price-cutting and wildcat labour unrest. By 1936, 35 separate industrial codes had been

GM women on strike, 24 April 1937. General Motors did not hire married women, and the women it did hire worked in segregated areas. Some 500 women worked in the upholstery department. When GM workers struck in 1937, only one woman, Gertrude Gillard, was on the bargaining committee. COTA Globe & Mail Coll. Item 44297.

established, but the government refused to act as an enforcer, leaving it up to the unions to police their own activities and deal with unfair employers. Strike activity increased. Between 1934 and 1940, the province averaged 88 strikes a year, almost exactly the number for the turbulent 1914–21 period. Strikes grew more violent. The struggle to establish industrial unionism and collective bargaining had been joined in Ontario, Canada's most industrialized province and the centre for most of

the nation's mass production industries.[18]

The most famous battle took place at the General Motors plant in Oshawa. In the 1920s, GM had bought out the McLaughlin Carriage Works and made its Oshawa facilities the largest GM assembly plant in Ontario. In early 1937, the company simultaneously announced record profits of $200 million, an assembly line speed-up from 27 to 32 vehicles per hour, the fifth wage-cut in five years, and new medical examinations that seemed to

A wartime nursery, 1942. Governments at both levels launched a variety of programs to accommodate working mothers. Childcare facilities were concentrated in areas where war industries were located: 13 of the 18
provincial nurseries were in Toronto; the rest were in Hamilton, Brantford, St Catharines, Galt, and Oshawa.
Women working in other regions had to fend for themselves. AO ACC 10108-5.

threaten the jobs of older workers. The workers downed their tools and a spontaneous
strike swept through the factory. When the
Oshawa organizers asked the United
Automobile Workers in Detroit for assistance,
the UAW dispatched Hugh Thompson who,
opposed to disorganized, spontaneous strike
action, advised them to return to work.

Ignoring Thompson, the strikers formed

UAW Local 222, signed up workers, established
a negotiating committee, and presented a set of
concrete demands to GM's management. At its
plants in Flint, Michigan, GM in the United
States had just fought a long and bitter strike
with the UAW which ended in union recognition
and collective bargaining. GM Canada seemed
prepared to follow suit when suddenly Mitch
Hepburn, who opposed the establishment of

any CIO union in his province, stepped in. With the premier on the side of management, talks broke down in April 1937 and 4,000 GM workers in Oshawa struck. Why did Hepburn intervene? The explanation seems clear. Ontario's mining magnates, close friends and financial backers of Hepburn, feared CIO organizing drives in the north. Hepburn concluded that this threat might be avoided if the CIO could be prevented from establishing a foothold in the auto industry.

When he dispatched a special force dubbed 'Hepburn's Hussars,' or—among those of a different political perspective—'Sons of Mitch', to Oshawa, two of his cabinet ministers resigned in disgust. Hepburn then demanded that the federal government send an RCMP unit as well, but King refused. The GM workers were successful, but other breakthroughs in collective bargaining proved more difficult to obtain. In 1937, economic stagnation again gripped the province, and organizing drives in Ontario's other mass production industries faltered.

With the outbreak of war in Europe, 10 years of economic depression came to an end. As in 1914, the transition to wartime production, accompanied by an influx of investment capital, reinvigorated the sluggish economy and immediately generated new employment opportunities. By 1943, war production hit full stride and the province came closer to the ideal of full employment than at any other time in its history. New technologies, particularly in the chemical and metal industries, insured an explosion in productivity. Incomes increased as swiftly as productivity.

In 1939 Ontario's population stood at 3.8 million, of whom 72 per cent claimed British ancestry and 80 per cent had been born in Canada. As in 1914–18, Ontarians overwhelmingly supported the war effort. But there was a difference: in the First World War Ontarians had expressed their support for Britain; in the Second, they supported taking action against Germany 'out of their informed convictions that fundamental issues were at stake'. Among the few dissenters were many of Ontario's Native peoples (about 3 per cent of the population). Arguing that they did not enjoy the rights of citizenship, the Six Nations band 'strongly protested the imposition of 30 days military training upon the single men of this reservation', and though many of Ontario's Native people did enlist, their participation rate was far lower than it had been in the earlier war. Those of German and Italian origin (6 and 2 per cent of the population respectively) were deemed suspect by many Ontarians: in June 1940 the RCMP arrested 700 Italians and incarcerated them at Camp Petawawa. Many of German origin also ended up in one of the approximately 15 internment camps scattered across the province.[19]

As Canadian men enlisted—some 120,000 by 1941—their jobs went to women. In the Great War, the women who had gone to work were overwhelmingly young and single, but now married women with children also took jobs for wages. For some women, such opportunities were liberating. For others, especially working-class women with families to raise and husbands overseas, work was a necessity and far from glamorous. In some employment sectors, women continued to face discrimination and low wages. In others, such as teaching, married women benefited and maintained that advantage in the years following the war.[20]

'Bren Gun Girl', James Inglis Ltd., Toronto, 1941. This widely distributed government photo presented a glamorous view of women's war work. NAC PA1197600.

As in 1914, the federal government led Canada's domestic war effort. With bad grace, Hepburn conceded that role to King, who was convinced that the only way to avoid regional economic imbalances and inflation was through careful management of economic resources. King assembled a team of hard-nosed managers headed by industry minister C.D. Howe. Government procurement of war matériel proceeded with few hitches. When inflation threatened to get out of hand in 1940–1, the government imposed wage and price controls. Imports insured that some inflation was inevitable, but government regulators proved flexible and allowed prices to rise in a controlled fashion. Similarly, they allowed wages to rise either to pre-Depression levels or to industry standards. Cost-of-living bonuses made it possible to cope with inflation. Indeed, during the war wages rose faster than prices, a result of government policy and a marked increase in productivity.

Labour unions pressed their advantage, organizing mass production workers in all sectors. When a wave of strikes over union recognition threatened to disrupt wartime

Women at work at Stelco, Hamilton, 1940. The reality of women's wartime work is more apparent in this non-governmental photo. Hamilton Public Library, Industrial Coll.

production, King again intervened. In late 1943, a special Wartime Labour Board investigation recommended that the government introduce compulsory collective bargaining. Passage of the appropriate legislation, in February 1944, led to substantial gains for Ontario's industrial workers. Despite a population of only 12 million in 1946, Canada could rightly claim membership in the G-7 group of the world's largest economies. Ontario, the nation's most heavily industrialized province, provided the economic engine for modern Canada. By 1946, Ontario had embarked on a new era of affluence.

CHAPTER TEN

Modern Ontario: 1945–2000

*W*ar left little the same. It brought rising incomes and widespread personal tragedies. Virtually everyone had a friend or neighbour touched by the destruction and carnage abroad. A decade and a half of economic depression and war also affected longstanding attitudes concerning the proper relationship between government and society. The Depression had undermined public confidence in unfettered markets, while five years of economic management during the war spurred interest in the possibility of public economic planning. Hepburn's Liberals represented the old school in which government managed a public budget and, to some degree, regulated business practices but otherwise left the market to its own devices. As the new notions of Keynesian economics spread among Ottawa's economic managers, the provincial Tories rethought their traditional assumptions concerning the appropriate sphere for state activities. Over the next three decades, the 'Big Blue Machine' pursued economic management, including 'planning', with an openness and on a scale that few could have imagined when the war began.

The Depression, together with Hepburn's anti-Labour policies during the 1930s and the substantial growth in labour organizations and collective bargaining during the war years, encouraged the emergence of a socialist alternative in Ontario. Although Hepburn won re-election in 1937 on the basis of his anti-labour policies, by 1941 the CIO unions had formed a national federation, the Canadian Congress of Labour, which endorsed the CCF as organized labour's political voice. With labour onboard, the CCF challenged the Liberals. As the 1943 provincial election approached, provincial voters had three viable choices.

George Drew, the new Progressive Conservative leader, welcomed the challenge. Aggressive, autocratic, and outspoken, Drew had worked hard to rebuild his fractious party, centralizing control of constituency nominations and funding in the leader's office. Always fearful of 'socialism', Drew was nonetheless a pragmatist. He and other party members noted the great success enjoyed by the CCF, and they took freely from the left in preparing their own blueprint for the postwar era.[1]

The Tories' sweeping 'Twenty-Two Point

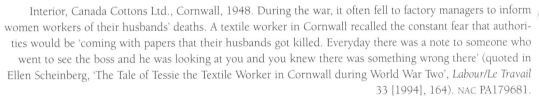

Interior, Canada Cottons Ltd., Cornwall, 1948. During the war, it often fell to factory managers to inform women workers of their husbands' deaths. A textile worker in Cornwall recalled the constant fear that authorities would be 'coming with papers that their husbands got killed. Everyday there was a note to someone who went to see the boss and he was looking at you and you knew there was something wrong there' (quoted in Ellen Scheinberg, 'The Tale of Tessie the Textile Worker in Cornwall during World War Two', *Labour/Le Travail* 33 [1994], 164). NAC PA179681.

Program' pledged support for the creation of a federal/provincial social security system.[2] It promised new infrastructure projects, new agricultural marketing boards, new commissions for forest resources, expanded education and health services, and tax and administrative reforms—aid to all sectors of the provincial economy. But the voters granted the Tories only four more seats than the CCF. During the final years of the war, Drew's minority govern-

ment bided its time, conceding the political lead to the Liberals in Ottawa. In the spring of 1945, with the war in Europe clearly won, Drew lost a vote in the legislature and immediately called a new provincial election. Emphasizing the 'Progressive' element in his own party's name, Drew equated the CCF with fascist Germany's National Socialism. 'The decision,' he warned, 'rests between freedom and fascism.' The scare tactics worked: in

1945, the CCF won only eight seats. Drew had his majority.[3]

The Depression laid bare a basic weakness of the Canadian federal system: the federal government had far greater financial resources, but the provinces had jurisdiction in labour and social policies. In both cases, this mismatch of money and jurisdiction hampered capacity to respond to economic crisis; Unemployment Insurance, for example, required a constitutional amendment to enact. After 1937, a federal Royal Commission on Dominion–Provincial Relations became a forum for centralists who advocated expansion of the federal jurisdiction at the expense of the provinces, and the war provided a golden opportunity for them to carry their ideas into practice. During the war, King used the War Measures Act to expand federal control over taxation while pressuring the provinces to share other jurisdictions.

In 1945 King's government called a Conference on Reconstruction to deal with the demobilization of Canada's wartime economy. Federal civil servants proposed that various wartime financial arrangements be retained during the postwar period. Most of the provincial governments, particularly Quebec, wanted a return to the prewar constitutional status, and most observers expected Quebec to take the leading role in the discussions. But King and Drew commanded centre stage. King called for a new 'co-operative' effort led by the federal government, but Drew, insistently asserting Ontario's traditional provincial autonomy, blocked the wartime drift towards a more centralized Canada. 'If,' federal spokespersons lamented, 'the selfish interests of the two principal Provinces [Ontario and Quebec]

are going to hamstring the Federal Government in its efforts to provide machinery which will permit it to fulfil the functions of a central government in this modern age, then Confederation is a failure and Canada cannot be a nation.'[4] That was not Drew's view. He transformed the conference agenda of tax transfers and social policy into a fight for the older federalism of Oliver Mowat.

Drew's election victory in 1943 began an astounding reign for the Conservatives. Drew had a tendency to bombast and flamboyance whereas his three conservative successors, Leslie Frost (1949–61), John P. Robarts (1961–71), and William Davis (1971–85), all projected bland images. In many other ways, however, they followed in Drew's footsteps. Their governments were 'progressive' but cautiously pragmatic. 'Government is business,' Frost liked to say, 'the people's business.' Robarts proclaimed himself to be a 'management man', a chief executive officer whose shareholders were the voters.[5] These premiers 'managed' economic and financial policies with a view to making Ontario attractive for private investment. Although dedicated to free market capitalism, they did not hesitate to intervene with major public initiatives whenever they saw an opportunity. In effect, they consciously maintained a centrist position, co-opting policies from the right and the left to attract new followers—renewing the party in the process. In the tradition of Mowat, all three took care to ensure that deserving party workers were rewarded. Finally, for these conservative leaders, social reform took a back seat to economic development. One reason for this was the fear that if Ontario took the lead in social reform, the province, under the federal

The 'Porcupine Express', a train on the Temiskaming and Northern Ontario Railway, *c.* 1910. Railways had always held pride of place in Canadian development programs. The provincially owned Temiskaming and Northern Ontario—later renamed the Ontario Northland Railway—was a crucial factor in Premier George Drew's plans to expand agriculture and develop the north's forest and mining resources. NAC PA119904.

equalization program, 'might become paymaster in one way or another in ensuring that the other provinces could follow suit.'[6]

Following the Reconstruction Conference in 1945, Ontario embarked on an aggressive expansion of its industrial and resource sectors. Infrastructure became the top priority. To improve northern rail service, the government made extensive improvements to roadbeds and signalling systems, promoted use of the region's lignite coal for fuel, and supported the conversion to diesel. Mining in the north grew rapidly, yet despite rising freight rates, the viability of the Ontario Northern Railway declined. Like railways throughout the coun-

try, the ONR became increasingly dependent on bulk freight as trucks and buses siphoned off passengers and regional freight.

Ontarians' love affair with the automobile created mounting pressure to widen, crown, pave, and drain the extensive system of roads that criss-crossed the province. In the 1930s, Hepburn's Department of Highways began an ambitious new series of major highways. The grandest, completed in 1947, converted the 'Middle Road', which ran parallel to Highways 2 and 5, into one of North America's first limited-access parkways, linking Toronto to Hamilton and continuing on to Niagara and Buffalo. The Queen Elizabeth Way offered a public vista resplendent with monuments such as the Henley Bridge, styled as an Egyptian barge decked with the emblems of all the provinces.

Between 1945 and 1975, vehicles registered in the province increased sixfold, to 3.3 million private cars and more than 600,000 commercial vehicles, necessitating massive public construction projects; these were aided by the federal Trans-Canada Highway program, which helped to further integrate the provincial and continental economy of the Great Lakes Region. Between 1950 and 1975, Ontario added 40,000 kilometres of highways and roads in a system centring on the Toronto region, which soon emerged as one of the continent's most densely populated metropolitan areas.

In the forest industry, skidder and truck were replacing horse and river drive, and forest companies built several thousand miles of roads in the north and northwest that increasingly served campers, naturalists, and sportspeople. Continuing a tradition, the provincial government responded more slowly to the north's needs than to the south's. To the frustration of northern residents, interminable discussions of cost-sharing with the federal government delayed significant highway construction until the middle and late 1950s.[7]

The ever-increasing numbers of vehicles and highways created traffic nightmares in the most densely populated urban centres and forced municipalities throughout the province to undertake capital-intensive new urban transportation projects. By the 1960s, the province had little choice but to step in with major new initiatives such as the Government of Ontario (GO) trains running between Pickering and Oakville. These highly subsidized trains did indeed divert commuter traffic, yet continuing growth in the numbers of cars meant traffic arteries were still choked at rush hour.

Promoting industrial expansion and fostering an inviting environment for investment, public infrastructure programs played a large part in the extraordinary economic growth of the postwar decades. Ontario was well placed to share in the boom in the Western economies that initiated, to use John Kenneth Galbraith's term, the 'Affluent Society'. By war's end, the majority of Ontario families earned incomes high enough to cover most of life's basics. Over the next three decades, the per capita personal income in Ontario in constant dollars more than doubled. Ontarians in the urban south enjoyed the highest incomes and those in the north the lowest. Personal expenditures on consumer goods and services had increased during the war; after it, they became the primary engine of Canadian economic growth. Between 1946 and 1956, spending on consumer durables in Canada more than tripled—spending generated growth, and as Canada's most industrialized province, Ontario benefited the most. Then consumer spending on services took the lead, climbing by 1971 to three and half times what it had been in 1951.[8]

Not all of Ontario's regions, of course, enjoyed equal per capita income: rates were highest in the urban south and lowest in the north. 'Eastern Ontario from North to South has a lower average income and a higher welfare rate than the remainder of the province,' government officials acknowledged in 1965, 'because the area lies within the Laurentian Shield whose rocky terrain and colder climate makes it less attractive to manufacturing and

Camp Franklin near Parry Sound, *c.* 1955. Fishing and hunting camps, many accessible only by seaplane, dotted northern Ontario. CSTM CN x41330. Photograph courtesy of the Canada Science and Technology Museum, Ottawa.

less profitable to agriculture.' Nor did the various Tory provincial governments take effective measures to distribute income more evenly across regions.[9]

Moreover, Ontarians, and especially rural Ontarians, were pragmatic about what they would give up for something new and untried. A modern electric stove would be nice, one rural householder admitted in the late 1940s, but a wood-burning stove gave better heat in winter. Even in the late 1960s, rural families were less likely than their urban counterparts to borrow in order to consume. For reasons that Oliver Mowat well understood, rural householders believed that credit was too costly, led to profligate spending, and, in sum, was simply morally wrong.

Although automatic washing machines held out the promise of efficient and easy wash days, many Ontario homemakers continued with their traditional wringer washers after their homes were hooked up to municipal water systems. The wringer washer gave the user greater control over the washing process and, as Mrs H.G.F. Barr of London explained in 1955:

I have been appalled at the amount of water that seems necessary to do a normal family washing in the new spin dry type of machine. I believe one brand boasted that it rinsed clothes seven times, and all of them threw the water out after one use. There is hardly a city or town in Canada that does not have some water shortage in summer months. Large sums are being spent on reforestation, conservation and dams. It would appear that this trend toward excessive use of water should be checked now.[10]

Among consumer goods, the automobile was in a class by itself. Already important before the war, the auto industry became even more central after it, boosting production of iron, steel, and auto parts and generating high-paying jobs that sustained the consumer economy. The provincial economy as a whole was becoming less dependent on primary and secondary production, but automobiles would continue to be Ontario's leading industry for decades to come.

Farm production and the related food industries remained extremely important to the province's economy. Nevertheless, the change that rural Ontario experienced in the postwar era was nothing short of revolutionary. Ontario's non-farm rural population has continued growing up to the present day, while its farm population has been shrinking. Between 1951 to 1996, dairy farms declined from 40,000 to 7,200 and hog farms from 93,000 to a mere 5,500. By 1971, farm acreage had fallen to about the level recorded in 1871. At the same time, average farm size increased. The era of factory farming—'industrial' farming, the government termed it—had arrived.

By the late 1990s, one-quarter of Ontario's farms accounted for three-quarters of total farm revenues, and a majority of farm families depended at least to some extent on off-farm income.[11]

The fastest growth in the postwar era was seen in the service industries, which by 1971 accounted for fully 57 per cent of output and 60 per cent of employment in the province. Much of this increase came in the public sector, with the expansion of health, education, and welfare. But as one would expect during a boom driven by consumer spending, both retail and wholesale activity also grew rapidly. Retail sales, meanwhile, relocated from downtown cores to the new shopping centres in the suburbs, with their vast expanses of free parking.

The financial sector also grew substantially. Banking and finance had always been highly concentrated in Toronto and Montreal. Of the two, Toronto had historically been a regional metropolis that played second fiddle to Montreal on the national stage. The latter, however, declined, particularly after the fiscal disaster of the 1976 Olympics, while Toronto, fed by booming regional and national economies, burgeoned.

Finance capital became more concentrated during the 1950s and 1960s. In 1955, the Bank of Toronto and the Dominion Bank merged to form the Toronto Dominion Bank. This led in 1956 to the merger of the Imperial Bank and Barclays, which in turn merged in 1961 with the Bank of Commerce to form the Canadian Imperial Bank of Commerce. Newer 'near-bank' financial institutions such as trust companies came on stream during the 1960s while insurance companies also expanded the range of their operations. Economic power

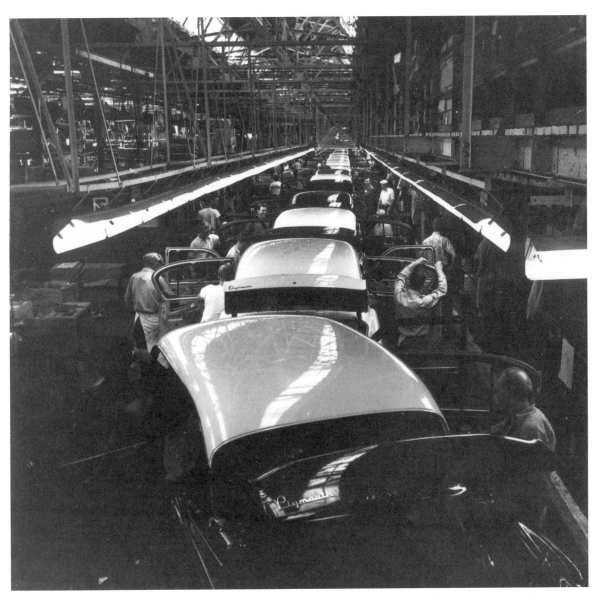

Chrysler assembly line, Windsor, 1953. Ontario accounted for 98.8 per cent of the nation's automobile production, 94.5 per cent of auto-parts production, and 77.4 per cent of primary iron and steel production. To protect the automobile industries, Ottawa negotiated the Auto-Pact Agreement with the United States in 1965. NAC PA205816.

became more and more concentrated in Toronto's boardrooms at the expense of Montreal and smaller cities, and by the year 2000, almost half of Canada's millionaires lived in Toronto.[12]

After the war, both Canada and Ontario

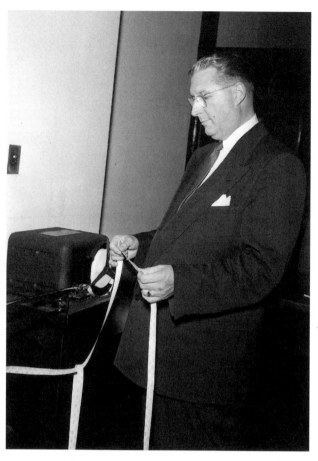

Stock ticker, Toronto Stock Exchange, 1952. Stock frauds centring on speculative mining issues plagued the Toronto Stock Exchange in the 1940s, despite the regulatory efforts of the recently formed Ontario Securities Commission. Postwar prosperity helped keep the political heat off the TSE for a while, but in the 1960s two particularly glaring scandals refocused public attention on the exchange. By 1975, however, the TSE had emerged as the heart of Canada's capital market. CSTM CN x37673 Photograph courtesy of the Canada Science and Technology Museum, Ottawa.

had opted for a modified welfare state. Depression and war demonstrated that older private and state-subsidized programs could not cope with the problems of modern indus-

trial society. The federal government took the lead with the development of Unemployment Insurance in 1940 (covering only 40 per cent of the workforce) and Mother's Allowances in 1945. But by the late forties and throughout the affluent fifties—a time of rising living costs and inflation—Ontario's poor were given little thought. As Louis Cecile, Ontario's minister of Public Welfare from 1956, admitted in 1965, 'to say that I have studied the topic [poverty] very deeply, I must confess . . . no.'[13]

Yet Ontario could not entirely ignore the issue: after all, welfare lay within provincial jurisdiction. As well, there was the problem of transfer payments. As a 'have' province, Ontario resented shared-cost welfare programs that transferred money outside of the province. As John Robarts informed Prime Minister Lester Pearson in the mid-1960s, Ontario was not 'a fat cat to be stripped'. At the same time, Robarts realized that transfer payments facilitated growth throughout Canada, and that Ontario, as the largest producer of goods and services, would profit nicely from enhanced interprovincial trade. Thus Robarts could assure the Ontario legislature that the problems were 'not so serious as to dictate the wholesale abandonment of . . . the system. . . . We are Canadians first and foremost.'[14]

In 1949, for every dollar of state assistance, families on welfare in Toronto received 11 cents from private charities. The older system of private charity was gradually supplemented by a public welfare system administered by municipalities and funded primarily by the province through transfer payments. But the nineteenth-century concept of poverty as a moral failure—caused by 'general subjective inadequacies', not by inadequate housing, education, or daycare—persisted. 'How far,' Robarts mused, '[should] society, through government . . . go to aid people who are not prepared to help themselves? . . . How far does one go in making sure they do not reproduce themselves?'[15] Such attitudes ensured that municipalities would continue to demand work in return for relief and left Ontario's welfare system chronically underfunded.

In 1961–2 Saskatchewan implemented Canada's first medicare program; in 1965 Pearson's federal government committed itself to national medicare; and in 1966 and 1968 the Liberals passed legislation that provided transfer funds to cover 50 per cent of the costs of provincial health insurance programs. Ontario was slow to respond. An unenthusiastic Davis created the Ontario Health Insurance Plan (OHIP) in 1972, under which Ontario residents would pay small regular premiums for medical insurance against virtually all hospital and doctor bills up to a minimum standard of care. In 1989, David Peterson's Liberal government substituted an employer tax for individual premiums.

The 1943 Twenty-Two Point Program had promised that 'every child in the province will have an opportunity to be educated to the full extent of their mental capacity, no matter where they live or what the financial circumstances of their parents may be.' The years between 1940 and 1975 witnessed a flood of new students, reflecting the postwar baby boom as well as rising participation; the number of students enrolled at the primary and secondary level jumped from 660,000 to 2 million, and the number of teachers increased from 22,000 to 95,000. During the heady days of economic prosperity in the 1950s and

Physiotherapist with a young polio patient, Sudbury General Hospital, 1953. Polio terrorized Ontarians in the immediate postwar era. A vaccine was developed in 1954. NAC PA116675.

1960s, local school boards not only built new schools but diversified programs. By the 1980s, the largest boards in metropolitan regions such as Toronto and Ottawa offered a wide variety of programs including French immersion and alternative education. The separate school boards also rapidly expanded their offerings, while French-language boards

Rusins Kaufmanis, 'Say OO . . . . Ohip', *Ottawa Citizen*, 1976. Not everyone was a fan of medicare; Ontario was one of the last provinces to implement a universal health program. Courtesy Rusins Kaufmanis. NAC C147960.

emerged within both the separate and public systems. By 1990, Ottawa—one of the province's most linguistically and culturally diverse communities—had no less than six local school boards, each offering a variety of programs.

In the 1960s, as the baby boomers neared high-school graduation, the Tories turned their attention to the post-secondary system. John Robarts and Bill Davis, each of whom came to the premiership after serving as minister of

education, now delivered on the post-secondary component of Drew's educational promises. Older universities, such as the University of Toronto, expanded rapidly. Private institutions, such as the University of Ottawa, became publicly funded. New institutions, such as Laurentian and Lakehead, expanded to serve northern Ontario.

The government's major new initiative came in 1965 with the creation of the Colleges of Applied Arts and Technology, which pro-

Roy Carless, 'The chef's not in the mood for foreign cooking. How about a nice Anglo-Saxon hamburg?' While
in Ottawa Tories as well as Liberals generally supported official bilingualism, in Ontario premiers Robarts,
Davis (pilloried in this cartoon), and later Peterson all maintained that such a policy would provoke an
English backlash and put other reforms at risk. Courtesy Roy Carless. NAC C147962.

vided vocational training to satisfy labour-market demands while at the same time offering a post-secondary option other than university. Within a decade, 20 CAATs operated in the province. Annual provincial expenditures on the CAATs, supplemented by federal transfer grants, increased from $2.5 million in 1966 to $63 million in 1971. Together with spending on primary and secondary education and health and welfare, this rapid expansion of the post-secondary system strained the province's fiscal resources, and per capita real funding for the system began to decline in the late 1970s, becoming the lowest in Canada over the following decade.

The postwar years also brought profound changes in the nature of Ontario's population. Ontario in general and the Tories in particular had to come to terms with increased cultural diversity. An assertive francophone community headed the list. In Quebec, sweeping postwar social and economic changes had found political expression in the Quiet Revolution ushered in by the Liberal Jean Lesage in 1960. Robarts considered Lesage a personal friend, and he understood Quebec's concerns about linguistic equality in the federal system as well as its assertive provincialism. In August 1967, Robarts announced new funding for French-language secondary public

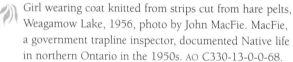 Girl wearing coat knitted from strips cut from hare pelts, Weagamow Lake, 1956, photo by John MacFie. MacFie, a government trapline inspector, documented Native life in northern Ontario in the 1950s. AO C330-13-0-0-68.

Mrs Echum of Moose Factory skinning snowshoe hare, 1959, photo by John MacFie. A rare glimpse inside a northern kitchen. AO C330-13-0-0-141.

schools to bridge the gap between primary and university education. Immediately, concerns were voiced about the potential loss of separate school supporters to the public system and the prospect of two French-language systems, one public and one separate. Education Minister Bill Davis was left to sort out these difficulties, and at the Confederation of Tomorrow Conference, Davis promised that Ontario would never revert to the 1912 policy of restricting the use of French as a language of instruction. After Davis himself became premier, in 1971, he gradually expanded French-language services throughout the province. Viewed from the government benches at Queen's Park, this progress may have seemed dramatic, but from the perspective of the fran-

cophone minority it was piecemeal and only grudgingly granted. Nevertheless, the Conservatives under Davis did make many parts of Ontario functionally, if not officially, bilingual.

Ontario's First Nations fared less well. In 1954 a provincial Report on Civil Liberties and Rights of Indians referred to their 'now almost imaginary disadvantages'. But as poverty-stricken Aboriginal people began to move off their reserves in search of employment, their deplorable living conditions became apparent to the wider population. Stigmatized as drunkards, vagabonds, prostitutes, and social threats, Native men and women were thrown *en masse* into local and provincial jails. Ottawa and Ontario argued over what to do and as a result did almost nothing. The First Nations continued to act for themselves. Reserves acquired greater administrative and fiscal autonomy. The development of museums, language courses, and traditional festivals throughout the 1970s signalled Native peoples' renewed interest in their own cultures. By the beginning of the 1980s, 18 Friendship Societies existed in urban areas throughout Ontario, and political associations bringing together bands from various Ontario regions began to press for economic, social, and political reforms.

During the 1970s, many of these groups began to press land claims and various issues of civil rights. One common protest tactic was the blockade. In the summer of 1990, Natives at Long Lake Reserve 58, northeast of Thunder Bay, blocked the CNR main line carrying banners saying 'Let's Get Canada Back on the Right Track.' Most such actions were peaceful. In 1995, however, a local band occupied Ipperwash Provincial Park, in southwestern Ontario, to protest against incursions on a traditional burial ground, and in an ensuing clash with police one of the protestors, Dudley George, was killed.

As they had in the past, the First Nations used the courts in their struggle for justice. The most celebrated case concerned the Teme-Augama Anishnabai who claimed ownership of more than 1 million hectares of land in the Lake Temagami region. They lost at the level of the Supreme Court in 1991. But in 1990, before the court handed down its decision, a 'Memorandum of Understanding' was signed with the provincial government which promised an ultimate 'treaty of coexistence'. In June 2000, Chief Doug McKenzie and Chief Raymond Katt of the Temagami First Nation

Rolls of birchbark being used to sheath a smoke house at Longlac, 1960, photo by John MacFie. Birchbark was used to construct everything from houses and canoes to the horns used to call moose. AO C330-13-0-0-147.

Hudson's Bay Company store at Sandy Lake, 1955, photo by John MacFie. Small trading posts like this one were scattered across northern Ontario, providing commercial links to the wider world. AO C330-13-0-0-205.

British immigrants arriving in Toronto, *c.* 1912. As late as 1921, immigrants accounted for fully 40 per cent of Toronto's burgeoning population, and three out of every four new arrivals came from the United Kingdom. Across most of southern Ontario, the sharp rise in immigration before the Great War reinforced the essentially British flavour of provincial culture. COTA SC 244 Item 103.

and Teme-Augama Anishnabai announced that after having 'spent the last century of the previous millennium in a struggle to obtain justice. . . . there is a light of hope that we may achieve some justice through a negotiated settlement within the first few years of the new millennium.' In the same year, the provincial government reported that 17 claims were in active negotiation, 10 others had been settled, and 42 were in the 'pre-negotiation' stage.[16]

Ontario has long been a destination for large numbers of immigrants. At the beginning of the last century, arrivals from continental Europe and the United States increased sharply, although the United Kingdom continued to provide 40 per cent of all new immigrants. Non-British European immigrants tended to settle in northern Ontario. In 1941, French Canadians represented the largest ethnic group in rural northeastern Ontario. British immigrants gravitated to the industrial cities and towns of southern Ontario.

Children in the Filipino heritage classes at St Mary's Separate School in Toronto attend a Christmas concert, *c.* 1970. AO F1405-14-16 MSR11867-2.

The first Temi-Augama Anishnabai blockade, 1 June 1988. Brian Back/Ottertooth.com.

The Toronto skyline seen from Algonquin Island. Photo Andrew Leyerle.

A lake freighter in port at Thunder Bay, 2001. Photo Andrew Leyerle.

The Caribana Festival attracts thousands of visitors to Toronto every summer. Photo John de Visser.

Abandoned gas station, Silver Islet, *c.* 1980. Photo courtesy of Bob Climie.

Black bear at dump, Sibley Provincial Park (near Silver Islet), *c.* 1980. Photo courtesy of Bob Climie.

After 1945, immigration to Canada increased sharply, from 22,000 arrivals a year to 282,000 in 1957. Although the annual total fell to 93,000 by 1963, the late 1960s witnessed more than 150,000 new arrivals annually. They were a highly diverse group of mainly non-British Europeans, and their arrival slowly altered Canada's demographic complexion. Historically the majority, British Canadians declined from 55 per cent of Canada's population in 1921 to only 45 per cent in 1971. By 1971, one in four Canadians was neither British nor French. During the 1970s and 1980s, large numbers of people arrived from developing nations in Asia—China, India, Sri Lanka, Pakistan, and Vietnam—the Caribbean, and the Middle East. Unlike the early twentieth-century wave of immigration, postwar arrivals settled in the largest numbers in the industrial cities of southern Ontario, especially Toronto, which had long been dominated by English, Irish, and other British ethnic groups.

Toronto's artists and cultural institutions—from Glenn Gould to Jack Bush and Michael Snow to the National Ballet—and its vibrant literary and publishing community were making a mark on the city, the nation, and the larger world, yet the city was still best known as 'Toronto the Good': conservative, safe, and staid. The new pattern of immigration dramatically changed that image. Over the last third of the century Toronto became truly cosmopolitan. Chinese, Italian, Portuguese, Greek, Caribbean, and South Asian communities, each with its own shops, markets, restaurants, entertainment, and festivals, dotted the city. This diverse cultural mix hugely enriched Ontario's social fabric. But social tensions also appeared.

The CN Tower, Toronto, 1976. A construction worker puts the finishing touches on the Observation Lookout. CSTM CN76102-1. Photograph courtesy of the Canada Science and Technology Museum, Ottawa.

Undercurrents of racism within the province made life difficult for many. Most of Ontario's social and economic institutions, from boards of directors of major corporations to labour unions to local police forces, continued to be dominated by individuals of British ancestry, and discriminatory hiring practices were common. Pressure mounted on economic and social institutions to respond to an increasingly multicultural community. In the period immediately following the war, horror at the Holocaust, and the United Nations' condemnation of discrimination, coupled with pressure from minority groups such as African Canadians, Japanese Canadians, and most particularly Jews led to the passing of important human rights legislation in Ontario. During

Byelorussian priest at the 20th Jubilee of St Eufrossinia Byelorussian Greek Orthodox Church, Toronto, 1969.
AO F1405-7-1 MSR8336-1.

the 1940s, Ontario passed more anti-discrimination legislation than any other province and in the same decade, the City of Toronto passed a model bylaw that required places of amusement to allow all customers use of the premises regardless of 'race, colour or creed'. Discriminatory land covenants, however, remained in place. In Hamilton in the 1940s, a typical covenant read: 'None of the lands described herein shall be used or occupied, let or sold to Negroes, or Asiatics, Bulgarians, Austrians, Russians, Serbs, Romanians, Turks, whether British subjects or not, or foreign born Italians, Greeks or Jews.'

In 1950, Frost's government, somewhat reluctantly, passed precedent-setting (for Canada) legislation prohibiting discriminatory covenants in any *future* land transactions. And in 1951, pressured by a coalition of human rights advocates led by Jews and including some 71 separate organizations from across the province, it introduced Canada's first Fair Employment Practices Act, which prohibited discrimination 'because of race, creed, colour, nationality, ancestry, or place of origin', and the province's first female equal pay legislation. Three years later, a Fair Accommodation Practices Act forbade the withholding of services on the grounds of birthplace, colour, creed, or ancestry. Frost defended these interventionist laws by assuring his small-town Orange colleagues that doing away with restrictions would benefit business by facilitating urban growth and community develop-

Kindergarten Sunday school, Chinese Presbyterian Church, Toronto, *c.* 1950. From the early twentieth century on, Presbyterian, Methodist and other churches commonly offered kindergarten classes for the children of new immigrants. The first such classes for Asian children were held in British Columbia in the late nineteenth century. Presbyterian Church of Canada Archives, G-1929-FC.

ment. Given the nature of his political support, Frost had no choice but to take an incremental approach to human rights. Nor were these laws perfectly enforced. Often an intransigent bureaucracy impeded adequate implementation. Despite pressure from more liberal-minded reformers, it was not until 1962 that the province consolidated all its anti-discrimination statutes into one code and established a commission to oversee its implementation, with powers to investigate and even prosecute. At the same time it is clear that Frost himself believed that the state had the right to legislate on human rights, a stance that moved Ontario's political culture further away from its nineteenth-century laissez-faire roots.[17]

From the 1970s through the 1990s, immigrant communities continued to pressure politicians to combat discrimination; as one commentator noted, 'all political parties . . . now scramble to attract the support of various new ethnic groups in the province.' New Canadians sat on school boards: in 1989, boards were required to provide heritage language instruction if 25 or more students petitioned for it. Many became active in labour

MISS AGNES MACPHAIL

YORK, EAST

Agnes Campbell MacPhail, 1944–5. Representing the Progressive party, MacPhail was the first woman elected to the federal House of Commons, in 1921. Two decades later, in 1943, she was one of the first two women elected to the Ontario legislature, representing the CCF. In 1951 she was responsible for the province's first equal-pay legislation. AO RG15-90-0-0-54, 2027.

unions: 'Sure we should get more money,' one Italian woman asserted. 'We work hard for it, we leave our kids, come home tired, do the dirty jobs.'[18] By the 1990s, public opinion polls found that most Ontarians wanted their government to develop programs to counteract racism. In 1992, after racial rioting erupted

in Toronto, the NDP government appointed former UN ambassador Stephen Lewis its Special Advisor on Race Relations, and it quickly endorsed his recommendations.

Women made significant strides towards greater social equality during these years. After 1945, some of the many women who had joined the workforce during the war left their paid jobs to become homemakers, but many did not. In 1941, fewer than one in five workers in the paid labour force were women. By 1961, the ratio was more than one in three, but not even a quarter of Canada's married women worked outside the home, and they had to defy 'expert' advice warning that their families would suffer. Together, Dr Benjamin Spock's child-rearing books and TV sitcoms like 'Father Knows Best' reinforced the message that women's proper place was in the home, a home often isolated in the burgeoning suburbs of the postwar era. The government dismantled many of the child-care programs established during the war and actively encouraged married women to abandon their jobs to make room for demobilized soldiers. In 1965, a government official admitted that trying to make do with the existing subsidized daycare spaces was 'like hoisting a small umbrella to shelter a stadium full of people in a downpour'. Fathers were increasingly advised to help with raising children, but they could not be expected to do housework. Dr Alistair MacLeod, a prominent Montreal psychiatrist, explained: 'Father no longer has opportunities for pursuing aggressive competitive goals openly at work. Some of his basic masculine needs remain unmet. Mother no longer feels she has a real man for a husband and becomes openly aggressive and competitive herself.'[19]

Despite such patriarchal rhetoric, women, including married women, increasingly worked outside the home. In response to this trend, the Robarts government in 1963 established the Ontario Women's Bureau. Following the new agency's recommendations, the government then passed legislation allowing unpaid maternity leave and prohibiting the firing of women upon marriage. It also took steps to discourage gender discrimination in job postings. Prior to 1940, women had been rigidly ghettoized in a small number of occupations, typically in areas that could be seen as extensions of domestic work—textiles and clothing in industry, teaching and nursing in the professions. Although the war had seen women performing many tasks, particularly in manufacturing, previously reserved almost exclusively for men, after 1945 the pattern of rigid gender segregation reasserted itself in many industries. But the range of occupations available to women continued to expand, and changes in the labour market came more rapidly as more and more women joined the workforce.

By the 1980s, the numbers of women in positions of some power and influence were still not large, but they were growing, and they helped to accelerate the pace of change. The Ontario government introduced a series of employment and pay equity laws, and human rights tribunals became ever more effective. As Ontario governments, including a one-term NDP interregnum under Bob Rae in the 1990s, waffled on many labour issues, they continued to support programs to insure gender equality.

For three decades, the Twenty-Two Point Program introduced by George Drew in 1943 served as the blueprint for Ontario's Progressive Conservatives. Following this blue-

THE OTHER WOMAN

MAY-JUNE '72   TORONTO   Vol.one No.one

25¢

A Revolutionary Feminist Newspaper

The first issue of *The Other Woman: A Revolutionary Feminist Newspaper,* May–June 1972. The feminist movement regained much of its lost vitality in the 1970s as activists forced new issues such as child care and abortion onto the political agenda. Feminists demanded greater recognition of women's rights and an end to discrimination in all its forms. Archives and Special Collections, University of Ottawa Library Network/CWMA Fonds.

print had given the party an unbroken record in power and made the provincial government a key player in virtually every aspect of economic life. In the 1970s, however, the party began to reassess its legacy.

The change in mood began with the economic difficulties occasioned by the Yom

Gay community activists, Toronto, 1978. The occasion for this protest was a speech by right-wing family-values advocate Anita Bryant. AO C193-3-0-3167, 78285-20, 5290.

Kippur War in the Middle East in 1973. Ten days after the war began, six members of the Organization of Petroleum Exporting Countries raised their oil prices by 21 per cent. As the oil crisis increased fuel costs, consumers turned to smaller, more fuel-efficient vehicles from Europe and Japan, and North American manufacturers began losing market share to the imports. The slack in industrial growth was quickly taken up by the expansion of the service sector, which became the primary creator of new jobs in the 1970s and 1980s. Increasingly, however, growth in public services—health, education, and welfare— increased government expenditures without increasing revenues. Now a neoconservative body of opinion began to coalesce around the notion that the public sector was not an engine of growth and prosperity, but a yoke on the free market. Beginning with critiques of top-heavy bureaucracy, government over-regulation, and intrusive public enterprises, neo-conservatives came to focus on government deficits and the 'tax burden'. The process began at the federal level when, in June 1982, Pierre Trudeau's Liberal government unilaterally suspended collective bargaining with its own employees and imposed wage guidelines;

it also advised the provinces to follow and extend guidelines to prices, rents, and fees. Ontario immediately announced a 5 per cent limit on wage settlements and a one-year moratorium on any public-sector strike action.

In 1984, the Conservatives under Brian Mulroney came to power in Ottawa on the strength of campaign promises to control debts and deficits, pursue closer economic ties to the US, and resolve the constitutional dispute with Quebec. The result was eight years of cuts and privatization—and debts that continued to skyrocket despite massive tax grabs such as the Goods and Service Tax. Moreover, the efforts of Ottawa's economic managers to defend the dollar and defeat inflation through the Bank of Canada's monetary policies kept interest rates artificially high relative to the US. As a result, every cut in program spending was wiped out by mushrooming debt service charges.

Ontario felt the full brunt of federal policy in the 1970s and 1980s. In 1977, Bill Davis had dusted off Drew's Twenty-Two Point Program and repackaged it as the Ontario Charter, but it would be the last hurrah for an interventionist Progressive Conservative party. In 1985, on the eve of a controversial extension of separate-school funding, he announced his resignation. Then he closed his party's member lists, effectively excluding new members and new blood. As its new leader the party chose Frank Miller, a small-town populist from its right wing who was widely seen (particularly in Toronto) as the last vestige of 'little Ontario'. Unable to manage the minority government he inherited from Davis, Miller went down to defeat in the legislature after only five months.

David Peterson, the Liberal leader, reached an accord with the NDP under Bob Rae, who agreed to support a Liberal minority government for two years in exchange for concessions on rent controls, environmental regulation, and public access to government. In 1985 Peterson won a majority and, prodded by the NDP, embarked on a major social spending agenda financed by hefty tax increases. For perhaps the first time in the twentieth century, Ontario became a leader in the implementation of social programs in Canada, increasing social assistance payments—welfare payments for a couple with two children rose by one third between 1986 and 1993—at the very time when the Mulroney government began cutting transfer payments to the provinces, especially Ontario, in these same areas.[20]

Another topic on which Peterson vigorously opposed Mulroney was free trade with the US. Given that Ontario had long benefited from the Auto Pact, the province's major business interests firmly favoured the FTA, and the US was the province's largest trading partner, some found that opposition hard to fathom. No doubt Peterson believed that the FTA would lead to extensive de-industrialization in the province; in addition, the Liberals and NDP alike believed that the deal posed a threat to Canadian culture, and that the social policies they were underwriting were threatened by the neoconservative social agendas of both the Canadian and American federal governments.

Peterson was as one with Mulroney, however, on constitutional issues. Brian Mulroney aimed to bring Quebec, which had not agreed to the Constitutional Act of 1982, on board. His first attempt, the Meech Lake Accord, which Peterson firmly supported, seemed a sure thing until it was defeated in the

Manitoba legislature by a single vote. Mulroney tried again, but in a 1992 referendum, the Charlottetown Accord was rejected by 55.4 per cent of Quebec voters and 54.2 per cent of voters nationally. Ontarians had voted yes by the slimmest of margins. Peterson's high-profile support for both Accords had linked him too closely to the federal Tories, and both suffered defeat at the polls. In Ontario, Bob Rae and his NDP were suddenly in power.

Peterson had enjoyed a buoyant economy within which to implement social reform—and even then he had increased taxes and debt. Rae entered power at the edge of a severe economic downslide with taxes already near a record high. Fiscally, he had little room to manoeuvre. To some degree, Rae owed his position to organized labour, and he quickly rammed Bill 40, a controversial new piece of labour legislation, through the legislature. Bill 40's many reforms included an increase in the discretionary powers of strike arbitrators and a ban on the use of replacement workers during a strike—the so-called 'anti-scab' provisions. Bill 40 drew fire from all business groups and was intensely unpopular with many middle-class Ontarians. Throughout the province, billboards went up condemning Bill 40 and promising its repeal at the earliest opportunity; many of them would remain in place for the entire NDP mandate.

In reality, Bill 40 was the least of the NDP's problems. The 1980s had seen numerous complaints that Ontario's competitiveness was declining because of high labour costs and excessive taxes. Liberals and NDPers argued that free trade would encourage manufacturers to move to low-wage, low-cost southern regions. Shortly after the North American Free Trade Agreement was signed in 1990, the Canadian economy went into a tailspin. As manufacturing jobs disappeared, the recession hit Ontario harder than any other region. The NDP reacted initially in Keynesian fashion by increasing government expenditures. They soon changed their minds.

The fiscal pressures of expanding social services had been building for years. OHIP, together with rapid advances in high-technology medicine, had dramatically increased government health expenditures. The added burden of nearly a decade of artificially high interest rates further increased budgetary deficits. As if the worst recession in years was not bad enough, Mulroney had also frozen transfer payments to Ontario. It did not take long for Rae and his colleagues to convince themselves that drastic measures were necessary. Having increased expenditures during their first year, the NDP launched an aggressive campaign of cuts. An 'expenditure control plan' required all transfer partners, including universities and schools, to cut spending drastically. When this was judged insufficient, the New Democrats turned on their most loyal supporters and introduced a 'Social Contract' designed to reduce compensation paid to public sector workers by $2 billion. A cycle of layoffs, fiscal crisis, budget cuts, and more layoffs began.

The Social Contract was certainly novel. At its heart were savings generated by requiring public-sector workers to take as many as 12 unpaid 'holidays' per year. Rather than simply impose budget cuts, Rae's government promised that workers and their employers would negotiate 'voluntary' agreements. In an astounding assault on the basic principles of

Rusins Kaufmanis, 'Acid Rain Damage Spreading', *Ottawa Citizen*, 1979. Not even Grant Wood's American classic was immune. NAC C147961.

collective bargaining, the legislation explicitly allowed employers to act unilaterally if workers had not 'voluntarily' agreed to concessions by the government's deadline. Only when that deadline was about to expire did the NDP realize that it was opening the way for employers to unilaterally change the terms of contracts even in areas unrelated to wages. It then modified the program to permit unions that opted for the 'fail safe' option of unilateral employer action to 'roll over' non-wage clauses in order to protect them from unilateral abrogation.

No Tory government had ever under-mined free collective bargaining so thoroughly, and labour—historically, the NDP's most reliable supporter—responded accordingly. The Social Contract split Ontario's labour movement as little else could. Some private sector industrial unions, such as the United Steel Workers, continued to back the party, but the Canadian Auto Workers—formerly stalwart NDP supporters—sided with the public sector unions in condemning the government; by the end of the decade, CAW President Buzz Hargrove was even promising to vote Liberal. Rae's problems were only exacerbated when a new federal government was elected in 1993 under Jean Chrétien. In an effort to address the federal deficit, the Liberals in Ottawa slashed transfer payments to the provinces for health, education, and welfare.

By 1995, it was clear that the NDP had lost the labour support it depended on, without winning over any replacements: business still preferred Conservative 'fiscal conservatives' to socialist ones. Waiting in the wings were Mike Harris's Conservatives with their 'Common Sense Revolution'. With Harris's election, the drift from Drew's Progressive Conservatives advocating state intervention to Frank Miller-style populists who believed Ontarians were all over-governed and over-taxed was complete. Although it explicitly targeted the deficit, the Common Sense Revolution clearly aimed to rein in government as well. Privatization was the new mantra, and it would go so far that by 2002 the government would be attempting to sell Ontario Hydro.

Typical of populists, Harris played on popular distrust of politicians. The polls indicated that people were willing to support parties that fulfilled their promises. The Tories delivered on their agenda, often in a highly doctrinaire fashion. Having promised to repeal the NDP's Bill 40, they passed Bill 7, which repealed not only the unpopular provisions of the NDP's labour legislation but even the ones business had supported. The Common Sense Revolution document indicated that $400 million would be cut from primary and secondary education through administrative reform and added vaguely that the post-secondary sector would be expected to 'contribute' to deficit reduction. When $400 million was cut from primary and secondary education, another

$400 million was slashed from post-secondary education without any acknowledgement that this represented a 16 per cent cut to universities compared to a 3 per cent cut to primary and secondary education.

A clear signal of the government's direction came with the introduction of Bill 26, the so-called 'Omnibus Bill'. The stated objective of this highly complex bill was to 'achieve Fiscal Savings' and 'promote Economic Prosperity through Public Sector Restructuring, Streamlining and Efficiency'. Its primary object, however, was to lodge enormous powers in the hands of the cabinet and allow the province to offload expensive responsibilities—such as regional roads—onto the municipalities while giving it more direct control over health, education, and welfare, whose funding was immediately cut. The same Bill created a Health Services Restructuring Commission with open-ended powers that was then used to close hospitals throughout the province. In the case of education, the province forced the amalgamation of many boards and then took direct control over funding, imposing a new formula based on 100 per cent operating capacity. This in turn forced local boards to begin closing schools. By the end of Harris's first term, school closings were the subject of bitter disputes between local school boards and parents, and public concern was rising over closed hospitals, overcrowded emergency rooms, and the amalgamation of municipal governments.

Like Peterson before him, Harris reaped the benefits of a rising economy. Unlike Peterson, he slashed social spending. In a sense, this put Ontario in the mainstream with most other governments in the English-speak-

Garbage dump, Toronto waterfront, 1922. Like all big cities, Toronto has long had trouble disposing of its garbage. NAC PA 84921.

ing world. Ontario's private-sector workers, thankful for a job, especially in the Golden Horseshoe area, and small-town fiscal conservatives, for whom small government was beautiful, re-elected Harris to a second term.

During the first 18 months of his first term and in the shadow of draconian cuts to welfare, education, and health, Harris had slashed funding on environmental programs and devolved responsibility for many environmental issues to the municipal level without providing any new funding to facilitate the transition. At the beginning of the 1980s, Ontario had taken the lead in pushing for an agreement with the US on air quality and acid rain agreement and co-operated with Ottawa over Great Lakes water issues. Moreover, through-

out the 1980s and 1990s, polls indicated strong public support for these policies. But the Harris government seemed oblivious to public opinion. Its curtailing of municipal recycling led to a proposal that Toronto should dump, over a period of years, 20 million tonnes of garbage down a mine shaft in northern Ontario. Its reluctance to provide adequate funding for public transportation, charged Eva Ligeti (the province's quasi-independent environmental commissioner), 'will only add to Ontario's excessive reliance on the automobile . . . the number one source of smog-causing pollution in this province'. These measures plus the general budget cuts led some experts to claim that Harris had made it impossible for the province to honour its commitments to the

Canadian and American federal governments concerning acid rain, clean air, and Great Lakes water management.[21]

Until May 2000, it seemed that Harris had dismantled environmental programs with quiet impunity. Then tragedy struck the town of Walkerton in southwestern Ontario. *E. coli,* possibly from livestock manure, had infected the local water supply and caused seven deaths. Ligeti herself had advised in 1997 that municipalities had neither the money nor the knowledge to test drinking water properly. Complaints about the environmentally unsound practices of industrial farming— Ontario's 3.4 million hogs produce as much raw sewage as Ontario's 10 million people— had been increasing. Regulations concerning manure management were few and inadequate despite municipal requests for provincial assistance in these matters.[22]

Like the politicians he had critiqued in order to get elected, Harris stonewalled before finally admitting that he and his government bore major responsibility for the tragedy. He had ignored government reports detailing the radically insufficient monitoring of local water supplies, documents reminiscent of the reports written by medical reformers in the late nineteenth and early twentieth centuries. Harris's stringent fiscal conservatism and rigorous downsizing of government were now seen to be far from risk-free. As the Sierra Club of Canada put it, '[The air] is as contaminated as Walkerton's water. Both suffer from an addiction to unregulated economic activity, cut backs and lack of commitment to protect health and the environment.'[23]

Furthermore, under Harris Ontario seemed to be shifting its focus, both in trade and in social spending, away from Canada and towards North America, becoming less a province than a kind of regional state. Before Harris assumed power, Ontario's vision of itself as the lynchpin of a united Canada had already been in question. Ottawa was no longer quick to side with Ontario on fiscal and constitutional issues, and it had failed to support the welfare spending programs Ontario had adopted under the Liberals and the NDP. With Alberta now the province with the healthiest income, it seemed that Ontario was no longer Canada's centre. In the early 1970s, fully half of Ontario respondents identified more closely with the federal than the provincial government, and only a third identified more with the provincial government. Ten years later, the figures were virtually reversed.[24] Pundits began to envision the possibility of an Ontario outside of Confederation.[25]

Yet just as the water crisis had a history, so too did the idea of a secessionist Ontario. The Annexation crisis of the late 1840s—occasioned by Britain's abrogation of protective trade and fiscal policies (an early form of government downsizing) is a case in point. One of the ways bourgeois politicians at that time deflected the crisis was by moving towards freer trade with the US. Goldwin Smith, a nineteenth-century neoconservative, was only one of many voluble advocates of a pan-North American union. Moreover, it was only after George Drew that Ontario began walking closely with the federal government. For most of its history until then, the province had stood at odds with Ottawa. The notion of a regional state has a history. Ontario and the nation of which it is still a part continue under construction.

NOTES

1: Change and Exchange: 9000 BCE–1500 CE

1. Tamara L. Varney and Susan Pfeiffer, 'The People of the Hind Site', *Ontario Archaeology* 59 (1995), 96–108.

2. Andrew Stewart, 'Relating Environmental Change to Cultural Behaviour in the Late Pleistocene Great Lakes Region', in R.I. MacDonald, ed., *Great Lakes Archaeology and Paleoecology: Exploring Interdisciplinary Initiatives for the Nineties* (Waterloo, 1994), 141–54.

3. W.A. Fox and R.F. Williamson, 'Free Trade in Prehistory: A Lesson from the Past', *Ontario Archaeological Society Newsletter* 89, 4 (1989), 9–11.

4. George R. Hamell, 'Strawberries, Floating Islands and Rabbit Captains: Mythical Realities and European Contact in the Northeast During the 16th and 17th Centuries', *Journal of Canadian Studies* 21 (1986–7), 72–94; D.W. Penney, 'The Origins of an Indigenous Ontario Arts Tradition: Ontario Art from the Late Archaic Through the Woodlands Periods, 1500 BC–AD 600', ibid., 37–55.

5. Conrad E. Heidenreich, 'History of the St Lawrence Area to A.D. 1650', in Ellis and Ferris, eds, *Archaeology*, 478; G. Warrick, 'Comment on Varley and Cannon', *Ontario Archaeology* 58 (1984), 99; William R. Fitzgerald, 'Contact, Contraction and the Little Ice Age: Neutral Iroquoian Transformation, A.D. 1450–1650', *KEWA* 92 (1992), 3–24; M. Annie Katzenberg, 'Changing Diet and Health in Pre- and Protohistoric Europe', in Rebecca Huss-Ashmore et al., eds, *Health and Lifestyle Change* (Philadelphia, 1992), 27; Mary Jackes, 'The Mortality of Ontario Archaeological Populations', *Canadian Journal of Anthropology* 5 (1986), 33–48; Bruce C. Trigger, 'Maintaining Economic Equality in Opposition to Complexity: An Iroquoian Case Study', in S. Upham, ed., *The Evolution of Political Systems* (Cambridge, 1990), 119–45.

6. For a provocative statement of the status thesis see Mima Kapches, 'Chaos Theory and Social Movements: A Theoretical View of the Formation of the Northern Iroquoian Longhouse Cultural Pattern', in A. Bekerman and G. Warrick, eds, *Origins of the People of the Longhouse* (Toronto, 1995), 86–96.

7. Celina Campbell and Ian D. Campbell, 'Pre-Contact Settlement Pattern in Southern Ontario: Simulation Model for Maize-Based Village Horticulture', *Ontario Archaeology* 53 (1992), 3–25.

8. Fitzgerald, 'Contact', 17.

2: Cultural Transformation: 1580–1653

1. Bruce C. Trigger, *The Children of Aataentsic: A History of the Ontario People to 1660* (Montreal, 1987), 218–19, 245; James W. Bradley, *Evolution of the Onondaga Iroquois: Accommodating Change, 1500–1655* (Syracuse, 1987), 110–11, 223, fn. 26; C.L. Miller and George R. Hamell, eds, 'A New Perspective on Indian-White Contact: Cultural Symbols and Colonial Trade', *Journal of American*

History 73 (1986), 311–28; G.R. Hamell, 'Strawberries, 72–94.

2. Ian K. Steele, *Warpaths: Invasions of North America* (New York, 1994), 72.

3. Wm. C. Noble, 'Tsouharissen's Chiefdom: An Early Historic 17th Century Neutral Iroquoian Ranked Society', *Canadian Journal of Archaeology* 9 (1985) and 'Historic Neutral Iroquois Settlement Patterns', *Canadian Journal of Archaeology* 8 (1984), 3–27; S. Jamieson, 'Economics and Ontario Iroquoian Social Organization', *Canadian Journal of Archaeology* 5 (1981); see also A. Rotstein, 'The Mystery of the Neutral Indians', in Roger Hall, W. Westfall, and L.S. MacDowall, eds, *Patterns of the Past: Interpreting Ontario's History* (Toronto, 1988), 11–36; and William R. Fitzgerald, *Lest the Beaver Run Loose: The Early 17th Century Christianson Site and Trends in Historic Neutral Archaeology* (Ottawa, 1982).

4. See Bradley, *Evolution*, passim; W. Engelbrecht, 'New York Iroquois Political Development', in W.W. Fitzhugh, ed., *Cultures in Contact: The Impact of European Contact on Native American Cultural Institutions A.D. 1000–1800* (London, 1985), 163–83; and W.A. Starna, 'Seventeenth Century Dutch-Indian Trade: A Perspective From Iroquoia', *Halve Maen* (Holland Society of New York) 69, 3 (1984), 5–8, 21.

5. Bradley, *Evolution*, 90.

6. T.D. Hall, 'Historical Sociology and Native Americans: Methodological Problems', *American Indian Quarterly* 13 (1989), 224.

7. Heather Pringle, *In Search of Ancient North America: An Archaeological Journey to Forgotten Cultures* (New York, 1996), 180–3.

8. John Webster Grant, *Moon of Wintertime: Missionaries and the Indians of Canada in Encounter Since 1534* (Toronto, 1984), 40.

9. First quote, Carol Devens, 'Separate Confrontations: Gender as a Factor in Indian Adaptation to European Colonization in New France', *American Quarterly* 38 (1986), fn. 11, 477; second quote, Olive Dickason, 'Campaigns to Capture Young Minds: A Look at Early Attempts in Colonial Mexico and New France to Remould Amerindians', *Historical Papers* (1987), 62.

10. Devens, 'Separate Confrontations', 468.

11. On missionaries and Native women see Karen Anderson, 'Commodity Exchange and Subordination: Montagnais-Naskapi and Huron Women, 1600–1650', *Signs: Journal of Women in Culture and Society* 11, 1 (1985), 59.

12. John Steckley, 'Joseph Chihoatenhwa: The Forgotten Martyr', in Steckley, ed., *Untold Tales: Four 17th Century Huron* (Toronto, 1981, 1992), 1–17.

13. Howard Vernon, 'The Dutch, the Indians and the Fur Trade in the Hudson Valley, 1609–1664', in L.M.Hauptman, ed., *Neighbours and Intruders: An Ethnohistorical Exploration of the Indians of Hudson's River* (Ottawa 1978), 204, 298–209; Olive Dickason, ed., 'Europeans and Amerindians: Some Comparative Aspects of Early Contact', *Historical Papers* (1979), 198–200. Francis Jennings, in *The Ambiguous Iroquois Empire* (New York, 1984), 71, speculates that the difference may relate to Champlain's early success in controlling the Mohawks, and the early Dutch failure to do so; however, Trigger, in *Natives and Newcomers*, 334, implies that the Dutch were also interested in colonization. See also Francis Jennings, *The History and Culture of Iroquois Diplomacy: An Interdisciplinary Guide to the Treaties of the Six Nations and Their League* (Syracuse, 1985). 132; Jan Piet Puype comments on the number of guns and gun parts focused on Seneca sites for this period in 'Dutch and Other Flintlocks from 17th Century Iroquois Sites' in C.F. Hayes III, ed, *Proceedings of the 1984 Trade Gun Conference* 1 (Rochester, 1985) 9, 90–81; Trigger, *Children*, 633; James Hunter, 'The Implications of Firearms Remains from Sainte-Marie among the Hurons A.D. 1639–1649', in C.F. Hayes III, ed., *Proceedings of the 1984 Trade Gun Conference* 2 (Rochester, 1985), 5–7.

14. J. A. Brandão, *'Your fyre shall Burn no more': Iroquois Policy Toward New France and its Native Allies to 1701* (Lincoln, Neb., 1997).

15. Craig S. Keener, 'An Ethnohistorical Analysis of Iroquois Assault Tactics Used Against Fortified Settlements of the North East in the 17th Century', *Ethnohistory* 46 (1999), 790–1.

16. Keith Otterbein, 'Huron vs Iroquois: A Case Study

in Inter-Tribal Warfare', *Ethnohistory* 26 (Spring 1979), 141–52.

17. Ibid.

18. Brandão, '*Your fyre. . .*', Table D1.

3: Contested Terrain and Cultural Mixing: 1653–1763

1. Richard White, *The Middle Ground: Indians, Empires and Republics in the Great Lakes Region, 1650–1815* (Cambridge, 1991).

2. Daniel Richter, 'Iroquois vs. Iroquois: Jesuit Missions and Christianity in Village Politics, 1642–1686', *Ethnohistory* 32 (1985), 16, note 72, and 8 (quote at 8).

3. W.J. Eccles, *France in America* (Markham, Ont., 1990), 66.

4. Stephen S. Webb, *1676: The End of American Independence* (New York, 1984), 287.

5. J.A. Brandão and W.A. Starna, 'The Treaties of 1701: A Triumph of Iroquois Diplomacy', *Ethnohistory* 43 (1996), 213.

6. E.E. Rich, *The Fur Trade and the Northwest to 1857* (Toronto, 1967), 55.

7. R. White, *The Middle Ground*, 130–2 (quote on 131).

8. Ibid., 130.

9. Peter S. Schmalz, *The Ojibwa of Southern Ontario* (Toronto, 1991), Chapter 3.

10. Daniel Richter, 'War and Culture: The Iroquois Experience', *William and Mary Quarterly* 40 (1983), 354–5; R. Hahn, 'The Problem of Iroquois Neutrality: Suggestions for Revision', *Ethnohistory* 27 (1980), 322–4.

11. Figures calculated from data in R. Cole Harris, ed., *Historical Atlas of Canada*, vol. 1, Plates 40 and 41. See W.J. Eccles, 'The Fur Trade and Eighteenth-Century Imperialism', *William and Mary Quarterly* 40 (1983), 355, note 66, for a cautionary statement concerning such statistics.

12. Charles Bishop, 'The First Century: Adaptive Changes Among the Western James Bay Cree between the Early Seventeenth and Early Eighteenth Centuries', in S. Krech III, ed., *The Subarctic Fur Trade: Native Social and Economic Adaptations* (Vancouver, 1984), 48; C.M. Judd, 'Sakie, Esquawenoe and the Foundation of a Dual-

Native Tradition at Moose Factory', ibid., 87–8.

13. Judd, 'Sakie', 93–4.

14. Dean Anderson, 'The Flow of European Trade Goods into the Western Great Lakes region, 1715–1760', in J.S.H. Brown, et al., eds, *The Fur Trade Revisited* (East Lansing, Mich., 1994), 93–116. Bruce White, 'The Woman Who Married a Beaver; Trade Patterns and Gender Roles in the Ojibwa Fur Trade', *Ethnohistory* 46 (1999), 109–47.

15. John Clarke, 'Sarah Ainse', *Dictionary of Canadian Biography*, 6 (Toronto, 1987), 7–9.

16. Harriet R. Gorham, 'Ethnic Identity Among the Mixed-Bloods of the Great Lakes Region, 1760–1830', unpublished M.A. thesis (Carleton University, 1985), 48–9.

17. Helen Tanner, 'The Career of Joseph La France, Coureur de Bois in the Upper Great Lakes', in Brown et al., *Fur Trade*, 171–87.

18. Ibid., 179.

19. R. White, *The Middle Ground*, 210.

20. Francis Jennings, *Empire of Fortune: Crowns, Colonies and Tribes in the Seven Years War in America* (New York, 1988), 191.

21. Percy J. Robinson, *Toronto During the French Regime* (Toronto, 1933, 1965), 136; Jennings, *Empire of Fortune*, 294–7, 313–21; Steele, *Warpaths*, 199–206 (quote at 205).

22. Steele, *Warpaths*, 199–200; D. Peter MacLeod, 'Microbes and Muskets: Smallpox and the Participation of the Amerindian Allies of New France in the Seven Years War', *Ethnohistory* 39 (1992), 42–64.

23. Donald B. Smith, 'Who Are the Mississauga?', *Ontario History* LXVII, 4 (1975), 218; Schmalz, *The Ojibwa*, 59–64.

24. Elizabeth Fenn, 'Biological Warfare in Eighteenth-Century North America: Beyond Jeffery Amherst', *Journal of American History* 86 (2000), 1552–80; all quotations, in text and caption, are from this article.

25. Jane Graham, 'Wabbicommicot', *DCB* 3, 651–2; Schmalz, *The Ojibwa*, 71–80.

4: The 'Men with Hats': 1763–1791

1. R. Preston, *Kingston Before the War of 1812* (Toronto, 1959), xi, note 15.

2. Bruce G. Wilson, *The Enterprises of Robert Hamilton:*

A Study of Wealth and Influence in Early Upper Canada, 1776–1812 (Ottawa, 1983), 17, ch. 3.

3. Victor Lytwyn and Dean Jacobs, 'For Good Will and Affection': The Detroit Indian Deeds and British Land Policy, 1760–1827', *Ontario History* XCII (2000), 9–29.

4. Clarke, 'Sarah Ainse', 7–9.; Fred Hamil, *The Valley of the Lower Thames, 1640–1850* (Toronto, 1951); Linda Sabathy-Judd, ed., *Moravians in Upper Canada; The Diary of the Indian Mission of Fairfield on the Thames, 1792–1813* (Toronto, 1999), 159, 297.

5. Anthony Hall, 'The Red Man's Burden: Land, Law and the Lord in the Indian Affairs of Upper Canada, 1791–1851', unpublished Ph.D. dissertation (University of Toronto, 1984), 53.

6. Donald B. Smith, 'The Dispossession of the Mississauga Indians: A Messy Chapter in the Early History of Upper Canada', *Ontario History* 73 (1981).

7. David McNab, '"The Promise That He Gave To My Grand Father Was Very Sweet": The Gun Shot Treaty of 1792 at the Bay of Quinte', *Canadian Journal of Native Studies* 16 (1996), 293–314.

8. E. Wright, *The Red, White and Blue: The Loyalists in the Revolution* (New York, 1976).

9. First quote from Norman Knowles, *Inventing the Loyalists: The Ontario Loyalist Tradition and the Creation of Useable Pasts* (Toronto, 1997), 37; second quote from M.E. Comfort, 'Disbanded Troops, Settled Loyalists and Emigrants in the Niagara District in 1887', *Families* 27 (1988), 231.

10. Janice Potter-MacKinnon, *While the Women Only Wept: Loyalist Refugee Women in Eastern Ontario* (Montreal, 1993).

5: Rural Life: 1791–1871

1. Cited in Norman Knowles, '"Sons of the Brave Remember Your Forefathers": Nostalgia and the Emergence of the Loyalist Tradition in mid-Nineteenth Century Ontario', unpublished paper (Canadian Historical Association, Calgary, 1994), 16.

2. Donald B. Smith, *Sacred Feathers: The Reverend Peter Jones (Kahkewaquonaby) and the Mississauga Indians* (Toronto, 1987), 27.

3. Schmalz, *The Ojibwa*, 106. Peggy Blair, 'Taken for "Granted": Aboriginal Title and Public Fishing Rights in Upper Canada', *Ontario History* XCII (2000), 31–55; Brian S. Osborne, 'Organizing the Lake Fisheries: Landscapes and Waterscapes', *Historic Kingston* 38 (1990), 82–4.

4. D.B. Smith, *Sacred Feathers* 32, 24.

5. E. Reginald Good, 'Mississauga-Mennonite Relations in the Upper Grand River Valley', *Ontario History* XXXVII (1995), 165.

6. Brendan O'Brien, *Speedy Justice: The Tragic Last Voyage of His Majesty's Vessel, Speedy* (Toronto, 1992), 34, 42, 44, 45.

7. D.B. Smith, *Sacred Feathers*, 30, quote from 32; Leo A. Johnson, 'The Mississauga–Lake Ontario Land Surrender of 1805', *Ontario History* 82 (1990), 234–5; Schmalz, *The Ojibwa*, 107–9.

8. Mary Quail Innis, ed., *Mrs Simcoe's Diary* (Toronto, 1965), 182–3 (10–11 June 1796). On the British taste for turtle see Sarah Freeman, *Mutton and Oysters: The Victorians and Their Food* (London, 1989), 271–8. I am indebted to Lorne Hammond for this reference.

9. Christopher Vecsey, *Traditional Ojibwa Religion and Its Historical Changes* (Philadelphia, 1983), quote from 4, 10.

10. Grace Rajnovich, *Reading Rock Art: Interpreting the Indian Rock Paintings of the Canadian Shield* (Toronto, 1994), 54, fig. 42.

11. L.A. Johnson, 'The Mississauga–Lake Ontario', 244.

12. Schmalz, *The Ojibwa*, 110; L.A. Johnson, 'The Mississauga–Lake Ontario', 236.

13. L.A. Johnson, 'The Mississauga–Lake Ontario', 249; Peter S. Schmalz, 'The European Challenge to the First Nations' Great Lake Fisheries', unpublished CHA paper (Calgary, 1994), 13; Brian S. Osborne and Michael Ripmeester, 'Kingston, Bedford, Grape Island, Alnwick: The Odyssey of the Kingston Mississauga', *Historic Kingston* 43 (1995), 94.

14. Michael Ripmeester, '"It is scarcely to be believed. . . .": The Mississauga Indians and the Grape Island Mission, 1826–36', *Canadian Geographer* 39 (1995), 159.

15. Ibid, 163–6. Sidney L. Harring, *White Man's Law:*

Native People in Nineteenth-Century Canadian Jurisprudence (Toronto, 1998), 118.

16. J.R. Miller, *Shingwauk's Vision: A History of Native Residential Schools* (Toronto, 1996); Thorold T. Tronrud, 'Frontier Social Structure: The Canadian Lakehead, 1871 and 1881', *Ontario History* LXXIX (1987), 154–5.

17. David Moorman, 'Roads and Rights: Public Roads and Indian Land in Nineteenth-Century Southern Ontario', *Ontario History* XCII (2000), 57–69.

18. Leo G. Waisberg and T.E. Holtzman, '"A Tendency to Discourage Them from Cultivating": Ojibwa Agriculture and Indian Affairs Administration in Northwestern Ontario', *Ethnohistory* 40 (1993), 175–211; Elizabeth Arthur, 'Orientation and Disorientation in Rainy River', *Ontario History* 73 (1981), 195–218. Kathi Avery Kinew, 'Manito Gitigaan: Governance in the Great Spirit's Garden Wild Rice in Treaty #3 from Pre-Treaty to the 1990s', in D.H. Pentland, ed., *Papers of the 26th Algonquian Conference* (Winnipeg, 1995), 183–94.

19. Schmalz, 'The European Challenge', quote from 20, 22; Victor P. Lytwyn, 'Ojibwa and Ottawa Fisheries around Manitoulin Island: Geographical Perspectives on Aboriginal and Treaty Fishing Rights', *Native Studies Review* 6 (1990), 1–29; Lytwyn, 'The Usurpation of Aboriginal Fishing Rights: A Study of the Saugeen Nation's Fishing Island Fishery in Lake Huron', in Bruce W. Hodgins et al., eds, *Co-Existence? Studies in Ontario–First Nation Relations* (Trent University, 1992), 81–103.

20. Cited in Penny Petrone, ed., *First People, First Voices* (Toronto, 1991), 60.

21. Ibid., 59–60.

22. J.R. Miller, *Skyscrapers Hide the Heavens: A History of Indian White Relations in Canada* (Toronto, 1989), first quote, 112; Donald B. Smith, 'John A. Macdonald and Aboriginal Canada', unpublished paper, CHA (Charlottetown, 1992), second quote, 17 fn. 42.

23. First quote from Susanna Moodie, cited in Elizabeth Hopkins, 'Susanna Moodie', in J.M. Heath, ed., *Profiles in Canadian Literature* 3 (1982), 39; second quote William McAlister to David Walsh (25 May 1831), in E.A.K. McDougal and

J.S. Moir, eds, *Selected Correspondence of the Glasgow Colonial Society* (Toronto, 1994), 39; third quote from Ruth B. Phillips, *Patterns of Power: The Joseph Grant Collection and Great Lakes Indian Art of the Early Nineteenth Century* (Kleinberg, Ont., 1984), 17.

24. Good, 'Mississauga–Mennonite Relations', first quote, 163–4; Norman N. Feltes, *This Side of Heaven: Determining the Donnelly Murders, 1880* (Toronto, 1999), second quote, 17–18.

25. Janet Foster, *Working for Wildlife: The Beginning of Preservation in Canada* (Toronto, 1978), 9; Clint Evans, 'The 1865 Canada Thistle Act of Upper Canada as an Expression of a Common Culture of Weeds in Canada and the Northern United States', *Canadian Papers in Rural History* 10 (1996), 138; J. David Wood, *Making Ontario: Agricultural Colonization and Landscape Re-Creation Before the Railways* (Montreal, 2000), 9.

26. Helen E. Parson, 'Reforestation of Agricultural Land in Southern Ontario before 1931', *Ontario History* LXXXVI (1994), 238; Celina Campbell and Ian Campbell, 'Pre European Horticultural Impact on the Forest landscape and Forest Succession of Southern Ontario, Canada', *Arch Notes* (July–Aug. 1993), 13; Wood, *Making Ontario*, 13.

27. Elaine Theberge, '"Fothergill": Canada's Pioneer Naturalist Emerges from Oblivion', *The Beaver* (1988), 12, 18; Kenneth W. Dance, 'The Pileated Woodpecker in Ontario—Then, Now and Tomorrow', in M.K. McNicholl and J.L. Cramner-Byng, eds, *Ornithology in Ontario* (Toronto, 1994), 261–6; Foster, *Working*, 10.

28. Michael Katz, *The People of Hamilton, Canada West: Family and Class in a Mid Nineteenth Century City* (Harvard, 1975), 94–111; C.J. Houston and W.J. Smyth, 'Geographical Transiency and Social Mobility: The Illustrative Odyssey of Irish Immigrant Wilson Benson, A Well-Known Canadian Unknown', *British Journal of Canadian Studies* 7 (1992), 345–55.

29. Terry Crowley, 'Rural Labour', in Paul Craven, ed., *Labouring Lives: Work and Workers in Nineteenth Century Ontario* (Toronto, 1995), 37.

30. Michael Wayne, 'The Black Population of Canada

West on the Eve of the American Civil War: A Reassessment Based on the Manuscript Census of 1861', *Histoire sociale/Social History* 56 (1995), 465–85.

31. Susanna Moodie, *Roughing It in the Bush*, cited in Lorna R. MacLean, 'Common Criminals, Simple Justice: The Social Construction of Crime in 19th Century Ontario, 1840–1881', unpublished Ph.D. dissertation (University of Ottawa, 1996), 147. Quote from Feltes, *This Side of Heaven*, 34–8.

32. Quote from McLaurin to John Scott (5 July 1825), in McDougal and Moir, *Selected Correspondence* 4.

33. Doug McCalla, *Planting the Province: The Economic History of Upper Canada, 1784–1870* (Toronto, 1993).

34. John Moodie to James Traill (8 March, 1836), in Carl Ballstadt et al., eds, *Letters of Love and Duty: The Correspondence of Susanna and John Moodie* (Toronto, 1993), 53; Ian Radforth, 'The Shantymen', in Craven, *Labouring Lives*, 204–74; Wood, *Making Ontario*, 13–14.

35. John I. Remple, 'The History and Development of Early Forms of Building Construction in Ontario', *Ontario History* 53 (1961), 10.

36. Harring, *White Man's Law*, 35–61; Wood, *Making Ontario* 96–9.

37. David Gagan, *Hopeful Travellers: Family, Land and Social Change in Mid-Victorian Peel County, Canada West* (Toronto, 1981).

38. Bruce S. Elliott, *Irish Migrants in the Canadas: A New Approach* (Montreal, 1988), 196–7, 216.

39. Radforth, 'The Shantymen', 212.

40. First quote from Moodie to Traill (8 March 1836), in Ballstadt, *Letters*, 42, 49, 50; second quote, John Carroll, *My Boy's Life* (Toronto, 1882), 212–15.

41. Chewitt quote from John L. Ladell, *They Left Their Mark: Surveyors and Their Role in the Settlement of Ontario* (Toronto, 1993), 85. Shirley J. Yee, 'Gender Ideology and Black Women as Community Builders in Ontario, 1850–1870', *Canadian Historical Review* LXXV (1994), 60.

42. Helen E.H. Smith and Lisa M. Sullivan, '"Now that I know how to manage": Work and Identity in the Journals of Anne Langton', *Ontario History* LXXXVII (1995), 254–69, quote from 257.

43. MacLean, 'Common Criminals', 60, 148.

44. McDougal and Moir, *Selected Correspondence* 40, 124; Robert Summerby-Murray, 'Statute Labour on Ontario Township Roads, 1849–1948: Responding to a Changing Space Economy', *Canadian Geographer* 43 (1999), 36–52; T.F. McIlwraith, 'The Adequacy of Rural Roads in the Era Before Railways: An Illustration From Upper Canada', *Canadian Geographer* 14 (1970), 344–59; Wood, *Making Ontario*, 121.

45. Ballstadt, *Letters* (1838–39), from 114 (Susanna to John, 11 Jan. 1839).

46. Lynne Marks, 'Railing, Tattling and General Rumours: Group, Gender and Church Regulation in Upper Canada', *Canadian Historical Review* 81 (2000); Susan Lewthwaite, 'Violence, Law and Community in Rural Upper Canada', in Jim Phillips, Tina Loo, and Susan Lewthwaite, eds, *Essays in the History of Canadian Law: Crime and Criminal Justice* (Toronto, 1994), 353–86; MacLean, 'Common Criminals', Chapters 2 and 4.

47. Crowley, 'Rural Labour', 31; Lewthwaite, 'Violence, Law and Community'.

48. Susanna to John (16 July 1839), in Ballstadt, *Letters*, 157–9.

49. Gordon Darroch, 'Class in 19th Century Central Ontario: A Reassessment of the Crisis and Demise of Small Producers during Early Industrialization, 1861–1871', *Canadian Journal of Sociology* 13 (1988).

50. Lewthwaite, 'Violence, Law and Community', 384, note 73; Crowley, 'Rural Labour', 100, note 239.

6:   Towards a Canadian Polity: 1791–1867

1. E.A. Cruikshank., ed., *The Correspondence of Lieutenant Governor John Graves Simcoe and Allied Documents Relating to His Administration of the Government of Upper Canada* 1 (Toronto, 1923).

2. Katherine McKenna, 'The Role of Women in the Establishment of Social Status in Early Upper Canada', *Ontario History* 83 (1990), quote at 180; Robert J. Burns, 'God's Chosen People: The Origin of Toronto Society', *Historical Papers* (1973), 213–29.

3. Sid Noel, 'Early Populist Tendencies in the Ontario Political Culture', *Ontario History* LXXXX (1998), 173–87, and S.R. Mealing, 'David W. Smith',

Dictionary of Canadian Biography 7 (Toronto, 1988), 811–13.

4. J.B. Walton, 'An End to All Order: A Study of Upper Canadian Response to Opposition, 1805–10', unpublished M.A. thesis (Queen's University), 1977; G.H. Patterson, 'William Weekes', and E.H. Jones, 'Joseph Willcocks', *Dictionary of Canadian Biography* 5 (Toronto, 1983).

5. George Rawlyk, *The Canada Fire: Radical Evangelicalism in British North America, 1775–1812* (Montreal and Kingston, 1994).

6. George Sheppard, *Plunder, Profit and Paroles: A Social History of the War of 1812 in Upper Canada* (Montreal and Kingston, 1994).

7. Carl Benn, *The Iroquois and the War of 1812* (Toronto, 1998).

8. Jane Errington, *The Lion, the Eagle and Upper Canada: A Developing Colonial Ideology* (Montreal and Kingston, 1987). David Mills, *The Idea of Loyalty in Upper Canada, 1784–1850* (Montreal and Kingston, 1988).

9. Paul Romney, *Mr. Attorney: The Attorney General for Ontario in Court, Cabinet and Legislature, 1791–1899* (Toronto, 1986).

10. Carroll, *My Boy's Life.*

11. Paul Romney, 'From the Types Riot to the Rebellion: Elite Ideology, Anti-legal Sentiment, Political Violence and the Rule of Law in Upper Canada,' *Ontario History*, LXXIX, 1987, 113–144.

12. Christopher Adamson, 'God's Continent Divided: Politics and Religion in Upper Canada and the Northern and Western United States, 1775 to 1841', *Comparative Studies in Society and History* 36 (1994), 417–46.

13. Cited in Carol Wilton, '"Lawless Law": Conservative Political Violence in Upper Canada, 1818–41', *Law and History Review* 13 (1995), 124.

14. Carol Wilton, *Popular Politics and Political Culture in Upper Canada, 1800–1850* (Montreal, 2000).

15. Colin Read and Ronald J. Stagg, eds., *The Rebellion of 1837 in Upper Canada* (Toronto, 1985).

16. Thomas Matthews, 'Local Government and the Regulation of the Public Market in Upper Canada, 1800–1860: The Moral Economy of the Poor?' *Ontario History* (1987), 79, 297–326.

17. Peter Baskerville, ed., *The Bank of Upper Canada* (Toronto, 1987).

18. Calculated from data in J.K. Johnson, *Becoming Prominent: Regional Leadership in Upper Canada, 1791–1841* (Montreal and Kingston, 1989).

19. Irving Abella, 'The Sydenham Election of 1841', *Canadian Historical Review* 47 (1966), 326–43.

20. Mary Larrett Smith, *Young Mr Smith in Upper Canada* (Toronto, 1980), 131.

21. Paul Craven and Tom Traves, 'Canadian Railways as Manufacturers, 1850–1880', *Historical Papers* (1983).

22. Ontario Archives, Charles Clarke Papers, McDougall to Clarke, 17 Sept. 1853.

23. Amelia Ryerse Harris Diary, 16 Feb. 1859, in Harris and Harris, eds, *The Eldon House Diaries* (Toronto, 1998), 92.

24. First quote, National Archives of Canada (NAC) Baring Brothers Papers, 4, John Rose to Thomas Baring; second quote, NAC, RG 19, C1, 1181, file 9, Lydia Payne to J. Browne, Sept. 1866.

25. Michael Piva, *The Borrowing Process: Public Finance in the Province of Canada, 1840–1867* (Ottawa, 1992).

26. William Westfall, *Two Worlds: The Protestant Culture of 19th Century Ontario* (Toronto, 1988).

27. NAC, Galt Papers, MG 27 I D 8, vol 1, Charles Robertson, Secretary, Toronto Board of Trade, to Galt, 3 Feb. 1859.

28. Ibid, E.J. Charleton to Galt, 20 Feb. 1859.

29. J.M.S. Careless, *Brown of the Globe*, vol. 1 (Toronto, 1959), 315.

30. National Archives, Macdonald Papers, M.G. 26 A 1 B 191, Brydges to Macdonald, 22 Feb. 1864 and 24 Feb. 1864. I wish to thank Michael Piva for sharing his insights into and work on the significance of trade matters, especially the importance of the 'two market' policy, and Brown's feelings on that issue, in the context of the Confederation movement. See also Piva, *The Borrowing Process.*

31. For attitudes to democracy see Bruce W. Hodgins, 'Democracy and the Fathers of Confederation', in E.G. Firth, ed., *Profiles of a Province: Studies in the History of Ontario* (Toronto, 1967), 83–91.

32. Cited in P.B. Waite, *The Charlottetown Conference*, CHA Historical Booklet 15 (Ottawa, 1963), 12–13.

33. P. B. Waite, *The Life and Times of Confederation, 1864–1867* (Toronto, 1962).

34. Cited in J.M.S. Careless, *Brown of the Globe: Statesman of Confederation* (Toronto, 1963), 171.

35. Macdonald Papers, Macdonald to M. C. Cameron, 19 Dec. 1864, cited in Waite, *Life and Times,* 123.

7:   Ontario in the New Dominion: 1867–1905

1. Joseph Schull, *Edward Blake: The Man of the Other Way* (Toronto, 1975).

2. Douglas Owram, *The Promise of Eden: The Canadian Expansionist Movement and the Idea of the West, 1856–1900* (Toronto, 1980).

3. S.J.R. Noel, *Patrons, Clients and Brokers: Ontario Society and Politics, 1791–1896* (Toronto, 1990), 253–6; Peter E.P. Demski, 'Political History From the Opposition Benches: William Ralph Meredith, Ontario Federalist', *Ontario History* LXXXIX (1997), 199–217.

4. Information on the Boundary and St Catharine's cases is drawn from Margaret Evans, *Sir Oliver Mowat* (Toronto, 1992); Noel, *Patrons*; Harring, *White Man's Law*; Donald B. Smith, 'Aboriginal Rights A Century Ago', *The Beaver* 67, 1 (1987), 4–15; Kathi Avery Kinew, 'Manito Gitgaan Governing in the Great Spirit's Garden: Wild Rice in Treaty #3. An Example of Indigenous Government Public Policy Making and Intergovernmental Relations between the Boundary Waters Anishinaabeg and the Crown, 1869–1994', unpublished Ph.D. dissertation (University of Manitoba, 1995).

5. Noel, *Patrons*, 263.

6. Cited in Joseph Schull, *Laurier: The First Canadian* (Toronto, 1965), 178.

7. First quote 'The P.P.A. in Ontario, History and Principles of the Organization' (n.p., n.d.), cited in James T. Watt, 'The Protestant Protective Association of Canada: An Example of Religious Extremism in Ontario in the 1890s' in B. Hodgins and R. Page, eds, *Canadian History Since Confederation: Essays and Interpretation* (Georgetown, Ont., 1972), 248. For changes within the Catholic leadership see Mark McGowan, *The Waning of the Green: Catholics, the Irish and Identity in Toronto, 1887–1922* (Montreal and Kingston, 1999), quote at 61 (my italics); Peter

Baskerville, 'Did Religion Matter: Religion and Wealth in Urban Canada at the turn of the Twentieth Century', *Histoire sociale/SocialHistory* 67 (2001).

8. Information on wholesale prices presented here is from F.H. Leacy, M.C. Urquhart and K.A.H. Buckley, eds, *Historical Statistics of Canada*, 2nd edn (Ottawa, 1983), Series G386–388, K33–43, and M228–238.

9. The 'terms of trade' measures the export price as a percentage of import price. See Leacy, Urquhart and Buckley, *Historical Statistics*, Series G386–388.

10. D. Lawr, 'The Development of Ontario Agriculture, 1870–1914: Patterns of Growth and Change', *Ontario History* 64 (1972), 239–51; Robert L. Jones, *History of Agriculture in Ontario, 1613–1880,* (Toronto, 1946), quote at 254.

11. Noel, *Patrons*, quote at 263. Agricultural statistic from W. Robert Wightman and Nancy M. Wightman, *The Land Between: Northwestern Ontario Resource Development, 1800–1990s* (Toronto, 1997), Table 2.1, 71.

12. Livio Di Matteo, 'Fiscal Imbalance and Economic Development in Canadian History: Evidence From the Economic History of Ontario', *American Review of Canadian Studies* (1999), 287–327; quote from M. Evans, *Mowat*, 283.

13. The classic work on this is H.V. Nelles, *The Politics of Development: Forests, Mines and Hydro-Electric Development in Ontario, 1849–1941* (Toronto, 1974). See also Noel, *Patrons,* 268.

14. Matteo provides estimates for dicennial census years for this period. He claims these years to be standard (i.e., not exceptional) in terms of income. Accordingly, for the purposes of the estimation in the text, I have assumed that the net income for the first five years in each decade was the same as that of the first census year (for the 1880s that would be 1881) and for the last five years the same as the second census date (for the 1880s that would be 1891); Matteo, 'Fiscal Imbalance and Economic Development', passim.

15. Ibid., 310–11; quote from R. Peter Gillis and T.R. Roach, *Lost Initiatives: Canada's Forest Industries, Forest Policy and Forest Conservation* (New York, 1986), 43. On northern lumberers see Wightman

and Wightman, *The Land Between,* 124–5. For Arbor Day see D. Diamantakos, 'Private Property Deforestation and the Clerk of the Forestry in 19th Century Ontario', *Scientia canadensis* 21 (1997), 29–48. For tourism in the north see Patricia Jansen, *Wild Things: Nature, Culture and Tourism in Ontario, 1870–1914* (Toronto, 1995).

16. Dianne Newell, *Technology on the Frontier: Mining in Old Ontario* (Vancouver, 1986), 77–89.

17. Craig Heron, 'Factory Workers', in Craven, *Labouring Lives,* 480; Carl Wallace, 'The 1880s', in Wallace and Ashley Thomson, eds, *Sudbury: Rail Town to Regional Capital* (Toronto, 1993); Eileen Goltz, 'A Corporate View of Housing and Community in a Company Town: Copper Cliff, 1886–1920', *Ontario History* LXXXII (1990), 29–51.

18. Heather Menzies, 'Technology in the Craft of Ontario Cheesemaking: Women in Oxford County circa 1860', *Ontario History* LXXXVII (1995), 293–304; Terry Crowley, 'Experience and Representation: Southern Ontario Farm Women and Agricultural Change, 1870–1914', *Agricultural History* 73 (1999), 238–51; M.J. Thompson, 'A Whey with Cheese', *This Country: Canada* 6 (1994), 69–72.

19. Margaret Derry, 'Gender Conflicts in Dairying: Ontario's Butter Industry, 1880–1920', *Ontario History* LXXXX (1998), 31–47.

20. Peter Baskerville and Eric Sager, *Unwilling Idlers: The Urban Unemployed and Their Families in Late Victorian Canada* (Toronto, 1998), Chapter 4.

21. Toronto *Globe,* 26 Feb. 1894.

22. The information in the last six paragraphs is drawn mainly from Baskerville and Sager, *Unwilling Idlers,* Chapters 6 and 7; John Bullen, 'Hidden Workers: Child Labour and the Family Economy in Late Nineteenth Century Urban Ontario', *Labour/Le Travail* 18 (1986), 163–88.

23. Gerald Tulchinsky, 'Hidden Among the Smokestacks: Toronto's Clothing Industry, 1871–1901', in David Keane and Colin Read, eds, *Old Ontario: Essays in Honour of J.M.S. Careless* (Toronto, 1990), 257–84; Robert McIntosh, 'Sweated Labour: Female Needleworkers in Industrializing Canada', *Labour/Le Travail* 32 (1993), 105–38.

24. Lynne Marks, *Revivals and Roller Rinks: Religion, Leisure and Identity in Late Nineteenth Century Small-Town Ontario* (Toronto, 1996), 58.

25. Thomas Conant, *Upper Canada Sketches* (Toronto, 1898), 195.

26. Edgar-André Montigny, *Foisted Upon the Government? State Responsibilities, Family Obligations and the Care of the Dependent Aged in Late Nineteenth Century Ontario* (Montreal and Kingston, 1997), Chapter 5 and passim; Stormie Stewart, 'The Elderly Poor in Rural Ontario; Inmates of the Wellington County House of Industry, 1877–1907', *Canadian Historical Association Journal* (1992), 217–34.

27. Peter Oliver, '"A Terror to Evil Doers": The Central Prison and The "Criminal Class" in Late Nineteenth Century Ontario', in R. Hall, *Patterns of the Past,* 206–37.

28. Peter Oliver, '"To Govern by Kindness": The First Two Decades of the Mercer Reformatory for Women', in Phillips, *Crime and Criminal Justice,* 516–72 (all quotes from here); Carolyn Strange, '"The Criminal and Fallen of Their Sex": The Establishment of Canada's First Women's Prison, 1874–1901', *Canadian Journal of Women and the Law* 1 (1985).

29. Harring, *White Man's Law,* 159–64.

30. Andrew Holman, *A Sense of Their Duty: Middle Class Formation in Victorian Ontario Towns* (Montreal and Kingston, 2000), 152, 210; M. Evans, *Mowat,* 201–7; Craig Heron, 'The High School and the Household Economy in Working-Class Hamilton, 1890–1940', *Historical Studies in Education/Revue d'histoire de l'éducation* 7 (1995), 221; Colin McFarquhar, 'A Difference of Perspective: Blacks, Whites and Emancipation Day Celebrations in Ontario, 1865–1919', *Ontario History* XCII (2000), 147–60.

31. Chad Gaffield and Gerard Bouchard, 'Literacy, Schooling and Family Reproduction in Rural Ontario and Quebec', *Historical Studies in Education/Revue d'histoire de l'éducation* 1 (1989), 201–18; Holman, *A Sense of Their Duty,* Chapter 6; Gordon Darroch, 'Scanty Fortunes and Rural Middle-Class Formation in Nineteenth Century Central Ontario', *Canadian Historical Review* 79 (1998), 621–59; R.D. Gidney

and W.P.J. Millar, *Inventing Secondary Education: The Rise of the High School in Nineteenth Century Ontario* (Montreal and Kingston, 1990).

32. Alison Prentice, 'The Feminization of Teaching', in S.M. Trofimenkoff and Prentice, eds, *The Neglected Majority* (Toronto, 1977); Bruce Curtis, '"Illicit" Sexuality and Public Education in Ontario, 1840–1907', *Historical Studies in Education/Revue d'histoire de l'éducation* 1 (1989), 73–94.

33. Holman, *A Sense of Their Duty*, 153–5.

34. The last two paragraphs are based on Peter Baskerville, 'Women and Investment in Late Nineteenth Century Urban Canada: Victoria and Hamilton, 1880–1901', *Canadian Historical Review* 80 (1999), 191–218; Baskerville, 'Gender, Family and Self-Employment in Urban Canada, 1901 and 1996', unpublished paper, Canadian Business History Conference (McMaster University, 1998); Sue Ingram and Kris Inwood, 'Property Ownership by Married Women in Victorian Ontario', *Dalhousie Law Journal* 23 (2000), 404–39; Lori Chambers, *Married Women and Property Law in Victorian Ontario* (Toronto, 1997).

35. Marks, *Revivals and Roller Rinks*, 95–101 (quote from here). Carol Lee Bacchi, *Liberation Deferred? The Ideas of the English-Canadian Suffragist, 1877–1918* (Toronto, 1983), 69, 85.

36. M.P. Sendbuehler, 'Battling "the bane of our cities" Class, Territory and the Prohibition Debate in Toronto, 1877', *Urban History Review* 22 (1993), 32–3.

37. Annalee Golz, '"If a Man's Wife Does Not Obey Him, What Can He Do?" Marital Breakdown and Wife Abuse in Late Nineteenth-Century Early Twentieth Century Ontario', in L.A. Knafla and Susan W.S. Binnie, eds, *Law Society and the State: Essays in Modern Legal History* (Toronto, 1995), 323–50; Bernadine Dodge, '"Let the Record Show": Women and Law in the United Counties of Durham and Northumberland, 1845–1895', *Ontario History* XCII (2000), 127–45.

38. See, for example, Lorna Ruth McLean, 'Home, Yard and Neighbourhood: Women's Work and the Urban Working-Class Family Economy', unpublished M.A. thesis (University of Ottawa, 1990), 60–8, 74–6; Ashley Thomson, 'The 1890s', in Wallace and Thomson, *Sudbury*, 39; Baskerville and Sager, *Unwilling Idlers*, 134.

39. First quote, Colleen MacNaughton, 'Promoting Clean Water in 19th Century Public Policy: Professors, Preachers and Polliwogs in Kingston, Ontario', *Histoire sociale/Social History* 32 (1999), 51; second quote, Heather A. MacDougall, 'The Genesis of Public Health Reform in Toronto, 1869–1890', *Urban History Review* 10 (1982), 6; for Sudbury see Thomson, 'The 1890s'. All other quotes are from Larry Sawchuck and Stacie D.A. Burke, 'Mortality in an Early Canadian Community: Belleville, 1876–85', unpublished paper (2000), passim.

40. Jamie Benidickson, 'Plumbing the Depths of Ontario's Environmental History: The Board of Public Health and Water Quality Protection', unpublished paper, Environmental History Conference (Victoria, 1996).

41. MacNaughton, 'Promoting Clean Water', 55; John Hagiopan, 'The Political Geography of Water Provision in Paris, Ontario, 1882–1924', *Urban History Review* 23 (1994), 32–51; Jeremy Stein, 'Annihilating Space and Time: The Modernization of Fire-Fighting in Late Nineteenth Century Cornwall, Ontario', *Urban History Review* 24 (1996), 3–11.

42. Quote from Rosemary Gagan, 'Mortality Patterns and Public Health in Hamilton, Canada, 1900–14', *Urban History Review* 17 (1989), 169; Sawchuk and Burke, 'Mortality'.

8: The Making of Industrial Ontario: 1905–1923

1. Quotation from Charles W. Humphrey, *'Honest Enough to be Bold': The Life and Times of Sir James Pliny Whitney* (Toronto, 1985), 122. Statistics calculated from Ian A. Drummond, *Progress Without Planning: The Economic History of Ontario: From Confederation to the Second World War* (Toronto, 1987), 401, 412–13, and Doug McCalla, 'The Ontario Economy in the Long Run', *Ontario History* LXXXX (1998), 99–100.

2. Terry Crowley, 'J.J. Morrison and the Transition in Canadian Farm Movements During the Early Twentieth Century', *Agricultural History* 71 (1997), 335.

3. Livio Di Matteo, 'The Economic Development of the Lakehead during the Wheat Boom Era, 1900–1914', *Ontario History* 83 (1991), 297–316; Donald Kerr and D.W. Holdsworth, eds, *Historical Atlas of Canada* (Toronto 1990), 3, Table 16.

4. Drummond, *Progress*, 364.

5. E. Brian Titley, *A Narrow Vision: Duncan Campbell Scott and the Administration of Indian Affairs in Canada* (Vancouver, 1986), 73; Jean L. Manore, *Cross Currents: Hydroelectricity and the Engineering of Northern Ontario* (Waterloo, 1999).

6. James Angus, 'How the Dokis Indians Protected Their Timber', *Ontario History* LXXXI (1989); Janet Chute, *The Legacy of Shingwaukonse: A Century of Native Leadership* (Toronto, 1998), 227–30.

7. James Miller and Edmund Danziger, Jr, '"In the Care of Strangers": Walpole Island First Nation's Experiences with Residential Schools after the First World War', *Ontario History* XCII (2000), 71–88; J.R. Miller, *Shingwauk's Vision*, 357–8.

8. Constance Backhouse, *Colour-Coded: A Legal History of Racism in Canada, 1900–1950* (Toronto, 1999), 103–31; J.R. Miller, *Skyscrapers*, 217; Neil S. Forkey, 'Maintaining a Great Lakes Fishery: The State, Science and the Case of Ontario's Bay of Quinte, 1870–1920', *Ontario History* LXXXVI (1995), 45–86; Stephen Bocking, 'Fishing the Inland Seas: Great Lakes Research, Fisheries Management, and Environmental Policy in Ontario', *Environmental History* 2 (1997), 52–73.

9. Alan Brookes and Catharine Wilson, '"Working Away" from the Farm: The Young Women of North Huron, 1910–30', *Ontario History* 77 (1985), 281–300, quotation at 282.

10. Carolyn Strange, *Toronto's Girl Problem: The Perils and Pleasures of the City, 1880–1930* (Toronto, 1995), 117.

11. Varpu Lindstrom, '"I Won't be a Slave": Finnish Domestics in Canada, 1911–30', in Franca Iacovetta et al., eds, *A Nation of Immigrants: Women, Workers and Communities in Canadian History, 1840s–1960s* (Toronto, 1998), 206–30; Dionne Brand, '"We Weren't Allowed to Go into Factory Work until Hitler Started the War": The 1920s to the 1940s' in Peggy Bristow et al., eds, *'We're Rooted Here and They Can't Pull Us Up': Essays in African Canadian Women's History* (Toronto, 1994), 171–91.

12. Graham S. Lowe, 'Women, Work and the Office: The Feminization of Clerical Occupations in Canada, 1901–1931', in Strong-Boag and A. Fellman, eds, *Rethinking Canada: The Promise of Women's History* (Toronto, 1991), 269–85; Veronica Strong-Boag, *'Janey Canuck': Women in Canada, 1919–1939*, Canadian Historical Association Historical Booklet, 53 (Ottawa, 1994), 5.

13. Joan Sangster, 'The 1907 Bell Telephone Strike: Organizing Women Workers', in Strong-Boag and Fellman, *Rethinking Canada*, 249–68; Cynthia Comacchio, 'Mechanomorphosis: Science, Management, and "Human Machinery" in Industrial Canada, 1900–45', *Labour/Le Travail* 41 (1998), 47.

14. Mercedes Steedman, *Angels of the Workplace: Women and the Construction of Gender Relations in the Canadian Clothing Industry, 1890–1940*, 78–85. See also Douglas Cruikshank and Greg Kealey, 'Strikes in Canada, 1891–1950', *Labour/Le Travail* 20 (1987), 107.

15. James Naylor, *The New Democracy: Challenging the Social Order in Industrial Ontario, 1914–25* (Toronto, 1991), 159–88, 205–7; Margaret McCallum, 'Corporate Welfarism in Canada, 1919–1939', *Canadian Historical Review* LXXI (1990), 46–79.

16. Toronto, *Minutes of the Council* (1912), Appendix A, 903, 1128.

17. Statistics on privies from Drummond, *Progress*, Table 13:1.

18. R.E. Spence, *Prohibition in Canada* (Toronto, 1919), 206, 579–80, cited in Graeme Decarie, 'Something Old, Something New . . . : Aspects of Prohibition in Ontario in the 1890s', in Donald Swainson, ed., *Oliver Mowat's Ontario* (Toronto, 1972), 155.

19. Nellie McClung, *In Times Like These*, Introduction by Veronica Strong-Boag (Toronto, 1972), 77; originally published in 1915.

20. Quotations from Humphries, *Sir James Pliny Whitney*, 126, and 101.

21. First quotation, Hamilton *Spectator* (December

1899), cited in Kenneth C. Dewar, 'The Early Development of Hydroelectricity in Ontario', *Canada's Visual History*, vol. 31, Illustration 6; second quotation, Nelles, *The Politics of Development,* 219.

22. The last two paragraphs draw from Nelles, *The Politics of Development*, 215–306, quotation at 248–9; Humphries, *Sir James Pliny Whitney*, 151–68, 218–20.

23. Humphries, *Sir James Pliny Whitney*, 128; Naylor, *The New Democracy*, 77–80.

24. Quotations from Humphries, *Sir James Pliny Whitney*, 19, 221.

25. Cited in Peter Oliver, *Public and Private Persons: The Ontario Political Culture, 1914–1934* (Toronto, 1975), 39.

26. On recruiting see Paul Maroney, '"The Great Adventure": The Context and Ideology of Recruitment in Ontario, 1914–17', *Canadian Historical Review* 77 (1996), 62–98.

27. London *Free Press*, (10 Dec. 1915), cited in Barbara M. Wilson, *Ontario and the First World War, 1914–18* (Toronto, 1977), xxxvii.

28. Derry, 'Gender Conflicts in Dairying', 31–47; Crowley, 'Experience and Representation', 238–51.

29. Linda Ambrose and Margaret Kechnie, 'Social Control or Social Feminism?: Two Views of the Ontario Women's Institutes', *Agricultural History* 73 (1999), 222–37; Cecilia Reynolds and Harry Smaller, 'Ontario School Teachers: A Gendered View of the 1930s', *Historical Studies in Education/Revue d'histoire de l'éducation* 6 (1994), fn 7,155, 168.

30. The section on the UFO and the UFWO has benefited from Crowley, 'J.J. Morrison,' quotation at 343; Charles Johnston, *E.C. Drury: Agrarian Idealist* (Toronto, 1986); Margaret Kechnie, 'The United Farm Women of Ontario: Developing a Political Consciousness', *Ontario History* 77 (1985), 266–80; Pauline Rankin, 'The Politicization of Ontario Farm Women', in Linda Kealey and Joan Sangster, eds, *Beyond the Vote: Canadian Women and Politics* (Toronto, 1989), 309–32.

31. The last four paragraphs have benefited from Naylor, *The New Democracy*. See also Cruikshank and G. Kealey, 'Strikes in Canada', 85–145; Craig Heron, 'The Crisis of the Craftsman: Hamilton's Metal Workers in the Early Twentieth Century', in Michael Piva, ed., *A History of Ontario: Selected Readings* (Toronto, 1988).

32. Bruce Kidd, '"Making the Pros Pay" for Amateur Sports: The Ontario Athletic Commission, 1920–1947", *Ontario History* LXXXVII (1985), 110.

33. Crowley, 'J.J. Morrison', 349.

34. Oliver, *Public and Private Persons*, 39.

35. James Struthers, *The Limits of Affluence: Welfare in Ontario, 1920–70* (Toronto, 1994), Chapters 1 and 2; John Bullen, 'J J Kelso and the New Child Savers: The Genesis of the Children's Aid Movement in Ontario', *Ontario History* 82 (1990), 107–30; Margaret Little, 'No Car, No Radio, No Liquor Permit': *The Moral Regulation of Single Mothers in Ontario, 1920–1997* (Toronto, 1998), 1–75; Comacchio, 'Mechanomorphosis', 51–3.

36. For international context see Joel Mokyr, 'Why "More Work for Mother?" Knowledge and Household Behaviour, 1870–1945', *The Journal of Economic History* 60 (2000), 1–41. For a national perspective see Veronica Strong-Boag, *The New Day Recalled: Lives of Girls and Women in English Canada, 1919–1939* (Toronto, 1988), Chapter 4; Joy Parr, *Domestic Goods: The Material, the Moral and the Economic in the Postwar Years* (Toronto, 1999); Kerr and Holdsworth, *Historical Atlas of Canada*, 3, Plate 29.

37. Naylor, *The New Democracy*, 225–9; Rankin, 'Ontario Farm Women', 316–17; Richard Harris, *Unplanned Suburbs: Toronto's American Tragedy, 1900–1950* (Baltimore, 1996), Chapter 4.

9: Boom, Bust, and War: 1923–1943

1. Peter Oliver, *G. Howard Ferguson: Ontario Tory* (Toronto, 1977), 313–14; Struthers, *Limits of Affluence*, 65.

2. Oliver, *Ferguson*, 78, and Chapter 12; Oliver, *Public and Private Persons*, 92–125; John T. Saywell, *'Just Call Me Mitch': The Life of Mitchell F. Hepburn* (Toronto, 1991), 40; Reynolds and Smaller, 'Ontario School Teachers', 151.

3. Oliver, *Ferguson,* 116, 155–6, passim; Saywell, *Mitch,* 141; Little, *'No Car'*, 83.

4. Oliver, *Ferguson,* 208ff; Mark Kuelberg, '"We Have Sold Forestry to the Management of the Company": Abitibi Power Paper Company's Forestry Initiatives in Ontario, 1919–29', *Journal of Canadian Studies* 34 (1999), 187–209.

5. The material in the last four paragraphs is drawn from Struthers, *Limits of Affluence,* Chapter 12 and Table 13:1; Stephen Davies, '"Reckless Walking Must Be Discouraged": The Automobile Revolution and the Shaping of Modern Ontario', *Urban History Review* 18 (1989), 123–38; Gerald T. Bloomfield, 'No Parking Here to Corner: London Reshaped by the Automobile, 1911–61', *Urban History Review* 18 (1989), 139–58; Comacchio, 'Mechano-morphosis'; and Oliver, *Ferguson.*

6. Saywell, *Mitch,* 84–7; Scott Vokey, 'Inspiration for Insurrection or Harmless Humour? Class and Politics in the Editorial Cartoons of Three Toronto Newspapers During the Early 1930s', *Labour/Le Travail* 45 (2000), 147; W. Peter Archibald, 'Distress, Dissent and Alienation: Hamilton Workers in the Great Depression', *Urban History Review* 21 (1992), 3–32; Terry Crowley, 'The New Canada Movement: Agrarian Youth Protest in the 1930s', *Ontario History* LXXX (1988), 311–25; Sally M. Weaver, 'The Iroquois: The Grand River Reserve in the Late Nineteenth and Early Twentieth Centuries, 1875–1945', in E.S. Rogers and D.B. Smith, eds, *Aboriginal Ontario: Historical Perspectives on the First Nations* (Toronto, 1994), 250.

7. Gerald Killan and George Warecki, 'J.R. Dymond and Frank A. MacDougall: Science and Government Policy in Algonquin Provincial Park, 1931–54', *Scienta canadensis* 22–3 (1998–9), 131–59.

8. Ivar Nordstram as told to Satu Repo, 'Lakehead in the Thirties: A Labour Militant Remembers', *This Magazine* 13, 3 (1979), 42.

9. Archibald, 'Distress', 24; Archibald, 'Small Expectations and Great Adjustments: How Hamilton Workers Most Often Experienced the Great Depression', *Canadian Journal of Sociology* 21 (1996), 393.

10. Last quotation from Lita-Rose Betcherman, *The Little Band* (Ottawa, 1982), 166–7.

11. Toronto *Daily Star* (1 Oct. 1933), cited in Irving Abella, 'Oshawa, 1937', in Abella, ed., *On Strike: Six Key Labour Struggles in Canada, 1919–1949* (Toronto, 1974), 97.

12. Saywell, *Mitch,* 179–81; John Manley, '"Starve Be Damned!": Communists and Canada's Urban Unemployed, 1929–1939', *Canadian Historical Review* 79 (1998), 479.

13. Carmela Patrias, 'Relief Strike: Immigrant Workers and the Great Depression in Crowland, Ontario, 1930–1935', in Iacovetta, *A Nation of Immigrants,* 322–58.

14. Patrias, 'Relief Strike'; Nordstram, 'Lakehead', 44; Archibald, 'Distress'; Drummond, *Progress,* Table 10:1; Greg Kealey and Douglas Cruikshank, 'Workers' Responses', in Kerr and Holdsworth, *Historical Atlas of Canada,* 3, Table 45.

15. Little, *'No Car'*, chapter 4; Margaret Hobbs, 'Equality and Difference: Feminism and the Defence of Women Workers During the Great Depression, *Labour/Le Travail* 32 (1993), 201–23; Ellen Scheinberg, 'The Tale of Tessie the Textile Worker: Female Textile Workers in Cornwall During World War Two', *Labour/Le Travail* 33 (1994), 161; Patricia Bird, 'Hamilton Working Women in the Period of the Great Depression', *Atlantis* 8, 2 (1982–83), 126–36. Reynolds and Smaller, 'Ontario School Teachers', passim; Joy Parr, *The Gender of Breadwinners: Women, Men, and Change in Two Industrial Towns, 1880–1950* (Toronto, 1990), 87–90.

16. Struthers, *Limits of Affluence,* Chapter 2.

17. Nordstram, 'Lakehead', 40; Archibald, 'Small Expectations', 395. Crowley, 'The New Canada Movement', 320.

18. Calculated from D. Cruikshank and G.S. Kealey, 'Canadian Strike Statistics, 1891–1950', *Labour/Le Travail* 20 (1987). Table E. On the Industrial Standards Act see Marcus Klee, 'Fighting the Sweatshop in Industrial Ontario: Capital, Labour and the Industrial Standards Act', *Labour/Le Travail* 45 (2000), 13–51.

19. First quotation, Terry Copp, 'Ontario 1939: The Decision for War', *Ontario History* LXXXVI (1994),

269; second quotation, NA, RG 10, V. 6768, file 452–20, Pt 4, S Devlin to MacInness, 2 Oct. 1940, cited in Michael Stevenson, The Mobilization of Native Canadians During the Second World War', *Journal of the Canadian Historical Association* 7 (1966), 209. For an account of one interment camp see Sylvia Bjorkman, 'Report on Camp "W": Interment Camp "100" North of Lake Superior in World War Two', *Ontario History* LXXXIX (1997), 237–43. See also John Zucchi, *Italians in Toronto: Development of a National Identity, 1875–1935* (Kingston, 1988), 192.

20. Scheinberg, 'The Tale of Tessie'; Ruth Roach Pierson, *'They're Still Women After All': The Second World War and Canadian Womanhood* (Toronto, 1986).

10: Modern Ontario: 1945–2000

1. Robert Bothwell, Ian Drummond, and John English, *Canada Since 1945: Power, Politics and Provincialism* (Toronto, 1981), 92; Keith Brownsey, 'Opposition Blues: Policy and Organization in the Ontario Conservative Party, 1934–43', *Ontario History* 88 (1996), 280.

2. *Globe and Mail* (10 July 1943); Kenneth J. Rea, *The Prosperous Years: An Economic History of Ontario, 1939–75* (Toronto, 1985), 18–19.

3. Quotation from Terry Crowley, *Agnes MacPhail and the Politics of Equality* (Toronto, 1990), 188.

4. Bothwell, Drummond, and English, *Canada Since 1945*, 96.

5. Sid Noel, 'The Ontario Political Culture: An Interpretation', in Graham White, ed., *The Government and Politics of Ontario* (Toronto, 1997), 60.

6. Thomas J. Courchene with Colin R. Telmer, *From Heartland to North American Regional State: The Social, Fiscal, and Federal Evolution of Ontario* (Toronto, 1998), 13.

7. John C. Van Nostrand, 'The Queen Elizabeth Way: Public Utility Versus Public Space', *Urban History Review* XII (1983), 11.

8. Nancy M. Wightman and W. Robert Wightman, 'Road and Highway Development in Northwestern Ontario, 1850–1990', *Geographica* 36 (1992), 366–80.

9. Rea, *Prosperous Years*, 84–5.

10. Struthers, *Limits of Affluence*, 223.

11. Parr, *Domestic Goods*, last quotation, 240; see also 33, 107.

12. For primary production see Rea, *Prosperous Years*, 83, Table 15; for rural non-farm population see M. Toombs, 'Rising Concern in Rural Ontario Re Swine Production', web site, Ontario Ministry of Agriculture, Food and Rural Affairs (OMAFRA) (8 March 2000); farm decline calculated from Rea, *Prosperous Years*, 136, Table 31, and 'Ontario Census Farms Classified by Total Farm Area, 1991 and 1996', web site, OMAFRA; farm acreage from McCalla, 'The Ontario Economy', 103; hog and dairy farm decline from 'Discussion Paper on Intensive Agricultural Operations in Rural Ontario', web site, OMAFRA; percentage of total farm revenue from 'The Protection of Ontario's Ground Water and Intensive Farming: Special Report to the Legislative Assembly of Ontario', Environmental Commissioner of Ontario (27 July 2000), web site, Environmental Commissioner of Ontario; farm income calculated from 'Ontario Census Farms Classified by Total Gross Farm Receipts', web site, OMAFRA; off-farm income from 'Rural Ontario Demographic Trends and Factors', web site, OMAFRA.

13. See Rea, *Prosperous Years*, Table 15, 83.

14. *Globe and Mail* (29 Aug. 2000), A16.

15. Struthers, *Limits of Affluence*, 123, 141, 213.

16. Ibid., 209–10.

17. Ibid., 146, 200, 218, 256.

18. See note 2 above.

19. Leacy, Urquhart, and Buckley, *Historical Statistics of Canada*, 2nd edn. W121 and W170.

20. Rea, *Prosperous Years*, 112.

21. Last three paragraphs based in part on Struthers, *Limits of Affluence*, 226–30; Manore, *Cross Currents*; Harvey McCue, 'The Modern Age, 1945–1980', in Rogers and Smith, *Aboriginal Ontario*, 377–417; David T. MacNab, 'Aboriginal Land Claims in Ontario', in Ken Coates, ed., *Aboriginal Land Claims in Canada* (Toronto, 1992), 73–99; Anthony Hall, 'Treaties, Trains and Troubled National Dreams: Reflections on the Indian Summer in Northern Ontario, 1990', in

Knafla and Binnie, *Law, Society and the State*, 290–320; Joan Sangster, 'Criminalizing the Colonized: Ontario Native Women Confront the Criminal Justice System', *Canadian Historical Review* 80 (1999), 32–60; quotation from web site of the Ontario Native Affairs Secretariat, Temagami Land Claim (21 June 2000).

22. Ross Lambertson, 'Activists in the Age of Human Rights: The Struggle for Human Rights in Canada, 1945–1960', unpublished Ph.D. thesis (University of Victoria, 1998), 278 (note 14), 261–9, 407–22; James W. St G. Walker, *'Race', Rights and the Law in the Supreme Court of Canada: Historical Case Studies* (Toronto, 1997), 172, 222–6, passim.

23. First quotation Rand Dyck, 'The Socio-Economic Setting of Ontario politics', in G. White, *Government and Politics*, 43; second quotation Franca Iacovetta, 'From Contadina to Worker: Southern Italian Immigrant Working Women in Toronto, 1947–1962', in Strong-Boag and Fellman, *Rethinking Canada*, 390.

24. Veronica Strong-Boag, 'Home Dreams: Women and the Suburban Experiment in Canada, 1945–60', *Canadian Historical Review* 72 (1991), 471–504; Struthers, *Limits of Affluence*, 243.

25. Courchene, *From Heartland*, Chapter 5.

26. See J.M. Bumsted, *A History of the Canadian Peoples* (Toronto, 1998), Table 11.1, 'Results by Province of the 26 October 1992 Referendum on the Charlottetown Accord', 387.

27. *The Labour Relations and Employment Statute Law Amendment Act, 1995* (Bill 7) introduced 4 Oct. 1995.

28. *The Savings and Restructuring Act, 1995* (Bill 26).

29. First quotation cited in Robert Paehlke, 'Environmentalism in One Country: Canadian Environmental Policy in an Era of Globalization', *Policy Studies Journal* 28 (2000), 166; second quotation from 'Ontario Environmental Commissioner Reports Decline in Environmental Protection', web site, Environmental Commissioner of Ontario, news release (28 April 1999).

30. 'The Protection of Ontario's Ground Water and Intensive Farming: Special Report to the Legislative Assembly of Ontario', Environmental Commissioner of Ontario (27 July 2000), web site, Environmental Commissioner of Ontario; 'State of the Industry: Pork', web site, OMAFRA.

31. Eighth Annual Environmental Report Card, web site, Sierra Club of Canada.

32. H.V. Nelles, 'Red Tied: Fin de Siècle Politics in Ontario', in Michael Whittington and Glen Williams, eds, *Canadian Politics in the 1990s* (Toronto, 1990) 94.

33. Courchene, *From Heartland*, passim.

INDEX

PLEASE NOTE: Page numbers in italic type refer to illustration captions.